My Father's *Writings*

An Inspiring Journey through Life, Love and a Lifetime of Memories

JIM DURHAM

BALBOA.
PRESS

A DIVISION OF HAY HOUSE

Balboa Press books may be ordered through booksellers or by contacting:

Balboa Press
A Division of Hay House
1663 Liberty Drive
Bloomington, IN 47403
www.balboapress.com
1-(877) 407-4847

ISBN: 978-1-4525-4903-3 (e)
ISBN: 978-1-4525-4904-0 (sc)

Library of Congress Control Number: 2012905287

Printed in the United States of America

Balboa Press rev. date: 05/18/2012

Contents

Cover Photo: Paige M. Durham
Author Photo: Hilary Rochelle

I want to thank everyone who has encouraged me to write—not because the results are so great, but because I enjoy it so much. Your support has been a real gift to me. This collection of writings only exists because a lot of people were willing to read early drafts and share their feedback. It also exists because Jennifer spent endless hours turning a mess of papers into a cohesive document, and because Kate and Lizzie did their best to edit a book of informal writing. Clearly, my family and closest friends need to be thanked for putting up with my passionate embrace of the Universal Spirit and all possibilities. That is not always easy to be around.

Chapter One

GLIMPSES OF LIFE ON THE INSIDE

When my dad's plane crashed the writings they found in the general area of the wreckage included a book he was reading, story ideas scribbled on napkins and a hint that one of his greatest concerns was that his son (that would be me, Andrew) might not realize his creative potential. This hint came in the form of a handwritten note on the back of an old business card that said: "If only his mother and I had given Andrew an 'A' in life; he would be following his dreams." I have since learned that this is a reference to the inspirational words of Ben Zander, but more on that later.

So it makes perfect sense that I would seize the opportunity to pull together my father's writings, and to share his insights and observations with a broad audience. Although being his son for 22 years has given me a pretty good understanding of my father's thoughts and gifts, I decided to go beyond just collecting and publishing Dad's ubiquitous piles of paper; I collaborated with some of his friends to get even more insight into his soul, and to more fully understand what some of his writings might mean.

Of course, it wasn't supposed to be like this—me writing about (and for) my father, with him gone at too early an age. But for whatever reason—tribute, grief-management, holding on to memories, or maybe just to fulfill his expectations of me, I have given myself the task of assembling, sharing and, to some degree, interpreting my father's words. Since some of the writings I found were little more than skeletons of ideas, I used my best judgment to explain his thinking and speculate on where he was going with them. Essentially I am just doing the work he posthumously assigned to me; an assignment for which I know he would give me an "A" no matter how it turns out.

This book is a collection of insights, essays, sermons, random chapters, and poems, captured on a plethora of notes scattered in and among drawers, files, folders, briefcases . . . and, unfortunately, wreckage. The writings of my father are really just the thoughts and dreams of us all. He believed in trying to make his own life right so he could do more to help others. He worked toward perfection, but was learning to be okay with never getting there; he believed we were in the world to serve others—whether as the general manager of a business, a salesman, a parent or a friend. But it is also clear to me that he did not learn until late in life that we need to serve ourselves as well—to say "yes" to our hearts and our intuition.

Now I understand why he was always trying to get me to read the stuff he read and the stuff he wrote. He used to send me large envelopes full of articles he had torn out of magazines and newspapers. We called it my bathroom reading . . . . Now I also see what he saw in my own writing that gave him hope that I, too, might explore my creative side; that I "might discover the marrow of life before the bone was spoiled." (That phrase was recorded as a quote in his scribbled notes, but I think it was just my dad's interpretation of Thoreau's statement: "I wanted to live deep and suck out all of the marrow of life.")

Ironic isn't it, that it was the death of my brother Casey 19 years ago that first opened my father's eyes to all possibilities—to his gifts of writing, preaching and inspiring. Now it is my father's death that is leading me to explore my own creative potential. I hope, over time, that I can find less painful ways to open up my feelings to others the way Dad did. (One of his sermons ended with: "Open your hearts to yourself and those you love, and you just might find your purpose and your joy. Amen.")

But all of what follows would be pretty confusing to those of you who didn't know the Watson clan if I don't give you just a little context. A simple roster, although we are quite a collection. Dad, as you will learn as you move through his writings, grew up in the wilds of Michigan, with no real understanding of the world outside of Baldwin. He was not even planning to go to college until a chance meeting with a guy who interviewed students for Harvard changed his life course. He still has a bit of that Midwestern hayseed in him, but he has found a way to be equally at home working in the biggest cities, in the highest levels of business. It is his life journey, I think, that informs his perspective, and gives him so much to say in what he writes.

He married my mom when he was in his twenties, but they were only together for about 7 years, so I grew up very much in two homes. While it was definitely challenging as a kid, I can now appreciate how much it has shaped my life to have known some adversity, uncertainty and conflict growing up. I hate the cliché "if it doesn't kill you it will make you stronger," but there is some truth in it. If you learn to adapt at an early age, those skills serve you well as you get older.

Then there is my special brother. Soon after Dad remarried an amazing woman named Nancy (who always treated me like her own son), they had twin boys, Casey and Brian. Casey had to undergo open heart surgery when he was just three days old, and was expected to live a normal life. But Casey died of a blood clot after a routine catheterization when he was not quite four months old. That was tragedy enough, but in the meantime they had learned that his brother Brian was born with an underdeveloped brain, so he was destined to a life of limited mental capacity! That is an awful lot to deal with, especially for a couple who had been married less than two years. But they beat the odds (most families who have a child die get divorced), and they are still together today. You will see as you read the many things Dad wrote how they managed to make it all work.

One of the writings I put near the front of this collection is the Homily that Dad delivered at the memorial service for Casey. It was a real 'coming out' for him. He put himself out there with emotion and vulnerability in a way that few men would, I think. But you can draw your own conclusions when you read it.

Then there is my amazing sister, Lindsay. She is almost ten years younger than I, but we are very connected. She is wise beyond her years, and is flat-out fun to hang around with. I have no doubt that she was profoundly influenced by growing up with a brother who had special needs. The way she responded is revealed in the various Holiday Letters that are reprinted throughout the book. I do not need to write much more about any of the family here, as you will get to know them through what Dad wrote in this collection.

Even though my father was a so-called "marketing guy" at a consulting company, he would accept any opportunity to speak, whether it was to get people to open up their hearts (and wallets) at a fundraiser, to deliver a sermon at church, or to be the keynote speaker at a conference. In the years just before his death, Dad would do almost anything to get his message out. And he would never miss an opportunity to write poems or letters to friends and colleagues. He also wrote an inspirational Holiday Letter every year for 13 years. If you have any doubt about whether he could write, check out the last letter he wrote.

HOLIDAY LETTER

"Me happy now." Brian, our 18-year-old with special needs, says these three beautiful words whenever he hears or does something that strikes his fancy. Learning that "Kaboom" (America's Funniest Videos) will be on Sunday night, or that his big brother, Andrew, will be home from college for a visit; going to his sister, Lindsay's, school to "push me please" (Brian's words for swinging); or just hearing that I will be home from work in time for dinner—any one of these events is enough to trigger the phrase.

I was wondering *what* would make most of us say *me happy now*. Getting a promotion, a raise or an unexpected day off? Getting flowers or a massage? Taking a trip with someone we love? Reading (or writing) a good book? Reconnecting with an old friend? Closing a huge deal? Visiting a family member whom we haven't seen for a while? If these are the things that make us happy then it seems that we should be doing them, or, at least, working toward doing them. There is nothing wrong with focusing on a little happiness in the midst of our sometimes crazy over-scheduled lives, right? I would really like to declare 2008 'the Year of Joy!'

Many of you probably heard about Randy Pausch, the young professor at Carnegie Mellon who was told he had just a few months to live earlier this year. A father of three small children, he chose to use his remaining time to make a positive impact on the world and to establish an exemplary legacy for his children. He called the diagnosis "a gift" saying: "to actually know how much time I had left on this earth gave me a chance to plan carefully how I used every minute." His Final Lecture has been viewed by millions of people on YouTube, and he has truly made a positive difference in many lives. My favorite point in Randy's presentation is that brick walls are put in our way not to stop us, but to give us something to break through. He talks a lot about childhood dreams, and enabling the dreams of others. These are the kinds of wonderful things that a dear friend and his amazing family focused on in his final months, after a year-long battle with a brain tumor. God bless them for the gift they gave us in their message at the memorial service "to live like you're dying."

Albert Ellis, whom *Psychology Today* once described as the "greatest living psychologist" (before he died, of course), was fond of quoting the Greek stoic philosopher, Epictetus, who essentially said: 'It's **not events,** *but* **our opinions of them**, which cause us suffering. The challenge is to be able to change our opinions and mental habits so that we become robust and self-accepting enough to withstand external events that used to cause us suffering, such as getting rejected by a woman or getting fired.' So as we face the inevitable challenges of daily life, maybe our response to whatever happens around us should be *me happy now* . . . not only when Lindsay makes a full-out diving save in a soccer game, but when she lets a soft goal slip past her—*me happy now* that she is able to play and be part of such a great team. When I think of Andrew graduating from college in May it makes me smile, but I still need to be happy even if he says he may not move back to Boston. I am typing with a stiff neck and wearing a brace right now, but Brian keeps kissing my neck saying "bubba better?" Even with this pain, how can I not be happy now?

Where else can we find Brian's wonderful perspective in our lives? How about when loved ones beat the odds of an illness and get a good bill-of-health; when I receive a wonderful book like *Season of Life* (thanks, Kathy) and I like it so much that I send a bunch of copies to my high school football friends; when Nancy tells me she got a "Big W" in their team tennis match; when Lindsay says she really likes her teachers; when we learned that our 6-month kitchen renovation project would be done (almost) on time; when we heard that Andrew's first snowboarding runs of the season were a blast; when thinking about our annual trip to Florida with the Jacksons; going to a World Series game in Denver; or when a family welcomes us into their home on Thanksgiving. *Me happy now.* How about a weekend on Nantucket, a vacation in Florida with great friends, sharing my collection of poems with those willing to read them, or hearing Lindsay sing in the school chorus. What about weekend getaways with my wife Nancy, or going to a yoga class (my new favorite workout), or winning our flight in the member-guest at my brother's club. There is real joy in seeing the rapport and connection Nancy has with her brothers . . . and what about my brother and sister-in-law having *another* baby! *Me happy now.*

I am reminded of the movie *Being There* in which Peter Sellers' character shares simple insights (mostly gleaned from TV) that catapult him from being a recluse gardener to a Presidential advisor. "If you give the flowers water, they will grow . . ." Simplicity. No agenda. No political clutter and no ego. Here, simple, honest phrases are interpreted as genius and loving kindness—a lot of lessons in a simple movie.

There are a number of life lessons encapsulated in Brian's simple little phrase, too. We are blessed to have a loving caretaker who spends a lot of quality time with Brian. But someday we will need to introduce Brian to a home where he will be with peers and full-time caretakers. We will plan and make the move sensitively, but leaving him there for the first time will be devastating emotionally. Our strength at that moment will not come from within, though; it will come from Brian when he looks around his new digs for the first time and turns to us with his disarming smile and says *"me happy now."* We will draw on his capacity to accept profound change, appreciate life's constants and connections, and his willingness to openly express his feelings . . . now that, my friends, is inspiration.

So why is there so much focus on Brian this year, when we have two other wonderful children? Partly it's because no matter how you interpret the Bible, its insights about children are priceless. The psalm says: "Come as a baby weak and poor to bring all hearts together." God has blessed us with someone who, in many ways, will always be a child. "Whomever welcomes this little child . . . welcomes God." Brian doesn't rely on hype or phony positivism to enjoy life; he just enjoys what he enjoys; he seeks it out and drinks it in. Even something as basic as bedtime prayers (which he calls "God Bless") or riding in the front seat of the van or seeing a UPS truck in front of our house gets it done for him. I want to learn from that perspective what joys I might be missing in everyday life . . . .

Talking about Brian also gives me a chance to talk about Nancy— she who for 17 years has never once—not once—complained about how much work it is to bathe and feed and dress Brian; no complaints about trips to the doctor or spilled water. Like other parents who raise children with special needs, this unselfishness is the true definition of 'motherhood.' Thank you to all who give care and comfort to those in need or less fortunate. It represents the kind of giving that I want to be reminded of this holiday season.

We can slice and package 'time' any way we want, and it may seem artificial to say we are at the end of a "gift;" but we are at the end of another year, and that is a gift for which I am truly thankful. Let 'the first gift of Christmas' this year be hope for more time together to live, and to give and to love.

Merry Christmas, Happy Chanukah, and a Great New Year to all from the Watsons.

This Holiday Letter led to a "Me Happy Now" movement to raise funds for an organization that supported special needs children. By sending out hundreds of "Me Happy Now" bumper stickers along with the text of the Holiday Letter, people flocked to Dad's website to get more. Dad's hope was to get on the Oprah show with this message. But the draft letter he wrote to her was still in a folder when he died. This is what it said:

Dear Oprah,

Holiday Letters are much maligned, but I have been writing one for 13 years—and your name has been mentioned prominently in several of them. Why? Because you (along with Pat Sajack, Bob Barker and SuperNanny) hold a special place in the life of my special needs son. Yes, you made the "Top 5" list of things for which he is most thankful at Thanksgiving time.

Brian was born 17 years ago with development problems that destined him to be mentally retarded. (He was a twin, but his brother died of heart complications at three months old.) Despite Brian's limitations, he knows only joy. When I wrote about his beautiful love for life in one of my Holiday Letters, and his favorite phrase, "Me Happy Now," people responded with incredible passion. One friend created the enclosed bumper sticker that is now being used to raise funds for a local support group for retarded citizens. Someone suggested to me that Brian and his message should be featured on the Oprah show. When I saw your "pay it forward" episode I was compelled to write.

A national (international?) campaign of "me happy now" could do a lot for morale in these difficult times, and possibly raise a lot of money for people with special needs. Whether Brian could ever meet you or not, a mention of his story, and the offer of a 'me happy now' bumper sticker for a modest donation (or just a visit to your site to get more information) could have a profound positive impact on those with special needs. Brian's message of seeing the beauty in all aspects of life can also be a gift to those among us who have simple human needs for love, peace and appreciation.

I recently completed a simple children's book, with the story based on Brian's eternal optimism. A copy is enclosed in case you have suggestions for the draft. It would be wonderful to have you as a co-author! Forgive this bold intrusion into your busy life and business, but you have been like a part of our family ever since Brian discovered your show many years ago. So, at least, accept this letter as a "thank you" for all of the good that you do in the world, and the joy that it brings our son to be able to say "Oprah be on."

What a shame that my father never got to send that letter. It was a long shot that he would get a response, but who knows. I guess I should start working on that, too . . . .

★ ★ ★ ★ ★

There was also a videotape that Dad had recorded as a 'leave behind' for our family. He so loved the book *Tuesdays with Morrie* (he played and replayed the book-on-tape in his car) that he referred to his own secret recordings as "Tuesdays with Love." (He recorded only on Tuesdays.) It was an interesting challenge for him to make a tape for posterity that he did not want anyone to find; but he had to hide it just well enough so it *could* be found after he died. I can't really figure out how he managed to set up the camera in our basement and videotape these "talks" without us ever catching on.

There were at least five sessions on tape, each about 20 minutes, during which Dad said pretty much everything you would say to your loved ones if you knew you were going to die. Well, I guess we all know we are going to die at some point, but you know what I mean. He used the videos to thank us for all of the joy and blessings he said we had given to him over the years, and there were little stories about us that made me realize how much he was actually paying attention to every aspect of our lives. In one part of the tape he talked about the one time he thought he caught my stepmother flirting with someone at a party many years ago—he told her how beautiful she still looked, and to not be afraid to use her obvious charms to find a new beau.

He told me to be sure to say prayers with my brother when I was with him at bedtime, as it was something Brian really loved even as a 19-year-old. Dad praised my sister for being such a wonderful, non-judgmental friend to everyone at school, and implored her to "stay nice." He even mentioned in the video that he had considered trying to produce a one-man, one-act play about a father leaving a video message for his family, but said he just couldn't find the time. I found an outline of the proposed play, however. Here is what it looked like; I think it actually could have been produced in some modest community theater.

Idea for a one-person, one-act play.

It opens with a song by the Bee Gees: "In the event of something happening to me, there is something I would like you all to see."

A man on stage is organizing a room while the song plays. He finds:

- Pictures of his kids that he props up
- A child's great school report
- A list of who gets what special things after he dies, and why
  o Best friends
  o Kids
  o Brothers
- He recites portions of ideas he has written for what might be said at his funeral—the song he wants played at his service: *Another Day in Paradise*
- He finds stuff he has hidden away from the kids (and wife?) and talks about each item as he looks at it
  o Private writings
  o Movies (some borderline appropriate)
  o Old magazines with interesting covers

He drifts into a soliloquy (a little like the therapist at the beginning of the play, *Equus*) about what his life has meant, what it has lacked and why he wants to leave a tape of his thoughts for posterity. First point: "Like most of us, I want to find the purpose in my journey."

- Later, the man starts going through the myriad stuff in his wallet; holding each thing up and commenting briefly:
  o Three Angel Cards that say: "Integrity," "Harmony" & "Adventure"
  o A scrap of paper that says: "Whitney, the Greatest Love of All"
  o A golf handicap card

o   Old business cards (from cool companies he had worked for)
o   A card that says: "What would you do if you knew you could not fail?"

He props up posters of motivational phrases, and is talking out loud to himself saying, "this needs to go here, and this there, so I can get it on camera." The posters say:

Would Jesus have done this for money? For a nice house?

Are the demands of our lives our "Purpose" or "Burden?"

Good works = the amount of love you bestow on others

He finds a big poster board with the word "Temptation—why, and what does it mean?" He starts discussing the concept of temptation.

The theme for the play will be that there is nothing genius or magical or special about him or his actions in life (or death); but that there is much to learn from ordinary events (and words), and, mostly, the theme will be that we are all simply born to love.

This play is something that Dad would have been able to pull off on stage. Given his obsession with making a difference, and his apparent obsession with death, I wish he would have completed it. It could have been titled "The Memorial." But how much can one man do when the arts are just a hobby, not his life work (or profession)? I bet if he had it to do over, Dad would have made the arts his life!

Dad's reference to *Equus* is significant. Sadly, I'm afraid, he could identify with some of the most painful parts of the therapist (treating a boy who had blinded eight horses), and the young boy grappling with the conflicts of religion and life. Dad saw the play four or five times.

As I rummaged further through my dad's incredible collection of things written, I realized that you can learn a lot about a person not only from his writings, but also from what he read. The pages

11

he had folded over and the notes he had made in the *Esquire* he was (apparently) reading on the plane before it went down, tell a story about his thinking. As was typical of my father, it appears from notes scribbled during that final flight, that he was flipping back and forth between *The Good Life,* a book by the Reverend Peter Gomes of Harvard, and *Esquire* magazine! That was soooo my dad.

The dog-eared pages in his *Esquire* revealed his A.D.D.-like approach to life. One page featured a martini recipe (he was always trying to improve his martini making skills), and on another there was a circled blurb (an endorsement actually) of "toasted coconut donuts." Dad didn't usually eat donuts, but when he did he didn't worry about being politically correct—he went for the goo. I bet he secretly loved finding this donut recipe.

Then there was the list marked on page 72 of *Esquire*: "The 10 Things You Don't Know About Women." He was head-over-heels in love with Nancy (my stepmother), and he worked hard at being a good husband. He had underlined some fun stuff in the list—some of which was a bit edgy, so I will spare you here. And he had drawn stars next to the phrases "give her flowers for no special reason," and "always ask 'what can I do to help?'"

A bookmark that remained intact in Reverend Gomes' book showed that Dad was on page 301—close to the end. That's a real tribute to the author since Dad seldom finished any book he was reading. His margin notes on page 283 of *The Good Life* show that he was particularly moved by the passage: "The good life is not to be found wrapped up and waiting for us like the Dead Sea Scrolls or some ancient artifacts from a culture that once flourished but is now long gone. Not at all. The good life, whose object, like that of hope, is a future good, difficult but possible to obtain, enables us to live now that which we seek."

Reverend Gomes was one of my father's heroes. I have included later in this book a transcript of Dad's remarks the night he met Peter. Dad described the experience of sharing a podium with him as "a triumph for the Midwestern hayseed."

Back in Dad's messy home office I found the beginning of his next Holiday Letter, even though he had told us he wouldn't write any more. It is just one paragraph, but it is intriguing, thought provoking, and exemplary of Dad's broader thinking. It's actually a bit of a tease, but here it is:

I did a search online for "Ram Dass" one day, sensing that there was something special about his life; what little I knew of him spoke to me. A set of CD's called "Conscious Living" popped up on the computer screen during my search, and I knew immediately that I needed to buy them. After listening to them once, I realized that they provided a form of meditation that I desperately needed. So I loaded them on my iPod, which was a gift from a former client who had become a dear friend. This allowed me to listen to these motivational passages over and over during my daily commute on the train. The meditations confirmed everything I have ever believed about the great moral scorecard. (Everything that you give to others you give to yourself; the more you give the more you receive, and we are all connected by love.) Some of what I heard on those CD's . . . .

This is as far as Dad got. He seldom completed a thought—never mind something he was writing—without interruption, so this wasn't surprising to me.

But now, after wading through Dad's voluminous piles of papers, thoughts and ideas, I understand what he meant when he said he had to stop writing the annual Holiday Letter because "it was just too hard to put everything he wanted to say into two pages." In the brief blurb above, he had already filled nearly a quarter of a page just introducing the ideas he wanted to expand upon that year.

My stepmom told me that Dad's way of writing the Holiday Letter had always been to put scraps of paper with ideas on them in piles "all over the house . . . in places you can't imagine." The top sheet of paper on each pile would simply say "Holiday Letter" or "H.L." somewhere on the page. But she said the last Holiday Letter he completed (the one you already read) was done spontaneously.

She said he just sat down on a Saturday morning and started writing without notes! He was done with the initial draft that day.

I realize that Holiday Letters are usually no big deal. In fact, the first one Dad wrote in 1994 was pretty typical fare ("what we did on our summer vacation"). But, these letters evolved into Dad's most pervasive form of "ministry." The themes always included: hope and all possibilities, gratitude, love, reflection and compassion. I thought it would be worthwhile to share some of them with you. As you read them you will see not only the consistent themes of warmth and love that emerge, but also an intriguing sophistication in his writing. If I had a dollar for every time a person said that his annual letter "made their Christmas" or "touched their heart" or "made them cry with joy," I would never have to work again. The other 12 years of Dad's Holiday Letters are reprinted throughout this book in no particular order; I think you will find them a real pleasure to read. But if they are not your cup of tea, you can just skip them.

Frankly, I have organized this collection in such a way that you can read all or only part of it and still find some entertainment, enlightenment or motivation. If you really don't like poetry, skip the chapter about poetry (although the way Dad wrote about poetry might surprise you). If homilies are not your thing, then you need not spend much time reading the pieces in the Chapter "In the Pulpit." I have no doubt that you will find what you need here, however, if you just proceed with an open mind and a dash of imagination.

Chapter Two

MY "ASSIGNMENT"

One of the writings I found in Dad's cluttered home office was titled "Chapter 1," so I guess Dad had planned (hoped) to write a book of some kind. Many of his other writings also started with the word "Chapter." I knew he always wanted to write a book, but I think he struggled with the idea of settling on a subject. He wrote (and self-published) books for lawyers and marketing people, but he never followed through on his idea of writing something inspirational. Here is one of his modest efforts to start such a book. The following words were found in his barely legible handwriting.

One of the many useful aphorisms, or, more fairly characterized, life-guiding tools, found in Steven Covey's *Seven Habits of Highly Effective People* is: "Begin with the end in mind." I have found those words to be incredibly valuable in planning my life and my business, and in consulting with businesses that want to change.

On the most profound level, beginning with the end in mind means thinking about what people would say about you at your funeral if you died today. This thought both inspires and haunts me. It did, however, provide much of the motivation for this book. [Note: I never realized how much Dad thought about death . . .]

I have tried to subscribe to the notion that the most important thing I can do in life (which will give my family something to hold on to upon my death) is to live with exemplary values: love and respect for all people; hard work balanced by good play; and a belief in all

15

possibilities. (A belief I hope my children might absorb.) Somehow it seems inadequate to aspire to "just live well." I feel compelled to share my vision and beliefs more broadly. I am not sure whether I am driven by ego, love of writing, or calling, but I really want to write about life as I understand it.

For many years I have tried to capture the essence of life in the context of a fairly typical (but not "painfully" typical, I hope) Holiday Letter. But as much as I tried to focus on character and calling, it still felt like the letters were too much of a recountation of Andrew's first home run, Lindsay's first violin recital or Brian's first complete sentence. If my goal was to inspire and teach, that format is simply too limiting. Moreover, distribution of the letter is limited to our family mailing list, and that seems like a pretty limited contribution to mankind if I fail to reach out further.

At first I thought the notes, essays and observations I had written over the years would someday just get thrown out with my business receipts, half-read magazines and the rest of the clutter that surrounds me. Then I had this vision (a fantasy of sorts) that a couple of my more-enlightened college friends would find and publish my body of writings years after I was gone. The light really went off, however, when I thought of how wonderful it would be if my teenage son were so inspired (impressed?) by his father's writing (and thinking), that he would make it his passion to collect, edit and publish my work. Not wanting to take that chance, though, I think I should probably try to pull together my writings myself. (My son is a brilliant writer and creative thinker, but seems to have some life interests that extend beyond his father's obsession with self-examination and a search for enlightenment.) I must admit that I get a certain sense of satisfaction pretending that people might actually want to read what I have written.

This is admittedly self-indulgent, but a new level of self-awareness seems to have come to me after reading the book: *You Will See It When You Believe It.* In my first conscious experience of synchronicity, I pulled this tattered paperback off the shelf of a wall full of mostly business books, and I began reading it out of curiosity.

I had never heard of Dr. Wayne Dyer at the time, but I had heard of a book called *Your Erroneous Zones* which he also had written. Simply stated, *You Will See It When You Believe It* got me thinking about life in a new way. But some would say my drift toward enlightenment actually started several years earlier when my infant son, Casey, died at just 3½ months old. Something extraordinary happened to me emotionally in response to this tragedy—most of which is explained in the homily titled "Coping with Adversity."

By reading this draft book *Introduction,* I learned that my assignment—to collect and publish my father's writings—was actually given to me over a dozen years ago. This piece was written in the late 90s. Fortunately, the collection of material he wrote in the ensuing years gave me a lot with which to work.

Since Dad mentioned the death of my brother Casey in many of his Holiday Letters, and in the draft book chapter above, I want to share here the Homily he wrote for Casey's memorial service which, in many ways, jump-started his passion for writing (and reflection).

Imagine a father being called upon by his powerful intuition to reveal at his son's memorial service the deep pain that had been hiding in his own soul for a lifetime. Imagine the cosmic tug that was going on as he thought about putting himself in front of friends and family in an effort to turn something tragic into something positive. But Dad went for it. Hundreds of people showed up that day. They came by the bus load. The pieces were all in place for the amazing emotional challenge my dad was facing on that cold December day.

On a random piece of paper Dad referred to the experience of delivering the Homily at Casey's service as: "The First Beginning: A new way of thinking and living for me." I was too young to remember much about the service, but reading the words he spoke at Casey's service blows me away today. I was not quite five years old, and Dad later said that having to tell me Casey died was one of the hardest things he had ever done in his life. I cannot recall my exact emotions at the time, but I will never forget the pain reflected in Dad's voice and his facial expressions when he delivered the news.

How Dad had the courage to deliver this Homily to a church full of friends and family may be hard to imagine, but you didn't know my dad! In subsequent years he shared the Homily with others who experienced the death of a child—he would even send it to strangers when he read about their loss in the newspaper. (They always wrote him back and thanked him.) The portion in *italics* below was an introduction Dad wrote a couple of years after the service to put the Homily in the proper context. That's when he added the title: *Coping with Adversity.*

Coping with Adversity

On a chilly Saturday night in early December, my son Casey died suddenly and without warning. He was three-and-a-half months old. Although he was in the hospital recovering from a routine heart procedure, my wife and I had been told that he was fine and that we could bring him home the next day. The doctors and nurses, whom we had come to know all too well, suggested that we go out and enjoy ourselves. After all, it was the weekend, and Casey's twin brother was in the same hospital room. He too, was recovering just fine from an apparent virus, and would also be coming home the next day.

With our little boys in the care of the finest children's hospital in the world, we decided to go out on a date for the first time in over five months. We spent a festive evening with friends, but when we returned home, there were several telephone messages from the hospital that would change our lives forever. Casey had died from an inexplicable blood clot.

To cope with this tragedy, my wife and I had to reach into our hearts and souls deeper than we ever imagined possible. And when I decided to deliver the Homily at Casey's memorial service, I had to call upon every ounce of strength and inspiration that God could give me.

My hope was to make something positive flow from something that was devastatingly painful. I also wanted to give others a framework to help them cope with all kinds of difficulty and to appreciate the many blessings that are often taken for granted.

I was told by many who attended the memorial service that the words I spoke were not only a tribute to my son, but also a source of great comfort and guidance for them. It was the feedback of these friends that made me decide to share these words with a wider audience. I hope that you derive some comfort and inspiration from them.

The Homily

When my son, Casey James Watson, was born, it was important to me that his middle name was "James." We had known for quite some time that he was going to be born with a very dangerous heart condition, and I think I believed, somewhat boldly I guess, that by sharing my and my father's name with him, he would be too strong to die in the face of what we knew to be some tough odds.

But, as Casey's death illustrates, our abilities as mere mortals are somewhat limited—a higher order has intervened, and we must now focus our energies on renewal. Our own strength is now being tested. But make no mistake about it—Casey was very strong in the face of a difficult crisis—he was taken from us in peace, not in weakness. He was one tough little guy.

As many of you know, right after Casey was born, he underwent heart surgery. Nancy and I were distraught, but hopeful. We were hopeful, in part, because of the love and support that came from the people in this room. In a sense, each of you has been with us at his bedside.

But despite our strength and our hope, there was a point, soon after Casey and his twin brother Brian were both home from the hospital for the first time, when I wondered aloud to Nancy whether the unbelievable joy that children brought to us was worth the potential pain that we could suffer as parents.

I was thinking of my other son Andrew, and how devastated I would be if he so much as broke a toe; I was thinking of friends who had experienced the loss of a child or faced some frightening childhood ailments—and, of course, I was thinking that my new twin boys were not completely out of danger.

When I expressed my concerns to Nancy, she looked at me in her ever perfect way, and said "The only way to avoid the pain you fear is to never really love anyone absolutely and unconditionally." Then it all seemed too simple to me. The greater our love for someone, the greater the pain we feel when something unfortunate happens to that

19

person. A pain born of love is not the kind of pain we should seek to avoid.

As I look out at this large crowd, I see a great deal of pain in this room today. The outpouring of love to me and my family over the past few days has been immeasurable. In fact, at times it has seemed that the level of pain we have seen and the sympathy we have received from others were almost too great to have been evoked by the death of such a little boy who had been on this earth for such a short time. Then I realized that this fountain of hurt and caring wasn't just for Casey—it was for Nancy and me.

We know that by being here today, you are not fulfilling some moral obligation. Rather, you are saying that you care about us, and for that we want to say openly and honestly that we thank you.

Last Saturday afternoon, just a few hours before Casey died, I was up at the hospital alone with my twin boys who were scheduled to come home from the hospital the next day. We were having a grand old time. I was pushing two strollers around the halls, much to the delight of the onlookers and my tiny passengers. I had three of my foursome together and I was really into it!

When we got back to their hospital room, Brian decided to take a nap, so Casey and I were just hanging out watching the Army-Navy football game. I thought it might be nice to look at the newspaper for a moment—that's not something you get to do very often when you have a busy career and two babies. I picked up the *Boston Globe* and noticed an article that discussed the way children view religion.

I did not want to ignore my little guy for even a few minutes, so I decided to read the article to him. I propped him up in my lap and began to read the article aloud. Casey's nurse, Kathleen, one of the many wonderful medical professionals who have treated our boys—some of whom are here today—caught me reading the paper to Casey and made me promise that I wasn't reading him the stock prices or the Business Section. I assured her that that was not the case.

Actually, the article I was reading said that the important thing for children in religion is not what Jesus or Elisha or anyone said—what matters to them is ***how these spiritual leaders acted and what they did.*** I concluded in my own mind that to children "religion" is watching and emulating model behavior.

Casey was staring at me as I read these words aloud to him. He was totally calm, and he seemed to be completely captivated as he listened with what seemed like the attentiveness of a serious student.

Intuitively, I knew at that moment how important it was for me to be a role model for him, but the thought of that responsibility also scared me. I know it may surprise some of my friends to hear this, but this person standing in front of you right now has always harbored an excessive amount of self-doubt; so the concept of having to act as a role model for Casey was troubling. There was some *real* power in that hospital room that afternoon. I reflected back on the scene soon after Casey died.

I realize now that to be a true role model *is to be Christ-like*—it is to be the best person you can possibly be, and to fulfill whatever purpose and potential you may have. Nature expects and demands personal greatness from each of us, and we must strive to fulfill our unique purpose on earth.

I felt inspired to be a role model for Casey even in his death. And yet, during the first meeting here at the church with Reverend Martin, when he asked Nancy and me who would deliver the Homily at Casey's memorial service, there was something inside of me that said, "You can't do it," an awful voice said, "let one of your more eloquent friends tell everyone how tragic this situation is, and how good you and Nancy are."

But when we got home from that meeting at the church, I told Nancy I was being drawn, almost mysteriously, into an extra room in our house that is sometimes referred to as my office. I told her I felt like I was going to find something important there.

So, I went upstairs and stood in the middle of the room. I just looked around for a moment until my eyes fixed upon a box full of old papers. The box was mostly filled with pages of notes, thoughts, stories, poems and other things I had scribbled over the years. As I flipped through the papers in the box, one page in particular caught my attention. This is what it said:

"*To write words is to dream aloud.*

To read the words of others is to expand the experience of your mind.

> *To read your own words is to examine the condition of your soul.*
>
> *To study your own words is to understand the essence of your nature.*
>
> *To criticize your own words is to appreciate the limits of your ability.*
>
> *To share your own words with others is to expose the depth of your character."*

I am sure several years had passed since I scribbled those words on a piece of notebook paper, but the last two lines leaped out at me like a thunderbolt.

> **"To share your own words with others is to expose the depth of your character."**

Suddenly it was clear to me that I had been drawn to my office and to this piece of paper because Casey was challenging me to reveal "the depth of my character." He was asking me to be a "model," to not be afraid to share my words with you by delivering this Homily. I was challenged to reach for my best in the face of the most difficult tragedy I have ever faced. I hope I am displaying the kind of character that will make him proud.

But since many of us, rightly or wrongly, judge character by looking at specific accomplishments, and since Casey was never given the opportunity to share his words with us, let's look quickly at what one child accomplished in less than four months on this earth. Let's look at the depth of Casey's character. In his brief lifetime:

- He has brought together and held together family and friends in an outpouring of love and, in some cases, forgiveness.
- He has taught Nancy, Andrew and me to appreciate more fully every single moment we have with Brian.
- I believe he has pushed many of you to appreciate more fully the blessing that your own children represent.
- He has virtually redefined the words "smile," "spirit" and "compassion."

- He has shown Nancy and me that our relationship and our faith is stronger than any obstacle with which life can confront us.
- He has given many of us the motivation to look for inspiration in the face of tragedy, and to speak of joy in the face of despair.
- He has taught us the limitations of modern medicine, and the lesson of perseverance; he has reminded us that it is better to love and lose, than never to have loved at all.

Casey James Watson's accomplishments display qualities we should seek to emulate.

We have entered the holiday season. Hanukkah and Christmas are upon us. These are times not only to reflect on your faith, but also to share joy and give gifts in celebration. Nancy and I do not wish for Casey's death to be a dark spot on these important times. So we have asked that your gifts in Casey's memory be in the form of donations to the *Globe Santa*. Whatever your religious persuasion, the idea of a child waking up to no gifts on Christmas, or the pain of a parent having to explain why, must hurt beyond description. So now, with our request for donations to a charity that delivers Christmas presents to needy children, we are hoping that Casey will be allowed to touch other children's lives in this holiday season. We have to wake up Christmas morning without Casey, but if we know that dozens of children are waking up to presents because of him, it will add something very special to our day.

When my wife and I were planning this service Monday morning, a package was delivered to our door. It was addressed to Casey and Brian. The box contained two adorable outfits that had the words "Christmas is for babies" sewn in front. But while those words reflect a sweet sentiment, I believe there is another way to look at it. Babies don't receive gifts—babies are gifts.

In a weak moment—a moment of frustration—a couple of months ago, I made a foolish comment to Nancy. I said something about small babies taking so much from us, and being able to give back so little. God was I wrong. Babies just give and give and give, in return for which they ask for only one thing: unconditional love. In the short time Casey was with us, he knew unconditional love and I know he felt the caring and sacrifice that flowed from his family and from each of you. Casey was a Christmas gift to our family that came early and the way he touched our lives was magnitudes greater than anything that can be wrapped up with bows and put under a tree. Babies really do give.

In closing, Nancy and I would like to thank our parents for their uncompromising support, and thank Reverend Martin for inviting us into his church. We also ask that each of you go away from here today with a sense of renewal and with a determination to:

- Do kind things for children, and spend time with them
- Tell people you appreciate them
- Be role models in all your actions
- Face challenges with strength, and think about testing the limits

And, perhaps most importantly, we urge you to gather together with those you love and watch *It's a Wonderful Life*. Even though real life doesn't always have perfect movie endings, life really is wonderful; and with all of you here today, I feel a little bit like George Bailey right now.

To each of you we say: "Thank you and we love you."

And for Casey I have these words: "This was the hardest thing I've ever done in my life, thank you for pushing me." Amen

This Homily was, indeed, a *New Beginning* for Dad. (That is the title he gave to a poem that you can read a few pages from now.) By delivering this message at Casey's service he went public for the first time with his faith, his vision of life and his belief in the healing power of love. I have talked to many of Dad's friends who were there that day, and they describe hearing his homily as a profoundly moving experience. I remember that I was in the third row of St. John's Church for the service, but, as I mentioned before, I was too young to remember his words. One of Dad's friends told me my father "hosted a Communion of the Saints" that day.

So, maybe I want to write this book not so much because my dad "assigned" me the task, but because I know how many people would like to read his private collection of insightful and motivational words. You see, as silly as it may seem, Dad's tradition of writing the Holiday Letter actually created a small, but passionate literary following. He also had created a modest fan base from speaking at numerous events, by sharing his poems with neighbors and friends, and by writing heartfelt letters when the occasion warranted it. When he announced in one of his Holiday Letters that it would be his last one, he got an avalanche of protests—some bordering on hate mail! But, as I said before, Dad reached out to people in many ways.

For example, a man and woman in our community found each other after tragedy and challenges had left them both single again. On the flight home from a business trip to attend their engagement party he wrote the following poem for them. (Of course, it took him about a year to get it framed and deliver it, but well, that's just how it was with Dad.)

By writing a loving and timeless poem that could be read in times of change (and in times of challenge) in any of our lives, it is clear that Dad truly felt and celebrated this couple's new-found joy and connection.

New Beginnings

New Beginnings, fresh and exciting,
filled with passion and joy.
Like new seasons, unpredictable and strangely
perfect in time and tone.
Like a new song born of love, notes flowing freely,
with rhythm, beauty and wonder.
A new message sings out a story of compassion;
loving opportunities unfold to be explored together.
A New Beginning is anticipation and forgiveness; it is
hope and radiance—it is life at its best.
In a world of questions and fears, our hearts embrace
all possibilities when we are blessed with
New Beginnings.

Another example of "Dad being Dad" can be found in the letter he wrote to his aunt and uncle (over 20 years ago) when his cousin Roger drowned in a river in Arkansas. Roger was Dad's true-to-life "Hillbilly" cousin, with whom he speared frogs, shot guns and 'cruised' the streets of Harrisburg, Arkansas in a pick-up truck with a 6-pack of Pabst Blue Ribbon on a Saturday night. I cannot tell you how many times Dad said that scenes on television and in movies reminded him of his experiences with Roger. He told "Roger stories" a lot. (Dad particularly liked that Roger let him shoot his 357 Magnum which, according to Dirty Harry, was "the most powerful handgun in the world.")

Dad felt awful that he could not afford to go to Roger's service (a decision he has forever regretted). Instead, he sent this letter a few days before the funeral. Essentially, this was Dad's first homily (although it was delivered in absentia). He was told by a family member that the letter arrived just in time, and was used by the minister as the message for the service. Here is a copy of the letter (reprinted in the exact form in which I found it).

May 19, 1986

Dear Uncle Larry and Aunt Charlotte,

I know that nothing I say can take away the pain you are feeling right now. I, too, feel sadness that I cannot describe.

I wish I could be with you today not just to give some of the comfort you need and deserve, but to reflect on all of the wonderful memories that no one can take away from us.

Roger and I always had a very special relationship. In many ways we grew up together. During every trip to Arkansas we each taught the other a little something about the world. But I feel as though I got the best end of that deal.

Roger had more energy, more ideas and more talent than anyone I've ever known. And during his visit to Boston last year I finally had a chance to tell him how much I admired all that he could do.

I'll never forget the good times we had and how much I admired Roger.

My thoughts are with you. You are wonderful parents. I know you are (and always will be) proud of your son.

Love,
Jimmy

There was nothing too profound in this letter, but it is a nice example of my dad's loving heart and his willingness to be expressive and compassionate. It is also a good example of what I have pulled together for this eclectic collection—*My Father's Writings*.

This book could have had a dozen titles; one that I almost used was: *Novel Observations on Life: Words of Strength and Inspiration*. As you will realize as you proceed, this book can make you think, smile, cry or just reflect. It really could have been titled so many different ways; and Dad's writings could have been compiled in a dozen different ways, too. I did my best to organize them in a reasonably logical fashion, but it wasn't easy. This next piece was written many years ago after my father travelled to Michigan upon learning that his brother had a brain tumor and needed surgery. It has no title, but it is filled with raw emotion. He invites you into his heart and his struggle with this beautiful writing.

I have been a workaholic since I found out. I have been an alcoholic since I found out. Somebody once told me about a book titled, "When Bad Things Happen to Good People" or something like that; now I wish I had read it.

I tried cracking jokes with a few people on the plane. It helped, but then they made me get off the plane and they left me alone too long. The weight of the journey was unbearable by the time they found a seat for me.

Everyone was interested in my broken finger. I guess they couldn't see my broken heart. "But what about my brother," I wanted to say. I just couldn't. I hinted, but no one really knew—except for one flight attendant.

I broke the ice by asking her for the change she had forgotten to give me; I broke the real silence by asking for some assurance that I would make my connection—it appeared unlikely—and all I wanted in the whole world was to make that connection.

"You see," I finally managed to say after she responded with standard avoidance, "my brother is having brain surgery at 8 o'clock in the morning, and I have to be on that plane to Grand Rapids tonight." What I did not say was that because of what struck me as needless confusion and delay at the airport several hours before I might never get to talk to my brother again.

She heard me and pulled the ticket out of my pocket. She unlocked the door to the cockpit and disappeared behind it.

Having to ask this favor brought the reality of the situation home to me. My 27-year-old brother, with two adorable little boys and a loving wife, had a large tumor in the middle of his head. My "Rock of Gibraltar" father would be a quivering mass, my all-too-strong mother would surely break down at some point, and I would hold my sweet nephews before they went to bed that night, without their knowing that the next morning their daddy's life would be in the hands of a man they did not know. I, of course, would not cry in front of the kids lest they should suspect that their lives could change drastically in the next few hours.

By the time the flight attendant returned from the cockpit to tell me that they were going to hold my connecting flight, tears were streaming down my face and I was too choked up to say thank you. Instead, the gravity of the circumstances again overwhelmed me, and I began to sob—I think until we landed in Pittsburgh. As I exited the plane I managed to say thank you to the flight attendant who smiled and wished me good luck.

I don't even remember who picked me up at the Grand Rapids airport. I just remember walking into Mark's room and trying like hell to make the NCAA finals seem like an important topic—anything to cut through the anxiety that was floating around in that room. We all tried to make it sound like this surgery wasn't that big of a deal, and we sort of believed that until the doctor showed up a few minutes after I arrived.

He asked me and my family to leave the room while he and his assistant explained the risks and the realities of the procedure to my brother and his wife. It didn't seem like the doctor was in there all that long, but Mark and Angie were visibly upset when we returned. My mother, of course, had a lot of questions for the man who was going to try to save her son's life. The doctor exuded personal confidence, while refusing to be too positive in light of the difficulty of the operation. He said that acoustic neuromas are often removed in a matter of three or four hours. He cautioned us, however, not to have any preconceived ideas because each situation is unique.

I don't recall how I slept that night. I don't recall what I ate or what anyone talked about. I just remember arriving at the hospital at about 6 o'clock in the morning to have a few minutes with Mark before the anesthesia kicked in. I don't remember what he and I talked about that morning, there just seemed to be so little time for us between doctors and nurses coming and going.

As the various medications kicked in it brought to bear the harshness of what was about to happen. I recall the sense of helplessness and despair I felt growing as Mark became more and more groggy. I also felt that he was being far too strong—typically. He deserved better, but he didn't bring a victim's attitude to the hospital. Besides, for the first time in several weeks, the anesthesia brought him some real calm in the face of a life threatening ordeal.

No one really looked at each other very much as the families and their ministers sat around in those early morning hours. There was a sense of inevitability about the time passing, and yet it seemed to be taking an eternity for everything to get started. They finally wheeled Mark's bed down the hall and through the swinging doors that led to the operating room. He was out of sight, but the ounce of relief that came from knowing things were underway could not overcome the sense of fear and wondering that consumed me.

Whatever speculation I had about the early morning proceedings was blown away by the first visit from the operating room nurse (who happened to be a high school classmate of mine—thank God someone we knew was in there with him). She informed us, approximately 2 hours after Mark was wheeled through the swinging doors, that they had finally positioned him properly and were about to make the incision. By this time, in my (and I'm sure in the collective) mind the able doctor was well on his way to removing the large mass that was weighing on each of us much like it was pressing against Mark's brain. Hearing that the doctor had not yet really begun was a substantial setback.

We fidgeted, changed seats, went for walks, got more coffee, went for breakfast, opened our magazines, and speculated about how long we might be there. That pretty much describes the balance of the day and early evening. There was another setback, however. At about 2:00 p.m. the same nurse informed us that the doctor was using a special laser machine to remove the tumor—this machine, we had been told, would only be needed in the most delicate or difficult situations.

That was probably the third time that I went for a walk alone. Why was I so afraid to cry in front of people who felt the same way I did? I think each time I found my way to the end of the hall I wished someone had followed me so I could tell them how I felt. But no one did.

My other brother and I had lunch outside the hospital (during which time we visited a friend of his in another hospital and shopped at a sporting goods shop to break up the wait). We talked a little bit about "being brought together" by all this, but I couldn't really imagine what Gary was thinking as the brother who never seemed to understand him lay near death. Maybe I didn't fully understand the situation, but I think he was confused and terrified.

Sometime around 8:00 p.m. the doctor finally emerged to tell us that Mark was in recovery, that the operation had gone as well as could be expected under the circumstances, and that we should be pleased, but cautious, for the next 24 hours. The relief we felt was jostled immediately, however, when the doctor was paged to call a certain number; his able assistant whispered into his ear that it was "recovery." I was the only one who heard her. My chest felt frozen as the two of them dashed off to the room where I knew Mark lay in a fragile state. No serious alarm, he said when he returned moments later, a catheter adjustment was required in Mark's arm. He was alive, groggy, but awake, and already cracking jokes. Within a few minutes we would be able to see him.

Dad's brother continues to live a joyful and healthy life. (And, yes, those two little boys got to grow up with a father.) What an emotional experience it must have been to cry openly on a plane, and be somewhat panicked about possibly never getting to see your brother alive again. Reading this makes me wonder whether it was at all humiliating to have to speak through public tears, and ask a flight attendant to see if a plane can be held just for you. As someone with a brother I adore, I think it's safe to say that most of us would do whatever it takes at that moment to try to get a few precious moments with a sibling.

Next I want to share some of the other things that Dad left behind with the title of "Introduction" or "Outline." The very existence of these writings would seem to be *further* evidence that he planned to write more than one book some day. But before we get to those, I want to share another of Dad's Holiday Letters. This one is a good example of Dad's subject matter reaching beyond "what we did on our summer vacation."

Holiday Letter

Year-end retrospectives usually single out "watershed" events or so-called "pivotal" developments in our lives. Most of us can point to a few such events—a baby is born, a loved one dies, an unexpected bonus, a challenging illness, a child goes to college or gets married, an article is published, or you land a dream job. These events are easy to recognize. This holiday season, however, our hope is to better understand the incredible impact of more modest events—the kind that occur in our lives every day: thanking the hard-working counter clerk for keeping the popcorn line moving; telling a flight attendant that you appreciate his upbeat attitude; meeting with a friend's child who wants to learn more about the college you attended; letting your little one sleep in your bed on a rainy night; spending a day counseling someone whose spirit is bigger than her pocketbook; or looking your child or spouse directly in the eye and saying "do you know how much I love you?"

These simple acts of kindness and encouragement can have an impact on someone for a lifetime. Our hope is to define the coming year by these "little profound" events—the kind that touch lives in a gentle, meaningful way. My Baci candy wrapper said: "Happiness is all around us, we just have to find it." Being a parent (while certainly a blessing) presents a lot of opportunities to test this philosophy. But when people who know our children well tell us how great they are, we feel particularly blessed. The kind words of these teachers, coaches,

31

and parents bring us happiness, and make Nancy and me feel like the luckiest people in the world.

On Halloween, our daughter Lindsay walked into her kindergarten class and saw her teacher dressed up as a scarecrow. After a quick assessment of the situation, Lindsay approached her and said: "Mrs. Harvey, I love your costume . . . you are making everyone smile." It just doesn't get any better than that. Lindsay encourages and compliments other kids, as well. Her willingness to express her true feelings, without reservation, should be a model for us all. On politics and *Decision 2000* she said: "No one really wins, because there's no prize." I suspect that she might be a victim of my self-help obsession. The other day she said: "Nobody's perfect, right Dad? But everyone is okay just the way they are, right?" (How do you support and encourage such a loving attitude without misleading her about the reality that there are people who do "bad things" that are not okay? Ahh, the joys of parenting.)

Lindsay scored four goals in her first soccer game, seldom scored again, and then decided to retire before the season ended. She is taking gymnastics and violin lessons. While she really does a good job playing the violin, her classmate's father may have summed it up best when he said, "they really look well holding their violins." Our son Brian's idea of sports is to watch figure skating, gymnastics and other sports on TV. He was greatly conflicted when the Olympics (which he called: "mark, set, go") pre-empted Wheel of Fortune, his all time favorite show!

We continue to see modest, but meaningful progress in Brian's expressive language development. (He has always had good comprehension.) His teachers get a little gushy when they talk about Brian's amazing capacity to draw out love from those around him. According to one report, he is like the Mayor when he walks around the school. He continues to order people to hug each other, and he continues to show an incredible capacity for intellectual and emotional growth. He loves going to school. When he is home, he constantly says: "Cass" (short for his wonderful teacher, Mrs. Castle) while rubbing our arms gently. This is his way of indicating that he is being cooperative and gentle at school with his classmates and teachers. We believe that there is a lot of expression and insight that wants to come out of Brian, but it may take a miracle to really tap it all. (Prayers are welcome and appreciated.) The challenges of raising a child with special needs are many, but not even close to the joys. Then there are the challenges of raising a teenager. Yikes! Our other son, Andrew, continues his pattern of physical, emotional and personal growth. (When Lindsay draws family portraits, Andrew is always considerably taller than the rest of us. His shoe size: 13.) Andrew entered 9th grade with the typical questions and concerns of a kid making the move to High School, but so far he has managed it just fine. He has met a few modest goals, such as: doing well academically, starting at quarterback for the freshman football team, getting elected to the Class Council, getting on an AAU baseball team, and spending more social time with his friends. He was a power-hitter and 1st baseman on the 8th grade baseball team last spring, and he wouldn't mind playing for the varsity this year. (It will not surprise me if he makes it.)

Andrew's mom would probably trade a couple of touchdown passes for a couple more "A's," but I must say it was great fun watching him lead the football team through a solid season. In one particularly great win, he got hit on virtually every play, but he showed a toughness and resolve that made me—and his coach—very proud. He demonstrates an uncanny sense of humor, along with an ability to write with clarity, wit and insight. More importantly, perhaps, he managed his fantasy baseball team to a league championship, surviving a strong challenge from his grandfather—and *former* mentor . . . .

Nancy makes a living running Watson enterprises. She somehow manages to manage everything from the finances of my business, to the feeding, care and social lives of us all. Our home is beautiful, not just because she decorates it, but because she is in it. We probably depend on her too much around here, so it is good for us to share her with the rest of the world. Notwithstanding all that she does for us, she still has more to give. So, she can now be found on a variety of church and school committees, in addition to her existing involvement in The Women's Exchange and other volunteer efforts. Once again, she has created a wonderful Christmas of love and giving for us and for others. We could never thank her enough for all she is and all that she does—except, maybe, to give her a few days of sleep.

My year can be summed up by the fact that I have Executive Platinum status with American Airlines. (I am comparably admired by other airlines.) Actually, it was a terrific year for my training and consulting business. But the highlights of my year were many and varied. There was the Katz Bar Mitzvah, which was a genuine celebration of triumph and love; picking up Lindsay on the morning of her first sleep over; watching Andrew "stiff" a 4 iron to about 8 feet into a strong wind on a 183-yard ocean hole in Bermuda; a spontaneous Broadway musical review performed by Jill and Peter Stevens (and another talented friend) in their den during a beautiful evening in Dallas; flying with Andrew to Chicago to see the White Sox and Cubs play on consecutive nights; writing a poem for a couple I did not know; writing lyrics to a country song (anyone know a publisher?); attending all of Lindsay's wonderful school assemblies; listening to Brian utter new words; my trusted assistant becoming a mom; and discovering a great little poem ("Guiding a stray bee out of the house; enough work for one day.") Every moment I spent working and talking with my friend, Chris Sargent, was special. He is one of the most brilliant and courageous people I will ever know. Chris inspired me in my business, now he inspires me in my life as he lives life in a passionate and loving way.

In *The Legend of Bagger Vance* we are told that golf (like life) is not a game you can win. It is to be played and enjoyed, as you look for the one authentic swing that is in all of us. Thoreau said it this way:

"I went to the woods because I wished to live deliberately, to front only the essential facts of life, and see if I should not learn what it had to teach, and not, when I came to die, discover that I had not lived. I did not wish to live what was not life, living is so dear . . ."

Living is so dear! A friend of mine, who is going through a difficult divorce, recently told me of his discovery that a lot of happiness can be found in the midst of adversity. We shared the irony that we often need to go through hell to discover that Heaven is right here on Earth. If you read *The Four Agreements* you will discover that the ancient Toltecs believed they could find Heaven on Earth by: being true to your word, not taking anything personally, not making assumptions and always doing your best. It's a great book, and you can't go wrong with its teachings, but I think we can find Heaven on Earth by simply living the two greatest Commandments: 'Love the Lord thy God . . . . and love your neighbor as yourself.' What a wonderful world it would be.

I often wonder what those who have gone before us would say if they could speak to us directly. I think it would be something like: 'Live with genuine love, empathy and humility as you play your round of life; keep score with smiles and helpfulness; when you go out of bounds, recover; when you are in the sand, blast out with confidence. Take a caddy to help you find your way; don't try to do it all alone. Love yourself,' they might say, 'because you look glorious from up here.' Well, to those of you who have passed on I ask: did I get it right? We miss, but will always love, the dearly departed. After all, they are what Angels are made of.

Merry Christmas. Happy Chanukah. Happy Holidays.

Love, the Watsons

Chapter Three

BOOK INTRODUCTIONS, OUTLINES AND ARTICLE IDEAS MY DAD LEFT BEHIND

I found a document called "A Draft Book Introduction" on the hard-drive of one of my father's old computers. This short piece reveals a lot about Dad's thinking . . . and I continue to be amazed at how much he thought about death and his legacy.

A Draft Book Introduction

"It was just a little before noon, a month before his 21st birthday, when Ethan began the incredible process of orchestrating his life and death. He started writing a script for his memorial service. He had experienced the power of bereavement as a transforming tool, and he believed that the way to have the greatest impact in the world would be to die with a plan.

Ethan wasn't crazy really. Oh, he was obsessed, to be sure, with the idea that we all have an important role to play in the grand scheme of things. His vision was that he could do the greatest good for the most people by planning a life that would lead to a tremendous outpouring of spirit, love and compassion in a carefully planned death. What the heck, Ethan thought, we are going to die anyway, so why not do it right? Why not make every minute on this earth count toward leaving it a better place? No one questions the Dali Lama's life of sacrifice, he thought. This just ups the ante a bit.

Ethan was not the cult type. He didn't want to control people, just influence them. He believed that real change could come from unleashing widespread goodness and riding the wave of peoples' heartfelt responses to it.

He did not come to the decision of planning a profound death lightly or quickly. There was a history—a history that explains a lot, but not everything . . ."

This little cliffhanger makes me wonder if Dad actually had ideas for finishing the story, or if he just hoped inspiration would strike and he would return to it. Obviously, we will never know.

It is, of course, as revealing to know what someone reads, as it is to read what they wrote. Dad's book collection would give you reason to think he was a pop-culture, spiritual explorer, self-help junkie.

Looking at the books scattered across many shelves in almost every room of the house reveals that he was in search of something ranging from meaning and inspiration to acceptance and a better golf game. (It was probably all of the above.) A *very* small sampling of the books he had read all or part of include: *The Re-enchantment of Everyday Life; Do What You Love, The Money Will Follow; The Alchemist; The Path to Love; The Legend of Bagger Vance; and The Game of Life and How to Play It.* The presence of these books and others he owned makes it very clear that he was obsessed with stirring his Soul—and maybe the souls of others, too. Like mine . . . . check this out.

Recently at dinner with friends, the question was posed to me: "Do you believe in predestination?" Without even reflecting I blurted out that I believe we all have a destiny to fulfill, and that we will achieve it if we make all of our decisions based upon integrity and love. As the night went on, I pontificated a bit about the fact that I think we have the freedom to choose how we live and where we end up (literally and metaphorically) in life, and that all paths lead to the right place if we are true to our intuitive Spirit. My goodness, I thought as I sat there, I have turned into my father! Then I went home and found this poem that he had written.

On Apparent Predestination

Is it possible to fail to see
a script being written, the subject, me?
Without a voice,
I have no choice,
but to live with the hope
that I can cope
with the plot that leads me
through this life;
confident of no future strife.

Allowed to move within the frame,
trepidation flows from threatened fame.
So careful now to choose my way,
no doubt I have some modest say,
in what's to come and where
I've been,
but less with whom,
just how and when.

Why trouble self with plans and dreams
since life proceeds, or so it seems,
without my holding all the reins,
without avoiding all the pains
that live nearby in actions true.
No doubt some sign will let me heed
that moment where I embrace the sight
of where the path will lead
each night.

I like the signs, as paths unfold,
so much of what I see foretold
is true to prayers in quiet time,
of future spirit, so sublime.
If it were not so right and clear,
emotions would be lost in fear;
making days of joy less real

as doubts replace the trusting feel
of life without a God this night—
no care to know, as all is right.

I never imagined myself in a meaningful discussion about predestination—and I certainly never thought I would initiate such a conversation. But that is the kind of impact Dad had on me (and others). He caused me to love more deeply, question things reverently, and accept more compassionately. This poem still makes me think about so much that goes on in the world. I haven't really thought too much about it, but I think I may have a tad more intellectual curiosity than many people. Maybe I should thank Dad for that.

My father kept looking for "the Source;" for the beginning of his passion for spiritual and emotional exploration. Maybe it was divinely programmed before he came to be in this worldly body. Then again, maybe it started decades ago when he felt painfully alone as a child, starved for love, and spent much of his free time selling golf balls on the 6th tee at a golf course near his home.

Maybe the stirring started when he fell off a porch at age five and broke his nose—an event and an injury about which no one knew for days. Maybe the loneliness started when he fell out of the top bunk at age six and it was my aunt who consoled him, even though his mother was there. Yes, Dad had shared a number of stories of childhood loneliness with me over the years.

Writers from Freud to the present-day Pop Culture gurus write about how our childhood "programming" stays with us for life. If we felt love, comfort and safety as a child, we will bring love, confidence and courage with us into adulthood. If we experienced rejection and fear, and we grew up longing for unconditional love, then we will likely lead fearful lives. (And, yes, we will inevitably look for love in all the wrong places.)

If we all read as many self-help books as Dad did, we would likely become as confused as he was. Should we forgive and show great love to parents who did their best, but stumbled, trying to raise us without an instruction book? (Or does that pose the risk of further rejection?) Would it be better to cut loose emotionally and just move on, seeing our parents objectively as people we know and love, but in the same way that we know and love our neighbors? Should we talk to them about what they "did to us" or just let it go? Is there some choice other than facing it or burying it?

Dad's preoccupation with turning all experiences into life lessons certainly runs through most of his writings. As he mentioned in one of his draft book introductions, he struggled for decades to try to understand and find enlightenment in his parental relationships. He particularly wanted to better understand his mother. He just couldn't reconcile her apparent love and admiration for him with the more discernible criticism that he experienced.

If there is any truth to the idea that our childhood has an impact on our adulthood, however, then his mother should get some credit for having overcome her own significant difficulties in her early years—and again later in life. Between having a nervous breakdown as a teenager, and starting a battle with Multiple Sclerosis in her 30's, Grandma could have punted many times. But she didn't. She showed real resilience, and moved into a place of love as she grew older.

I guess my dad mostly wanted us to appreciate, understand, accept, and forgive the imperfections of those who raised us. Or so it seems from this essay I found in a folder labeled "Parenting." The document title was "Words that Might be Said at My Mother's Memorial Service." Should I be surprised that Dad chose a funeral setting to share some of his thoughts about his mom . . . ? Of course, when he wrote this, Grandma was very much alive.

Words that Might be Said at My Mother's Memorial Service

My parents had children at what we would say today was a very young age. They started a family in an era when childrearing was not complicated by Dr. Spock's concerns with hugs and self-esteem—an era when people were not quite so open with their feelings. The economic circumstances of our early years as a family were challenging—money was in short supply, and Dad had to work long hard hours doing multiple jobs to keep us fed and in clothes.

Think about most of the 21-year-olds you know today—how prepared are they *really* to demonstrate strong emotional stability, manage a household and make critical decisions about a child's development? Simply stated: Mom and Dad grew up with their kids. You could call this experience the ultimate form of on-the-job-training.

So why do I go back to my family's roots in what most of you would expect to be a straight-forward, loving tribute to my mother?

I mention the early years because they are relevant to our later years—mine and Mom's. Clearly, wherever we are in life is a reflection of everything we have felt, learned and experienced before. We are the product of our collective experience (and some genes, of course).

As we get older we learn that our parents weren't perfect. They weren't perfect in the way they raised us, and they weren't perfect in the way they lived their lives. Psychologists would probably say this should not come as a surprise to us, but doesn't that depend on where in our development this realization occurs? For some, it is in those tumultuous teenage years when the combination of raging hormones and the knowledge of your parent's imperfections result in rebellion. For others, the realization comes later in life; and for some, mom and dad probably never fall off the pedestal.

As we learn about the ways in which our mothers may have let us down, led us astray, or bruised our emotions, we can respond with anger and resentment, or we can offer understanding and forgiveness. The former comes from a place of bitterness, the latter from a place of love.

My hope is that in having a few minutes to share my thoughts and feelings with this group in the wake of Mom's death, we can find ways to make her passing lead you to find more love and forgiveness in your hearts for everyone in your lives who is imperfect—your parents, your spouses, your children, your grandchildren, your friends and, yes, even your enemies.

From the days of the Old Testament until today, we have heard a lot about the value (and reward) of loving our enemies and offering forgiveness to those who may have wronged us; I believe in the healing power of forgiveness, and so did Mom.

So here's the deal—Mom may not have hugged me enough or told me she loved me enough to satisfy my inner child. She might have scowled at me when I screwed up more than she smiled at me when I did well, but those things do not define her feelings or her love for me (or my brothers).

What defines her as a person is the whole package—what defines her as a mom was her courage, her caring and her spirituality.

Courage

How many moms had the courage to coach a kid's youth football team when none of the dads could step up to do it? How many moms had the courage to drive the family dog of more than a decade to the vet to have him put down without asking for help? I don't know of many moms who took their 14-year old son hunting and on a long train trip to Washington, D.C. I wonder how many moms in their 30's were strong enough to go back to school and get a high school degree in the 1960's when moms were not typically concerned with being educated? We could spend a lot of time listing examples of her courage. She had the courage to admit that God performed miracles in her life—slowing the pace of her MS after an intensely spiritual prayer session. There wasn't much that Mom was afraid of.

Caring

How great was it that Mom took my side in the family debate about whether or not as a 12-year-old I could buy my first stereo and join a record club with my summer savings?

She fought to get me on a little league baseball team even though it would interfere with our family weekend trips to the lake.

Mom persuaded my dad to buy a more expensive house than we could probably afford closer to the school so I could spend more time with my friends.

Mine was the mom who allowed me to experience as much of life as possible—though she struggled with the idea of me going off to college and reaching my potential.

Mom's caring nature showed when my friends turned to her because they were afraid to go to their own parents with problems;

she was the mom who opened up her home to my best friend in high school so he could finish his senior year with our class (after his parents moved away).

Of course, she (and Dad) were the parents who were always there. They were in the audience for every sporting event I ever played in, every speech I ever made, every award ceremony and team dinner; every school function. Oh, yeah, and she put dinner on the table every night without fail.

Spirituality

As many of you know, Mom was diagnosed with Multiple Sclerosis when she was 35 years old. She spent a lifetime walking normally, resisting the disease. She absolutely believed that it was her faith—her answered prayer—that held the deterioration of MS at bay. It started catching up with her much later in life, but her faith remained strong.

Indeed, as she got older, Mom grew even closer to God, discovering God's goodness in the wonderful people she met in the Baldwin Methodist Church.

Her faith—and her courage—were revealed profoundly in the testimony she shared with the congregation at that church. Mom was not inclined to do public speaking, but she trusted God to give her the strength to tell her story to the people she loved—and she did it.

Courage, caring (maybe a little too much) and spirituality all rolled into one. That was my mother. That is what I want to remember; the journey of learning we made together.

I remember my dad once saying he was "locked in an emotional battle" in his effort to figure out his relationship with his mother. Yet these words he has written here paint a rather clear and comfortable picture of a knowing connection to her. By digging a bit I learned that Dad had written these words about his mother soon after his mother-in-law had a stroke. I called her "Mrs. R," and she was someone both Dad and I admired a lot.

Dad thought it was curious that on the day he had set aside time to write "the things you might say at your mother's funeral," his mother-in-law suffered a serious stroke. (She died six days later.)

The following passages were found among Dad's stacks of notes. It is obvious that he was very fond of his in-laws. Not only had he saved these few words he had written about Mrs. R, but he also had written some beautiful reflections of his father-in-law to be read for the internment of his ashes (see below). Here's what was in the folder.

As we are planning this beautiful memorial service in Regina's honor, I heard what her three children planned to say, and I experienced the REAL emotion of a mother's death. It made me think twice about writing about my own mother's mortality, realizing that this is not a place I may wish to go in advance—voluntarily.

As we collected her children's writings for the service, I read one moving tribute after another, as Regina's children shared myriad memories of nurturing, support, guidance and values. My wife's heartfelt list of "things I will miss about Mom" made people alternately laugh and cry. They reflect so much of the wonderful and unique person she was. Someone I grew closer to every passing year. She was an amazing woman. Here is Nancy's list:

Nancy's List of The Things She Will Miss About Her Mom:

I will miss a Mom who was so concerned about being fair that she counted the jelly beans and the green beans

I will miss Mom's brown sugar brownies and cherry squares—and the precise way she cut them

I will miss how fast she walked, her beige clothes, her perfect handwriting

I will miss our shopping trips to Talbots (I tried to be patient)

I will miss Mom's very special "Mimi" relationship with [her special needs Grandson] Brian

I will miss just barely beating Mom at ping pong

I will miss working with Mom to prepare holiday dinners filled with family traditions

I will miss a mom who actually let me do cartwheels in the house

I will miss how Lindsay [one of her Granddaughters] could warm Mom with her open heartfelt expressions of love

I will miss overhearing Mom's telephone calls with Auntie Dorothy that were filled with laughter

I will miss Mom on Christmas Eve; she fit in so beautifully with our dearest friends

I will miss teasing Mom about how much time she spent at the grocery store

I imagine that it was pretty hard for Dad to be a part of this outpouring of emotion for his mother-in-law, without publicly expressing his own feelings for her. But Dad was not asked to contribute remarks for the memorial service. He told me once that he had written something just in case, but I could not find it. But I did find the warm and loving words of tribute that Dad wrote about his father-in-law, Paul. They were never read publicly, but they were buried with Paul's ashes; they reveal a lot about how much Dad loved him. Frankly, if I am ever in the role of father or father-in-law, it would be amazing if anyone would ever say anything so glowing about me!

Dear Paul,

I was proud to be your son-in-law. I was proud to introduce you to my friends; and I wanted to include you in my life as much as possible. But I wasn't just proud of you, I also loved you—I loved spending time with you, just doing guy stuff. I loved your stories, no matter how often you repeated them. I am going to miss you terribly.

I appreciated the way you welcomed me into your family and accepted me for who I am. I learned so much from you about seeing the best in people, about playing by the rules and about having fun in almost any situation.

I want to thank you for raising a daughter who embodies all that was great about you—I am the luckiest guy in the world to have her as my wife.

Thank you for always being there when I needed some guidance, a golf companion, or even a short-term loan! There was no limit to your supportiveness.

Thank you for letting Andrew know you as "Mr. P"—you were a special grandfather figure to him. He said he wanted to hit a home run for you Wednesday night—a day after you died—and he did.

When you marry a man's only daughter, there is nothing you want more than to impress, or at least connect with, him. You were the kind of person who made that connection a breeze.

Whenever people would ask me about my father-in-law, I would say that he was the most decent man in the world—he was honest, ethical, easygoing, funny, accepting, humble, and grateful for the wonderful life and family he had been blessed with.

I am someone who looks for the presence of Spirit in every situation. One of my favorite examples of divine intervention occurred a few months ago when I visited you in the hospital.

The two of us were sitting in your hospital room, and you were really quiet and tired. You handed me the remote and asked me to see what was on. For you to give up the clicker was a profound spiritual event—but it gets better. As I started clicking around, I landed on a boxing match. I knew how much you loved boxing, even though you didn't follow it seriously.

Your eyes lit up. The color in your face got a little richer, and you even found the strength to lean towards me and say that the interns reminded you of a bunch of Boy Scouts that took themselves too seriously!

A guy's dream is to find a phenomenal woman as a companion—when you find her, and she comes with a wonderful family, it is a bonus; when that family includes a father-in-law like you, it's like winning the lottery.

You were as close to being a second father to me as anyone could ever be. There were no secrets, no qualms with expressing our feelings to each other, no limits to our comfort with each other.

I loved it when you retired and had business cards made which said: "no office, no phone, no money." I would add "no doubt, that life is good." Life was very good the way you lived it.

Lindsay called you "Ahbie," and she says "Ahbie is home" every time the doorbell rings or someone knocks. And while it's hard to explain to her what has happened, it makes me smile because she's right. There is a piece of you in everyone who arrives at the door; there is a part of you in the good that is in each of us.

I sometimes tell people to take a few seconds to think about those parts of themselves they most admire—the most decent parts; the parts that love most deeply and give most freely. Those are the parts of you that will always be with us. Although I will miss you, I know you are not really gone. You live on as the best parts of each of us—whenever I see something special in someone, I will see you.

There is a new bright shining star in the Universe. You have assumed your place in the heavens, where we will all join you one day. Keep working on your short game—I'll see you at the 19th hole. Yes, Ahbie is home.

With Love,
Jim

And the beat goes on, this time with Dad writing about his own father. I found a couple of pages of my father's writings that foreshadowed yet another book idea he had. He wanted to write a book in which he captured his own father's stories; yes, he hoped to write a book about his father's life. (I know this father-son thing is now getting really confusing, but bear with me.)

My grandfather owns over 100 acres of hunting land which he loves as much as life itself. He is happy when he walks the land, hunts, or just clears trees on the property. My dad wanted to sit in the woods with a tape recorder asking his father a bunch of questions about what it was like to grow up on a farm in Arkansas, moving to Michigan to work in factories and gas stations; were there any strange relatives? Pivotal events? Regrets?

As a child my dad overheard his father tell a lot of stories. He remembered hearing about picking cotton, daylong hunting trips with a 'coon hound' at his side; memorable foot races, American Legion baseball games Grandpa played in, and frozen bed warmers. Dad wanted to capture for posterity the experiences that his father had growing up. Ironically, it is *MY* father's memories that now need to be preserved, with Grandpa having outlived his son.

Frankly, some people found my grandfather's incessant storytelling painfully detailed. He could go on for 15 or 20 minutes about the simple act of oiling his log-splitter and cutting up an old tree. But many of Grandpa's stories from his childhood captured real – and amazing – experiences from a world most of us will never know. So Dad's idea of getting his father to talk on tape was terrific; it just never happened. What follows is, instead, an untitled story my dad had written about his father and his book idea. It is not Dad's best writing, but it is interesting.

The ability to tell a good story is a blessing; it's a skill that should not be left unused by those who have the gift. While growing up, I remember hanging on every word of my father's stories about his childhood, and his journey from the farms and fields of Arkansas to the factories of Michigan. When I got older I realized that the power of his stories was in the detail; and what sustained the listener's interest was the passion with which he would describe even the most mundane events.

If there is a subject for which no amount of passion would be sufficient to sustain an audience, however, it would be the linear recountations of a non-famous person moving from one stage to the next in a largely ordinary life. If, however, you could capture the most powerful emotions, the most challenging situations and the most thought provoking muses of this otherwise ordinary human being, it strikes me that a reader's interest might be peaked; and the story—if not bound by too much logic or order—could (like a good seminar) deliver some pearls of wisdom, some motivation and a little bit of entertainment.

It may seem unscholarly to simply turn on a recorder, ask my father questions about his life and just let it run. (God can he talk!) But if we start with the premise that in each of us there is some genius, some unique experiences that, when shared, can open up new ways of thinking for others, then I guess this idea is not one to be treated lightly. A published 'Q&A' with real people discussing issues we think about (or should think about) could be a good thing. The setting may change, and the themes may be different, but what will not change is the idea that experiencing new insights and feelings through shared experiences and literature can help us think differently and expand our worlds. It might come across as a little random, but what a ride it could be.

But to the extent that a book of conversation is *intended* to stimulate thoughts, actions, and memories, it is not "random" at all. (Although an element of randomness allows for the freedom to seize on the essential—like picking through a collection of unrelated short stories.) Everything you read in a book of conversations should seem real. You would decide where the boundaries lie and how the stories relate to you and your own life.

I once heard someone say that it was a writer's prerogative to exaggerate without accountability. But unless it's a novel, I do not completely agree. And I have learned that it is usually not necessary to exaggerate the real thoughts, real actions, and real feelings of the people we observe (or sometimes even imagine. I could argue that imagination is not exaggeration.)

The dictionary defines "provocative" as "tending to provoke or stimulate." I would define it as "something that causes us to think new thoughts, question assumptions and try new things." The equation might read "provocative = facts + creativity—the mundane." But where does that leave Alfred E. Neuman and his boyish face in the overall scheme of things? Maybe provocative is simply a word for the impact of myriad intense stimuli, not the least of which could be shared conversations and the observation of seemingly benign experiences and images applied to us.

But before I lose you on a trip to Never Land, let's pick up in the middle of another trip . . . a trip home from Pittsburgh in the middle of a trip through life.

Believe it or not, I actually know what my dad meant by that last sentence. (But I don't have a clue where the Alfred E. Newman reference came from. I recall Dad saying that he subscribed to *MAD* magazine as a kid, so some sick psychological connection to that experience must have bubbled to the surface.)

One of the best writings I found (IMHO) was what prompted him to reference "a trip home from Pittsburgh in the middle of a trip through life." That was the working subtitle for another of my dad's attempts at writing a novel. Back in the late 80's the convergence of my brother Casey's death and Dad's purchase of a MacPlus (complete with a 20 MB external hard drive) inspired him to continue writing after he had delivered the Homily at the memorial service. He was thrilled when he realized that he could actually "save" a document, go back to it, make changes, and save the new version, thus opening up a world of possibilities. He told me he used to put his Little League batting line-ups in that ancient computer (when he was coaching me), along with a resignation letter to his boss, expense reports, and more. He also used that first computer to start writing about the thoughts and experiences of a man sitting on a plane before take-off.

Dad subsequently lost the pages he had written; and, of course, he couldn't recall what he had written. He had only printed this kernel of a "manuscript" once. And years after that little old hard drive had been disposed of, he said he was sure those pages were gone forever. This actually hit him rather hard, not only because he liked what he wrote, but also because he had shared the writing with Nancy who looked up after reading the few pages he had written and said that she wanted more! Dad told me he could tell that she really meant it. That was high praise, because Nancy reads a lot of fiction.

Imagine how thrilled I was when, in my obsessive search for everything Dad had ever written, I found a folder that contained those magic words about sitting on a plane in Pittsburgh! Here they are. See if you think it would have been fun to have this novel continue . . . .

"REFLECTIONS WITHOUT BOUNDARIES"

It was one of those blustery winter days in Pittsburgh. The wind was throwing sleet against the airplane window as we awaited takeoff. My thoughts were still back at the hotel where I had just consummated a torrid two-day affair with a steamy French heiress. Someone tapped me on the shoulder and I was startled back to reality.

Why is fantasy always cut short? The frustration of life's events had driven me into a stranger's arms, and I wanted to linger there for a few minutes. Smoke, mirrors and dreams had turned the not-so-steamy accountant with whom I had romped, into the French heiress of my imagination. Besides, I wasn't with her for days, it was hours, and it hardly qualified as an affair . . .

The tap on my shoulder that spoiled my potentially wild dream was the act of another passenger pointing out that my checkbook had fallen to the floor near my seat. Little did this guy know that he had sabotaged my intimate reflection to save me from losing something that was of very little value to me—money. (I don't know whether the daydream was "valuable" or not.)

The leather-cased checkbook was a gift from an old girlfriend whose disappointment in my failure to commit fed me a steady dose of guilt like drops of medicine from a hospital tube. Intravenously administered pain is the worst kind; it nourishes some deep, destructive impulse that is stronger than our ability to break free emotionally.

The package is not the "thing." The check case was smooth, soft-leather, but had inside it something I cared little about. Similarly, I did not care enough for (or perhaps the better word is "appreciate") that which was inside the giver of the gift: a wonderful spirit and unconditional love. Her epitaph will surely say: "Here lies a person whose spirit, honesty, and sensitivity were unsurpassed" (. . . until recently).

I was never fair to her, and yet she never accused me of any wrongdoing. Her trust lengthened the relationship much more than pressure or accusations would have—it also magnified my discomfort with the all-too-abrupt ending brought about by my virtual blindness to what was right for me. All of this was even more real right now, as I waited on the runway to return to the mistake that triggered the guilt.

When I knew the giver of the checkbook, my unconscious, but passionate, search for status, power and the trappings of wealth—all of which were wrong for me, but not necessarily for everyone—insulated my heart from the loving and caring she offered. These things also strangled my own goodness and perspective. Does that make the checkbook a symbol? Is it, perhaps, a perverse, periodic reminder of those bygone years filled with unconscious insensitivity?

Since her reign as queen companion had clearly come to an end, why am I lingering on the subject? I think, but am not sure, that these ruminations work somehow to illustrate the depth—call it the tragedy—of my unconscious condition. Thinking these thoughts has the cathartic effect of a long overdue apology. And the string of these appreciative feelings helps to warm a hidden chill in my heart, by providing a sharp contrast to both the weather and the circumstances that currently surround my life.

You must understand that one does not generally "know" one's condition, we just think we do, at least I always thought I did. I can say definitely that my troubled condition (my loneliness and pain) was completely buried beneath layers of illusion and justification. ("Repressed" is probably the right word, but it is much too clinical, and I am not qualified clinically.)

I have this strange sense that many of my friends might identify with the gift giver; I fear that they, too, may feel cheated out of the reality of meaningful friendship. They could honestly claim that I never really let them know who I was, even though they gave me many opportunities to reveal myself. This is something I should reconcile both internally and elsewhere. In the meantime, however, I am driven simply to recount the pain and pose the questions, lest the voice speaking to me (surprisingly clearly at times) should fade, and the opportunity for deep reflection lost.

Speaking of fear, I have neglected to say that I have a rather substantial fear of flying. This seems almost oxymoronic though, since my real fear is of landing—perhaps it's because after landing, at least today, I will once again begin pretending. My current preoccupation with fantasy, change, passion, and self-improvement may well be driven by the underlying fear that when this plane leaves the ground I am prohibitively helpless in shaping the outcome of the flight, not unlike the subtle helplessness I all too often experience as I contemplate the outcome of my life.

The team of engineers, pilots, and controllers that were charged with getting this plane safely to its destination were trained extensively in reading radar screens, gauges and indicators of all things that mattered. Metaphysically and emotionally we are not nearly so well trained in the art of finding our way from here to there; but I suspect that there are many ways to deal with bleeps on the moral and mental screen. Therapy is certainly an option. But if you are dealing with any of the issues contemplated here, that is a road you should already be on.

Artistic expression, writing (an artistic expression in some forms), meditation, and religion are options (contemplative, involved religious activity—not religion by ritual). But what about fantasy?

If we knew for certain that unexacerbated, unruly fantasy was somehow good for us, then we would hope that this ultimate coping mechanism could be harnessed and directed. Just imagine your doctor telling you to go home and spend two days in bed thinking about punching out your least favorite relative or having sex with your favorite one . . . .

Where was this plane taking me anyway? I felt a little bit like someone who was awakened in the middle of the night and needed a few minutes to figure out where he was. An upbeat but gentle voice came over the sound system reminding me and the others on board that this plane was headed for Atlanta.

The announcement said we should notify a flight attendant if Atlanta was not our intended destination. I began to wonder if I would have spoken up if I had mistakenly boarded a plane to Hawaii or some other desirable geography where I might be able to disappear without a trace. Actually, I've always considered those who disappeared by choice to have committed suicide in a social sort of way. No personal tribulation, however painful, could ever push me to that extreme. But I must admit that the thought of being on the wrong plane, going to a great place—someplace where I could be a complete stranger—intrigued me right now.

Illusion and fantasy must play some positive role in the world. Otherwise, I, and others similarly distracted, are, at worst, subtly self-destructing, or, at best, wasting a lot of time. True magic would be in finding the ability to turn into reality only those dreams which were personally honest and morally correct; casting aside without remorse or embellishment those disreputable fantasies that serve as no more than a pressure valve for coping. Only the experts can tell you if such a formula would amount to "self-teasing," and whether a parade of anti-social dreams would invariably lead to anti-social behavior. (Maybe they just toughen the skin.) Relax, I'm not going to get into what is "moral." For now, just think of morality in terms of the basics: "thou shalt not . . ." 1 through 10.

The plane is now in flight. When it lands I will be faced with the real issue of where to hide and for how long—only partially certain of what I am hiding from.

For the moment, the world of the plane and the rush of my thoughts have created a small place of peace. The present has become too painful to contemplate, but I am finding my way out . . .

I know I keep saying this, but I think my father would have been able to write a novel. This raw and unpolished piece of writing shows signs of great imagination, and a clear ability to tell a story with the written word. But he was such a perfectionist! He said it would take him a lifetime to write a novel because he "wanted to get every detail right, and never miss a chance to make the story better or a description richer." But as we see throughout these writings, he had a lot of starts and stops.

Just as Dad was always trying to improve his writing, his golf game, his martini-making skills and his marketing savvy, he also worked hard at being a better father. I found the following piece, which I recognized to have been written about 18 years ago, as a result of an experience I had at a day care center. Dad came to visit me at lunchtime at least once or twice a week at New Horizons—even though the facility was all the way across town from where he worked. He also picked me up there a couple of nights each week.

One day at pickup time he learned that I had had "an issue" on the playground. Apparently, he was moved to write this essay, which I had never seen before. I find it interesting that it is written in the 3rd person.

Lessons from Parenting

Is there a chapter in one of those books about raising children that deals with "fighting back"? How do you teach a sweet three-and-a-half year-old boy, who has been taught that "it's not nice to hit," to screw protocol and whack the little sucker who just kicked him to the ground from the lower level of the climbing structure? The thought of this precious child hiding under a playground fixture "so no one else would kick me" (his words, not mine) tore at his father's guts. Or was it tearing at the dad because of his own childhood memories?

In a sense, the father's pain-filled response was both intensified and softened by the fact that he had been there himself. The boy seemed okay now, but what had he been through and was he really okay? And was it significant that the dad still never really fought back (not even against the sweet boy's not always sweet mother)? It's all quite complicated. Not just generally complicated, but specifically complicated.

First of all, by having not anticipated and prepared the good child for the attack by the not-so-good child, there was no planned response; there was no reaction blueprint giving either the victim or his father a framework within which to respond. Ergo, the father's response was purely from the heart and soul—an outward manifestation of what was going on inside. Perhaps that was true also of the child.

Second, the father has memories—not so pleasant memories—of his own childhood responses to bullies. Unfortunately, there is a gap, a lapse of details (from repression, perhaps) in the father's memory. Concealed somewhere was the event (or series of events) that had transformed the dad from childhood enforcer to a teenage wimp, and from a teenage wimp to an uncertain adult.

The complications multiply like mosquitoes in a marsh.

In stark contrast to his "jock" father, the good child has a rather pacifist mother. The mother cannot witness two minutes of a football game without expressing discomfort about the violence, and she passes out at the first sight of a good old-fashioned black eye.

The sweet boy lives in two homes; he's with this mother too much; he's not with her enough. He's not with his father enough, at least not in the real world that includes pain, suffering and bullies. The dad's household is far too calm, far too happy—what little anger there may be is typically concealed from the sensitive child.

And of course, the child is precocious.

This episode on the climbing structure has caused the father to revisit some tangled moments in his own early years.

When the dad was in first grade (and not particularly big), a third grader (who was not particularly small) bullied his best friend's (sort-of) girlfriend on the playground. He went at the guy like a big time wrestler and made quick work of him. This protective display of strength landed the dad back in the classroom, alone, for the balance of the lunch and for the next few recesses. But that didn't hurt so much. It was when his friend and the girl whose honor he had defended walked by the window and yelled "shame on you" that the dad turned away and cried. Perhaps at that point, aggression at school and fighting for principles became associated with loneliness and betrayal. Maybe it really is that simple.

A few years later the dad was confronted by some difficult classmates on the playground. When one of them threw a punch at him the dad went a little crazy and slammed one of the kids to the ground like Raggedy Andy. His assailant, turned victim, pleaded for his life. The suddenly vengeful father slowly lowered the clenched fist that was about to do facial damage to the object of his wrath; he got up, went into the school bathroom and sobbed.

So why the tears? No physical pain flowed from the one punch that hit his jaw. And he had swiftly disposed of yet another playground terrorist. Maybe the dad was feeling lonely; maybe he was feeling betrayed or just scared. Pain seemed to flow from the sense that someone could dislike him enough to lay in wait, leap out and throw a punch at his chin. Like the good child at the daycare center, the dad had not been prepared for this kind of behavior. He had not been programmed to respond with inner (and outer) strength. The dad knew all too well how lonely it could be as a child hiding under the climbing structure so no one else would kick him.

In the years following those winning playground fights, the once fearless, now confused, dad grew weaker in spirit even as he grew stronger in body. The three sport high school letterman never believed he was as good (or as strong) as he was. Oh, there were brief periods when he felt some confidence, but he just never "got it." Most importantly, in high school he lived for nearly two years with real fear as he was stalked by a jerk that smoked cigarettes, drank beer and hated the "good kids."

The dad was sure this bully must be a tough street fighter because he hung around with the mean crowd. The dad did not know, until many years later, how strong he, himself, was, or how easily he could have diffused this situation by pounding his chest a bit. The dad cannot remember what became of the bully—he only knows that the anguish of walking "the long way" to class just to avoid this menace in the hall went on for too long. Too bad the dad never found the confidence to display the strength that he now hopes for in his own child.

The good child will eventually know he is good, as the father now does. And hopefully, he will also find something at an earlier age that the father is only now discovering: *self worth*. The good child will understand that it is right to stand up for yourself; not necessarily in the rough streets of a big city or a rowdy bar, but in the day-to-day world in which he lives. He will respect himself. If he goes out of his way to avoid a confrontation it will flow from sensibility and intellect, not fear. If he confronts his nemesis, he will know that he has the strength to protect himself—in his body and in his heart.

Even though it didn't make it into this essay, Dad told me once that the high school stalker experience he mentions in this piece on parenting actually ended with a little bravado. In classic small town (Midwestern) high school fashion, everyone knew about the tension between my father and the supposed tough guy. His classmates were eager to be prurient observers after the protagonist put word out that he would fight my dad once and for all. The crowd gathered at the appropriate time and place. Dad said he showed up "scared shitless," but the other guy didn't show at all. Typically, Dad saw it as a relief, not as a victory, even though the kid never bothered him again.

Enough about fighting and fear. It seems like now would be a good time to revisit my father's "ministry." Let's read one of his Holiday Letters here; it will show how much he really enjoyed sharing his positive thoughts with the world.

Holiday Letter

One special evening will forever be etched in my mind. As I closed the door to Lindsay's room I said, "Good night. I love you," as was my custom. But for the first time, unprompted, I heard a sweet little voice in the darkness say, "I yuv you." These three simple words have changed many lives and that night I felt somehow changed.

And if "change" makes the world go 'round, then our world has been spinning at high speed. New schools, new jobs, new experiences, new challenges and new attitudes characterize our family's life over the past year.

Brian is attending a terrific new school where they really understand his special needs. He has adjusted beautifully, and the teachers and therapists all love him (no surprise there). His favorite part of every day is getting on the bus in the morning. We expect to see continued development as he enters his 6th year of brightening our lives. He has introduced his sister to Barney the Dinosaur, but there is still no joy like listening to his mom and Andrew recite the words and lyrics to every Barney tape ever produced! Brian has discovered a love for donut holes (which he calls "balls"—makes sense to me), and his innate ability to dribble a soccer ball is uncanny. He still eats more food than anyone in the family, and he nearly jumps on the table to get to his vegetables.

Andrew is changing from a boy to a man. Sure he is only 10, but he understands life, people, politics, sports—in other words, the human condition—way beyond his years. He continues to excel in school. He has an incredible group of good friends who, along with sports, piano and trumpet lessons, occupy most of his time. He made two critical first-down catches in this year's Turkey Bowl, and his fall baseball team again won the championship, with Andrew batting clean-up and playing first and second base with equal skill. (He had several clutch game-winning RBIs.) He is an excellent big brother, a delight around the house, and (for those of you tracking this statistic) his shoe size is now a man's 9.

Lindsay has probably changed the most. In one short year she has gone from being an innocent little baby, to an all-knowing "bossy pants" munchkin. Her strong will is exceeded only by her unbelievable charm and curiosity. Don't even think about helping her do something unless she asks for help; and don't you dare suggest that she eat a vegetable—thankfully she loves fruit. But if you ever ask her for a hug, you can expect to get a warm, cuddly one. She counts to 3, 4, or (with help) 10, depending on her mood, and she loves puzzles, singing the ABC song, reading books (over and over), and watching cartoon tapes (over and over). We realized that she was Harvard material when she saw a white tail deer bounding across the TV screen and quickly announced "horsy," followed closely by "moo."

Has Nancy changed? How could she? She is too busy helping all of us cope with change. She has started talking about escapes and outlets—emotional not retail! No one can raise a house full of kids—me included—and not need a break now and then. This past summer she rediscovered golf. (Her playing partners report that anytime she gets closer to the green than an 8-iron, panic sets in. Can you say "short game"? Not.) She reads more books and runs more miles in a year than I will in a lifetime. She has been the acting bookkeeper for my new business (although I think she prefers getting checks to paying bills). She keeps threatening to become computer literate, but Lindsay will probably teach her Windows NT before Nancy learns on her own. The support group she helped found for "Parents of Children Who Have Died" continues to provide a valuable service not only to members of our church, but to the broader community. The Bishop of the Episcopal Church presided at this year's memorial service, and we were touched by the fact that the service was held on the anniversary of Casey's death. All of you who know Nancy will agree that—simply stated—she has class, a great sense of humor and a great heart, all wrapped up in a delightful package. We are lucky she picked us to love.

Our lives also changed dramatically when we learned that Nancy's father, Paul, had some cancerous spots on his lungs. "Ahbie" (as Brian has taught Lindsay to call him), like his counterpart "Mimi," is too full of life and too much a part of our lives to be ill; and we certainly were not ready to give up on him. So we did what any loving family would do: we prayed and sent as much positive energy as possible his way. Along with the many wonderful friends that he and Regina have made over the years, we hoped for a "best case" outcome. With chemotherapy, surgery, and a lot of courage on the part of the patient and his wife, we got our wish. The cancer is gone, and we will be playing golf with "Ah-bie" for many years to come. (Assuming the pressure of co-owning a fantasy baseball team with me doesn't push him right over the edge.)

So, the entrepreneur in me is finally emerging. I have started a consulting company where I spend my time teaching people in the professional service business how to take better care of their clients. I also help law firms prepare for a future that will be very challenging. I teach sophisticated business development techniques like: "the more you give, the more you receive;" and "to ask is better than to guess." It's part therapy, part religion, and a whole lot of common sense disguised as consulting. I love it, and there is an incredible demand for what I do. Fortunately I have a client in Toronto, so I can watch Roger Clemens pitch in person this year.

I spend more time on airplanes than I do in my new office, but that's not all bad. It means business is good. Also, I have decided to use every take-off as a time to meditate. Flying can lead to a lot of metaphors, but this one came to me on a recent rainy flight to Australia: "If you rise above the clouds, the sun is always shining." Such a simple observation can provide great comfort in times of adversity.

A friend gave me a book titled *Golf is Not a Game of Perfect.* Whether you are someone who thinks golf is a metaphor for life or not, we should all take this message to heart. The next time we doubt ourselves or one of our loved ones, remember that 'life is not a game of perfect' either.

This year has, in many ways, been a spiritual one. I graduated from Sunday School teacher to Worship Committee member, and found myself in the pulpit on several occasions. But as we strive for more things, more work, more money and more excitement in the coming year, perhaps we should follow the words on the coffee mug I use every Sunday morning: "Live Well, Laugh Often, Love Much." Definitely!

God Bless and have a wonderful holiday season.

Chapter Four

A SERIES OF EMPLOYMENT
EXPERIENCES

My father had an amazing array of jobs—some great, some not so great. At one point in his teenage years he crawled up into the stainless steel ducts that exist above virtually all industrial kitchens to clean the grease vents; he sold insurance policies door-to-door right after college, and he even cleaned the dorm room of a celebrity classmate every two weeks in college for a while to make some extra money. He worked in the Admissions Office at college 15-25 hours every week throughout his four years there; and during two summers in his college years he worked on dangerous machines (that bend steel desk parts by slamming two dyes down on metal) at Steelcase. During another summer he loaded groceries on trucks at a food warehouse. (He was a card-carrying Teamster that year.)

Dad used to talk about his work in the grease vents with a combination of revulsion and pride. It was a high school job on which he worked with a crew of much older men who cleaned the grease vents mostly in college cafeterias ("it was hot and awful crawling around up in the ceiling," he said, "but I got $2.50 per hour, which was a fortune back then"); one summer during college he painted a lighthouse ("with a beer in one hand, and a paintbrush in the other"); he gave tennis lessons to a college Dean's daughter (until he crashed his bicycle into a car on the way to a lesson, missed the lesson and was fired); he umpired little league games in high school (and got $5.00 per game for covering both home plate and the bases); and he sold college class rings for a year-and-a-half before he went to law school.

Not your typical career history for an Ivy Leaguer, but Dad was always in a world of his own in many ways. As far as I am concerned, his two coolest jobs were working for a little company called Senior Golf Legends ("They still owe me $2,500 from 1991," he said once), and working for a company that built websites for professional sports teams. Either of these experiences alone could provide the basis for a book.

When Dad worked for the web company he had to be in New York City during most of the week. I was back in Boston with the rest of the family and I missed him terribly. He almost always made it back for my games and high school events, but it was still difficult having him so far away. Our late night "IM" exchanges, while he was in the office and I was avoiding my homework, were pretty cool. According to Dad, I first told him I loved him as a teenager at the end of one of our computer-based exchanges. He always signed off by saying: "Good night, I love you," and, apparently, one night I typed back "I love you, too."

But being in New York meant Dad was watching from his office as planes smashed into buildings, and as those buildings fell on September 11, 2001. As that day was for many of us, it was a life-changing experience for him. You will find references to this experience scattered throughout his writings.

Dad's experience at Senior Golf Legends inspired this next example of his writing. In that job he got to work with some of the greatest senior golfers of all time—and the not-so-senior (at the time) golfer, Judy Dickinson, who was in her 30's and President of the LPGA. Dad told great stories of traveling with Gene Sarazen, Doug Ford, Bob Goalby, Jerry Barber and others. He worked with Roberto DiVicenzo, Ben Hogan (though he never met him in person), Billy Casper and Byron Nelson. There were also the deals he did with Kathy Whitworth (whom he adored), Gardner Dickenson, John Brody (the former NFL quarterback) and, of course, Sam Snead.

Dad felt a special connection with Sam Snead. They traveled together a good bit when Sam did appearances, and the conversations were always memorable. Part of Dad's job involved hosting some of these senior golf legends at the Masters. The following story (which was rejected for publication by the *New York Times* magazine—Dad still had the rejection letter) was inspired by one of his trips to the Masters. You do not have to like Golf to love this story.

"The Greatest Golf Shot of My Life"

While growing up in a small Midwestern town, I often dreamed of standing on the plush green grass of the Augusta National Golf Club surrounded by the best players in the world as they pursued one of golf's greatest victories. I didn't play golf then, nor did I personally know anyone who did. Yet, for one weekend every year I would find myself magically drawn to the television to watch a golf tournament. It was, of course, The Masters.

Later, as a law student in Atlanta, I found the lure of The Masters pulling me towards truancy. Augusta, Georgia was only about 75 miles away, but some brutal irony in the golf gods' plans caused The Masters to occur just before spring exams each year. Reluctantly, I stayed home and studied, although, by this time, I had learned to play the game, and was mildly crazy (I wasn't good enough to be wildly crazy) about it.

I moved on to a big law firm, and out of the blue one day I told my wife that someday I WOULD go to The Masters. I had the wisdom to marry a woman who loved golf, so she realized the magnitude of my pronouncement, and expressed cautious optimism. But it was not long before a window of opportunity opened. I jumped at the chance to escape the traditional legal ritual without knowing it would actually move me closer to my dream.

A local businessman acted as an agent for well-known, senior professional golfers. His business was flourishing, and he needed some immediate help. The golf gods must have been with me, because he called (on a mutual friend's recommendation) and asked if I would consider coming to work with him. Within a week I accepted his offer to join a small group of entrepreneurs—three golf nuts, and one good sport—as a golf agent.

One day I heard two of my new associates talking almost casually about who would be staying with "us" at The Masters. Somehow I kept my composure. As casually as possible, I asked them to tell me a little bit more about their plans. In the next few minutes I learned that our company rented a house each year at The Masters, that a number of legendary professional golfers stayed at the house during the tournament and, yes, I would be able to attend. I nearly exploded with excitement.

I left on Tuesday of Masters week, and was told not to call our house in Augusta during the day because Sam Snead would be taking a nap and everyone else would be out—either picking up Bob Goalby at the airport or watching practice rounds. That's when it really hit me that I was going to be playing host to a very special group of house guests at a very special event.

When my associate met me at the airport late Tuesday evening, he was buzzing with stories about the events of the past two days. Names like Greg Norman, Gay Brewer, Billy Casper, Doug Ford, Nick Faldo and Gene Sarazen were rolling off his tongue as naturally as a waiter listing the available desserts. When we arrived at the house, Snead and Goalby were asleep, and I couldn't wait for breakfast.

Breakfast was all that I might have imagined. The "old pros" sat at the table telling great golf stories, while I sipped coffee and ate something that somehow stayed down amidst the butterflies in my stomach. After breakfast, we drove over to Augusta National with Goalby in a "Former Champions" Cadillac that had a Masters logo on the door.

My memories of the first day at The Masters are, for the most part, a blur—partly because I was on such a high and partly because the second day's events were even more extraordinary. I do recall, however, that goose bumps rippled up and down my entire body when I first saw THE golf course. I got a similar rush when I walked into the Champion's Room in the stately clubhouse to have lunch with former Masters champion, Doug Ford, on Friday.

On my second day at the tournament, we got up early to accompany Sam Snead to the course. Traditionally, he and Gene Sarazen officially start The Masters. Being in their 80's and 90's respectively, they represented many decades of great golf. (There was something truly moving about Snead teeing up Gene's ball so "The Squire" would not have to bend over.) I felt privileged to be among the gallery that assembled in the morning haze to watch these senior statesmen of golf, even if it was essentially an exhibition.

I was walking near Snead as he approached the infamous par three 12 hole. The 12th at Augusta National is rich in history. I had read about this phenomenal hole in *Sports Illustrated*. When a single golf hole is the subject of an entire *SI* story, that should give you an indication of its significance. Many Masters hopes and leads had been dashed there.

As we neared the tee, Snead turned toward me and mentioned that he once scored an 8 on this hole and then withdrew from the tournament. He then asked me what club I would use if I were taking a whack at it here. I told him that depending on the wind, probably a 7-iron. He said that anything too short would surely end up in Ray's Creek. I just nodded my head in agreement as I looked out at this devilishly beautiful golf hole.

On a number of occasions during this trip, I had pinched myself just to be sure I was really at the Masters and not in golf heaven. But when Sam Snead handed me his 7-iron and said, "See what you can do with it young man," reality tremors shot from my head to my toes. He mumbled something about lacking confidence on this hole, and said that any shot I hit had as much chance of turning out as "good" as any he would hit.

Every instinct in my body said *"decline this offer."* This was Sam Snead, a man with whom I was supposed to have an ongoing professional relationship. How could he ever respect me if I took the dreaded 20-handicapper divot and exploded mud all over myself and those nearby. (I did that once on the first tee at a fancy country club.) But I had also hit a lot of great 7-iron shots over the years, so another voice said, *"this may be your only chance ever to hit a shot at Augusta National."*

During these few seconds while the golf gods played tug-of-war with my instincts, I remembered having been told that one should accept valuable gifts with grace and appreciation. This offer was a gift of immeasurable value. Besides, mentally I had played this hole a dozen times (always at par or better), and I had always wanted to hit a golf shot with a fairway full of spectators.

So I winked at Sam and said I would try to get it close to the cup because I knew putting was not his favorite part of the game. This rather risky attempt at humor—putting is a sensitive subject with Sam Snead—was no crazier than the idea of me taking his tee shot on the 12th hole at Augusta National! It also loosened me up a bit as I stepped up between the markers.

My associates had been lagging behind the gallery, but now they had caught up and were looking at me with horror in their eyes. I kept waiting for some tournament official to come over and stop me; but I guess a legend like Sam Snead can do just about anything he wants in the sport he once dominated.

I had not actually hit a golf ball in over a month, but I often practice my swing while waiting for elevators. I also had studied Nick Faldo's form during Wednesday's practice round, and I had read just about everything ever written about golf. With that kind of preparation, how could I miss? I took a couple of practice swings that felt surprisingly fluid and compact. With what seemed like gallons of adrenalin flowing, suddenly it all seemed so simple.

I brought the club back slowly with an exaggerated twist, remembering that Snead says, *"for the swing to be right, you've got to get your [butt] out of the way."* I uncoiled with a confidence born of necessity, and for once I kept my head down, because I was terrified to see where the ball was going. As the crowd registered its approval and my associates let out an embarrassingly loud sigh of relief, I looked up and saw the ball heading for the green. It hit the green and stopped about 20 feet to the left of the cup.

I exhaled audibly, and quickly looked around the tee for Sam. I handed him his club and thanked him for allowing me to hit the shot. He said, *"Thank you son. What's your handicap, about a 12?"* "No," I said, *"About a 20."* He said, *"You must take a lot of peoples' money."*

Snead parred 12 and went on to finish his round several strokes under his age. I continued to walk in the gallery following him, but I felt a little taller now. Every once in a while someone would shout to me, *"Nice shot back there."* (One person even asked for an autograph.) Otherwise, there was no further fanfare and no further miracles took place in my life that day.

That night we hosted a barbecue at our Augusta house, with even more of the great names of golf in attendance. I flipped burgers, sipped beer, and mingled with the pros until late in the evening; then I went to sleep with a contentment for which one can only thank a romantic partner or the golf gods.

The next day I watched the second round of a wonderful Masters and did a little business. I felt like the luckiest person in the world as I headed for the Augusta airport at day's end. I arrived home with a suitcase full of official Masters memorabilia and a soul filled with memories. I had to watch the last two rounds on TV, since I had come home early for my son's fourth birthday party—someday he will appreciate it.

When I share golf dreams with my wife now I say, *"Someday I'm going to play a round of golf at Augusta National."* In her ever-supportive way she assures me that someday I will.

And, in case you are wondering, everything I've written here is true—well, almost everything. I actually had lunch in the Champion's Room, stayed with Snead and Goalby, flipped burgers for Ford and Casper, befriended Gene Sarazen and walked with the gallery as Snead and Sarazen played. I did not, however, hit Sam's shot on the 12th. He and Sarazen only played 9 holes, and Sam takes his golf a bit too seriously to give up the sticks.

But, who knows what will happen next year. There is nothing wrong with dreaming. Dreams really do come true. I should know, I've been to The Masters.

Everyone who has read that piece told me that they believed right up to the end that Dad had ACTUALLY hit a shot for Sam Snead! That, to me, is an example of what a great writer my father was. Here is one of Dad's early Holiday Letters. Still not the sophisticated stuff you read in some of the later ones, but a good advance over his first letter.

Holiday Letter

There is a friendly debate in our house about who has the toughest job. Nancy spends the bulk of her days with Brian and Lindsay – a very special 5-year-old and a wonderfully challenging 9-month-old. Nancy is constantly feeding, changing, entertaining, refereeing, bathing, driving, dressing, playing with, training and mostly loving these two little ones.

When Andrew and I are home, she makes our lives complete with meals, laughs, wardrobes and a whole lot of love, too. She monitors our collective health and keeps us all amused with her never failing sense of humor—well at least *she* thinks she's funny.

For my part, I end most days by walking into a warm and cozy house where children greet me by screaming some semblance of my name; there is **so much** to be appreciated there—have I said "thank heaven for little girls?" We cannot believe how awesome it is to have a daughter, especially one as sweet and healthy as Lindsay. She has a jack-o-lantern smile, she claps on command and she can sing, well sort of, but it seems to require the involvement of her entire face. (If you have seen those collectable Christmas carolers they sell this time of year, then you know what I mean.) Watching the way Andrew gushes over his little sister can send chills down your spine, and Brian yells "baby" almost as much as he yells "Mumma," "Bubba," "Mimi" and "Ahbie."

It is easy for me to forget that I am trying to start a new consulting business for my firm, while continuing my job as director of practice development. Oh sure, I am trying to write a book on marketing, produce a videotape for law school students (and another one for consumers of legal services), while dabbling with the idea of publishing a book of poetry. I have also scribbled the outline for a software product to help little league coaches manage their teams. But let's face it . . . . there is really no debate, I have the easier job.

Yes, for those of you who are wondering, Nancy is even thinner and more shapely than she was before the pregnancy—hard to believe isn't it! Not that I notice these kinds of things. After all, I am getting old. But to make sure she does not loose her great shape and attitude (and her mind, for that matter), I bought her a massage table for Mother's Day. By reading a book on massage, I have gotten pretty good at the art.

I spent my usual stints as a baseball coach for Andrew's teams, but our Fall League baseball team was anything but ordinary. We went undefeated, and Andrew was our star first baseman. His fielding was so good in the championship game that some of the parents on the other team were questioning whether he was too old for the team—he's 9 and the age limit goes to 12! He is now a dominant rebounder and scorer on our 4th grade basketball team. (His shoe size has increased to 8½!) In his first visit to the new FleetCenter he was impressed, but he still prefers the old Garden. And did I mention that he has an incredible collection of key chains? (All contributions welcome.)

Brian continues to sparkle. He has developed a passion for entertaining us with post dinner performances of silliness, for which he insists that we all sit attentively and clap when *he* decides it is appropriate! He is beginning to experiment with new sounds and he seems to understand almost everything we say. When he starts talking, we will probably learn a lot about ourselves from this little observer. He is constantly requesting that I give him massages (by untucking his shirt and rubbing his tummy), and he must be one of the few kids in the world who asks repeatedly to have his teeth flossed!

We live in a great neighborhood. As I walk to the train each morning, I am struck by the peaceful world of modest homes and friendly families. And while we appreciate this serenity, we appreciate even more the people with whom we share a portion of our lives in these pastoral blocks. This is about "friends." Not the rollicking group that amuses television viewers, but a caring and supportive group of neighbors who share their joys and challenges. It is rewarding to see such selfless giving in action. (And our occasional poker nights actually "rollick" somewhat!) To these special families we send a special blessing and thanks during this holiday season. In a passage from a song by a little known band called Lowen & Navarro, the band says:

"All is quiet tonight, the stars are in their places. The moon will give us light to see into each others faces. And I know the road is hard, but if we carry on together, we will get by." One evening Andrew turned to me upon hearing this song and said "Dad, that sounds like a song from a movie. The scene could be a dad and a son riding together in a car at night." What great insight! In fact, I find the passage to be reflective of many of our lives. With the pressure to do it all, be it all and know it all, there are truly a lot of challenges in just "getting by." Thank God we have tremendous love and support within our families and among our friends.

There have been births to celebrate this year and there will be more in the coming year—but not from us! We have, however, lost our dear friend, Ken Jensen. If ever there was an example of turning tragedy into triumph, it can be found in the incredible energy Ken put into focusing on the needs of others and advancing the cause of patient care, even unto his final days. We are thankful for his efforts and for the inspiration, love and courage that are his legacy. This is, after all, a season to celebrate Hope and to demonstrate love and appreciation by giving. I teach my clients that the more they give to others, freely and without expectation of reward, the more good things will come to them in their professional lives—I hope we can all go through the coming year with that in mind.

As we approach the fifth anniversary of Casey's memorial service I was inspired to write a brief poem in his honor.

To Casey

I look up to the sky, as I stand near your name
In the Garden where we shared your ashes with the earth.
You are larger than life, larger than all of us;
A child in boundless spirit from birth.

You know the peace to which we all aspire,
and you know the joy we can only imagine.
You know the love that we all desire,
and the heaven we continually seek.

You know the Angels we dream to embrace,
And the thoughts of a genius unknown.
You know the secrets of this human race,
and the splendor of God on a throne.

Be now in our midst as a constant reminder
Of the hope and serenity of life everlasting.
And help us be mindful of the love we can find here
in a word that follows God's teaching.

Have a Wonderful '96. God Bless and Happy Everything.

Chapter Five

OTHER LETTERS THAT MATTER

People don't seem to write letters much these days. Having grown up in an era of email and instant messaging, letters are a form of communication that my generation may never master. Except for the occasional "thank you" note, girlfriend apology, or letter home from camp, I am not sure I have ever actually written a letter in the traditional sense.

Dad, on the other hand, complained that he didn't have enough time to write all of the letters he wanted to write. But he still managed to write a few. I suspect that he wrote a lot of great personal letters, copies of which never made it into in his folders (and they were not on his hard-drive because they were handwritten.) He saved copies of a few of his letters, though, like the letter to his cousin Roger's parents that I shared previously.

Mostly his letters—like his writing generally—were about gratitude or encouragement. He also could write a killer letter of recommendation. He didn't write too many of these; he told me that was because they had to be sincere, so he would not write one for just anyone. The letters that follow are good examples of how he tried to communicate through this medium.

The first letter was written to a couple (among Dad's best friends) upon learning that their son had a brain tumor. Since Dad drew a lot of the content for this letter from the Homily he had written for Casey's memorial service, I didn't repeat the full letter here, but I love the openness he expresses in the few paragraphs that are repeated here.

Dear Steve and Janet,

I don't feel as though I always express my thoughts and feelings well in person, so I decided to write something—something about hope.

Because of who you are and what you have done in your lives, it really is a wonderful life for many of us. Steve made me feel like a part of his family way back in college when, in many ways, I was alone and I truly needed support. Together and individually I know you have touched many lives in many positive ways. Today, thinking of you two, I feel the concern one would feel for family members—but I also feel great hope for a healthy Jackson and an enriched future.

Please know how much I empathize, understand, and support you in these times. My prayers will continue.

Your friend always,

I recall my father trying to say something motivational at the end of each of the many seasons in which he coached my baseball and basketball teams. So it was fun to find this letter that he had sent to everyone on my Little League baseball team in the summer of 1994.

Dear Reds,

I have really enjoyed coaching this team. It was great to see the support you gave your teammates. You encouraged each other, and never said a bad word when someone made a mistake. Since most sports require teamwork, this will serve you well.

You have been a fun and competitive group; you have also been very "coachable." As you get older you will better understand the importance of being "coachable." It means you showed respect for the coaches' decisions, rules and instructions. You were willing to listen to our advice and learn from your mistakes. You will all have many coaches over the years. Please show them the same respect you have shown me and the other dads who helped this season.

All of you can play baseball well, but remember it's a long way to the pros. So be sure to have fun while you play little league over the years. Good kids make good ball players, and you are good kids.

Your Coach

This next letter really needs no introduction. It was just "Dad being Dad." Some kids would find this to be hokey, but even as a cynical teenager I had learned to appreciate my dad's open expression of feelings. I knew he wanted nothing more than for me to be happy . . . to have a genuine, fulfilled life. He handed this letter to me as I headed off for freshman orientation. It might not be a bad idea for those of you with college-age kids to share it with them. No matter how ready you think you are to be on your own, it is not easy to walk off to that first day of college, and knowing I had something special from my father in my pocket made it just a little bit easier.

A Letter to My Son as He Leaves for College

Finally, you are on your way! You are on your way to a college that was made for you, located in a place that is special like you. How can I not take this opportunity to share a few thoughts . . .

When you get to school, seek out friends who do good and interesting things; it is easy to find people to party with—it is harder to find friends who care about your soul. Make the effort to find them. They are like gold.

As you develop relationships with women, remember to distinguish sex from intimacy . . . you feel intimacy, you do sex. If your gut or heart says: "It's really fun to be with this person, and she thinks I am great the way I am," then hang around with her for a while. But there should never be any pressure to make it 'official' too soon. Be open, honest and fair in all of your relationships; remember that communication is the secret of great relationships.

From the time we are born as innocent children—filled with pure love and trust—much of what happens to us leads us to believe that 'we are not worthy' and that we are lucky to be loved at all. We find ourselves thinking we need to work hard to earn love. That is simply not true, Andrew. Please know that YOU ARE LOVE. There is within each of us, all of the love we need. You can help heal someone's pain with a gentle touch or a few kind words—I have seen you do it. Don't forget to turn that compassion inward; be sure to give the same loving consideration to yourself that you would give to a friend if you find yourself struggling. Don't *hear* a voice saying: "see, you are a screw up;" rather, *be* the voice saying to yourself, "wow, this is a tough situation, but you have a great heart and it will work out." Self-criticism is not authentic; it is a conditioned response from a world of critics. If you start thinking you are failing in any way, call me or talk to a friend; we will remind you of what matters.

On the fun side: Get lots of exercise; work out! Not so you will have a great physical body, but because it is great for your mind and soul. It will help you concentrate, and, by the way, you will live longer.

Play cards. Play for fun or for a few dollars. Don't ever bet more than you brought, and don't ever bring more than the cost of a pizza. And when it comes to gambling, don't even think about messing around on the Internet. Play darts—it's meditative. Play team sports, it's illustrative and fulfilling. Don't be afraid to try something new—that is one of the reasons for intramural sports. (If **I** could throw the javelin in a college track meet, **you** can do just about anything!)

Hike and bike and walk and talk. Many of the most lasting parts of my college education came from getting to know the new world I found myself in, and expanding my world by getting to know the people around me. Everyone has a purpose in our lives. Look for it; learn from them. They are all teachers—both the good and the bad.

Drinking and drugs will be commonplace. Don't make them a regular part of your life. Don't keep a "stash;" you can't afford it financially, and it is not a good investment emotionally. If it isn't readily available, you will use it less. There is an alcohol policy at your school, respect and observe it; it is for your own good, as well as the good of the community. Think about how far you have come, and how happy you are to be where you are. Ask yourself when confronted with the opportunity: "how much is that second beer worth?" How would probation, then suspension (without tuition rebate!) feel? More importantly, remember that you don't need any foreign substances to enjoy the richness of life. The sweetness of life is in you, and it is all around you every minute.

An essential part of my education came from ALWAYS going to class, and ALWAYS turning in my papers on time. (I didn't always have my reading up to date . . .) Remember that procrastination is driven by either a fear of failure or perfectionism; neither is a healthy motivator! There is no need for you to procrastinate; you are not perfect, and no one expects you to be. More importantly, perhaps, you cannot fail if you stay focused on what matters—loving *yourself* and others, and treating *yourself* and others with respect. You happen to have a great mind and great skills, so whenever you make a decent effort, the work you do will be really good. Just do it—a little each day. Don't let yourself get under water.

Read something that you have been assigned every day, but also spend a few minutes reading things that feed your soul. Recite the *Four Agreements*; have the kind of faith that is demonstrated in *The Game of Life and How to Play It*. Trust your instincts, like Fiver the intuitive rabbit in *Watership Down*. Remember what Bagger Vance said: we each have one authentic swing, you just have to trust it. If you get a chance to participate in a meditation class, do it. Profound things come out of the silence.

Call us . . . whether it is to say how beautiful the world looks from the top of a mountain, or for advice on how to deal with a noisy roommate. We will be thinking of you, but we don't want to drive you crazy with calls. Email your sister a couple of times a week; you are a great role model for her. (Thank you for that.) Think about Brian and the lessons he has taught us all about simplicity, and complexity and appreciation. You have been wonderful to him; he is better for having you as a brother. Continue to enjoy the wonderful relationship you have with Nancy; it is no secret that she has loved you like a mother, and you have been a special part of her life.

You know that you are my first-born son. That means I have to do fatherly things, like make sure you are doing what you need to do to stay on track, and help you make sometimes difficult decisions. But, you are also very much a "best friend" to me. I hope we can still find time to visit some more ballparks together, ride more roller coasters, throw a football around, talk about movies, play some golf and catch a few fish. You have turned out to be a son beyond what I could ever

have imagined as a father. I am very blessed by having you as a son.
God bless you as you start this new adventure.

When your father writes a letter like that to you it's hard not to
want to write yourself. So I find it flattering that my dad had saved
the following story that I wrote years ago about an experience I
had with my brother, Brian. My guess is that he figured one day
one of us might send it to Brian—when he was old enough to fully
understand it (which may be now or it may be never, as his special
needs make communication challenging). Although it doesn't really
fit in this collection, since it's not one of Dad's writings, I want to
share it here amongst his letters as a little extra connection to him.
I titled it "Together," because it was such an unbelievable bonding
experience for me and my brother.

Together—Andrew's Story about Brian

It was the end of August, the dog days of summer. It was a time
for sleeping, a time for playing, and a time for summer reading.
For the Watsons, however, the end of August signals the arrival of
jihad to the city that seemingly always sleeps. Welcome to Baldwin,
Michigan.

Located right next to the run-down, former hotspot known as
Idlewild, to Easterners, such as myself, Baldwin greets you like a
standard one-horse town. You've got your gas station, McDonald's,
and you've got your Dairy Queen. Beyond that, however, you are
hard pressed to do your shopping anywhere but the 'dime' store, the
Dollar Store or the Save-a-lot. But I digress. We don't go to Baldwin
to shop, we go to visit my grandparents.

Days are spent lounging around the cottage, basking in the warm
glow of satellite television, or, when you are feeling adventurous,
taking the paddleboat around the lake. Nights typically consist
of fishing with Grandpa, playing cards with Grandma, and, yes,
watching more TV. Meals are always fried, always filling, and always
delicious. This particular week had been nice, and very routine

up until Thursday; that is when I was called on to snap out of my vacation daze, and baby-sit.

Not only was I left in charge of my brother and sister, but also my three cousins. So there I was, responsible for five kids between the ages of six and twelve with the help of my grandparents who, at 70, were not as capable as, perhaps, they once were. My parents were out with my aunt and uncle, milking central Michigan for all the fun they could find at the casino in Manistee.

Truth be told, my only real project for the evening was entertaining my brother Brian who has special needs (the Cartoon Network was taking care of the rest of the group). After many books and songs, I got Brian ready for bed. He was rather reluctant to go to bed, as he is most nights in Baldwin, because it doesn't get dark there until almost 10 p.m., which is well past his bedtime. (Brian is a creature of habit, and is not accustomed to turning in while it is still light out.) It took a great deal of effort, and an even greater deal of tone-deaf singing, but Brian was finally in bed. Now I could just kick back and enjoy my evening with a nice cold Faygo Red Pop. Or so I thought.

Not more than ten minutes after I had put Brian to bed, he came strolling out of the bedroom. I wasn't terribly surprised, and I took him by the hand to lead him back to his bed. It didn't take me long, though, to see that he was in a great deal of discomfort. He and I sat on the side of his bed as he gouged his left eye, while moaning with a sense of panic. In about five minutes things went from bad to worse.

His left eye was now swollen almost completely shut, and my heart really began racing. It was becoming very clear to me now that Brian was having an allergic reaction to something. He is allergic to nuts, so I assumed that he had gotten into a nut product of some kind, but when? Where? These questions would have to be answered later. At this moment I had one goal: finding Brian's Epinephrine pen and somehow mustering the emotional strength to stick the gigantic needle into his leg. (The "Epi-pen" as we call it, is the antidote for an allergic reaction.)

I was having trouble with the nearly impossible task of holding Brian's hand away from his eye, while searching in vain for the Epipen, so I called on my cousin for assistance. With the help of my grandparents, we tore through every suitcase we could find, but to no avail. At this point I carried Brian into the bedroom to cover his eye with a cloth. I used this time to compose myself enough to think of a plan. Calls to my dad's cell phone went unanswered.

I sat there watching his condition deteriorate, his face went from pained to helpless, and I couldn't stand it anymore. It was time to call 911.

Right after my grandfather hung up the phone, I heard the call go out on my grandparents' police radio: "boy with special needs having allergic reaction." An overwhelming nausea overtook my body. I figured that Brian and I were on our way to the Traverse City Hospital, and who knows if people there are equipped to deal with this situation—especially for Brian who has other health issues to deal with, as well. I was thinking this over and over as I told Brian "it will be okay, it'll be okay;" I was trying to dispel his fears as well as mine. But he heard my wavering voice, and saw right through me. We were terrified together in the middle of nowhere, with nothing to hold on to but each other.

Our trance of fear was interrupted by my cousin running into the room with the Epi-pen in hand. Brian would live. The weight of the Universe was no longer resting solely on my shoulders. All that remained now was the challenge of sticking the pen in his leg; a challenge that proved to be too great for me. Brian wasn't the stuffed Sesame Street character I had practiced on – this was my brother, and this may be the difference between life and death. Just then I heard the roar of the ambulance as it pulled into the driveway. Once again I breathed a sigh of relief. Trained professionals are here, I thought. I'm off the hook.

Carrying Brian out to the ambulance was not an easy task either. When Brian heard those sirens, memories of a childhood spent in hospitals were revived, and he let out a howling cry. At this point I was holding back tears of my own. As they strapped Brian down to the bed and prepared to inject the shot, Brian and I looked at each other, wanting to be back home. Then, with a pop of the pen and a child's scream, it was done.

Brian fell asleep on my chest that night. I wouldn't have had it any other way. And while I watched TV into the wee hours of the morning, awaiting my parents' return, I knew my life had been changed as my brother's had been threatened. There was only one thing left to do on this vacation; get going on the Adventures of Huckleberry Finn.

★ ★ ★ ★ ★

My dad was so proud of what I wrote that he put an excerpt of this story in one of his Holiday Letters which appears later in this book (after the hunting article). But, since we are on the subject of great stories, here is the Holiday Letter from 2003. It contains some great stories, and it begins and ends with a reference to the very cool "Storypeople" website. Dad used to buy "Storypeople" books in bunches and give them as gifts—typical of his sometimes-quirky way of showing people how much he appreciated them, in a way that might inspire them.

Holiday Letter

If you have never visited www.storypeople.com you are missing a treat. It is filled with brief, insightful observations on life—the kind that make us think and smile. Here's one of my favorites: "There are many things you do because they feel right & they may make no sense & they may make no money & it may be the real reason we are here: to love each other & to eat each other's cooking & say it was good." Sort of like the Golden Rule; if we all lived by it, what a wonderful world this would be.

The Wonders of this year have been many. One life-lesson that was reinforced for me recently is the incredible impact our actions have on children. When Lindsay was putting our dog Sally's seatbelt on in the car one day, everything seemed to go wrong—it was tangled, she couldn't get Sally's leg through the right loop, and the latch was not working as it should. Silently and calmly Lindsay went about her business. When she was done, unprompted and very sweetly, she said: "See Dad, you don't have to get upset when things don't work right." If she had looked in the rearview mirror she would have seen a tear in my eye . . . here was a child teaching her father the patience he should have been teaching her.

Speaking of amazing daughters, we are thrilled to report that my brother, Gary, and his wife, Cindy, have a new daughter to join their three wonderful boys. Years of planning and anticipation were threatened by the SARS outbreak, as Jan waited for her family to come get her in China. But after some delay, all turned out well. Here is an excerpt from one of Cindy's emails chronicling the early days of the adoption process: "We received our Fed Ex package with some new pictures of Jan and a little more information. The Fed Ex lady came at 9:10 this morning, and I took her picture holding the package (my kids were so embarrassed they ran in the house, and wouldn't come out). I told her, through my tears, that she was delivering our baby! She gave me a big hug."

If you ever doubt how lucky we are to live in this country, and how special it is to be able to bring children here from remote Chinese orphanages, consider this email Cindy sent from China: "This has been a great experience and we are so glad we could come to China and experience Jan's birth country. Yesterday when we were out walking in the village an old man came up to Jan and told her 'good-bye and have a good life in America.' It brought tears to my eyes. We get stopped on the street many, many times and are told what a beautiful baby we have. They say 'she is a very lucky baby,' and I always reply we are the lucky ones to have her. God bless Jan, and God bless America."

Nancy and I spent three magical days in the city of Watson, England. What a beautiful and charming place (about 250 miles north of London). Obviously, it was cool to see our name on everything from dump trucks and pubs to courthouses and castles. Mostly, though, the rich history and the local hospitality were unbelievable. (And did I mention the pubs . . . ?) It was hard to call a taxi. When you say "the cab is for Watson," it turns into the Abbott and Costello skit of "who's on first;" the cab company just keeps saying "we **are in** Watson, but who are we picking up?" The **most** magical part of the trip was being in the extraordinary Watson Cathedral—built in 1097—where we participated in a beautiful Evensong Service sung by the Chapel Choir of St. Paul's School, York. Another highlight was when I stood in the pulpit of an empty 500-year-old church in London, imagining what it would be like with a full congregation . . . only to have the minister show up out of nowhere! Fortunately, he didn't seem to mind.

Check out the enclosed pictures. Take a good look at Lindsay's long locks, as she is committed to cutting her beautiful hair after Christmas. She will be donating 10 inches of hair to "Locks of Love" (for people who need wigs to deal with medical conditions). She has become a great player of Nintendo 64, thanks to her older brother Andrew's willingness to give her his video game system. She is thrilled about the upcoming 3rd grade play, and is still playing violin and piano. Lindsay teaches us life lessons every day, and brings great joy through her loving kindness to all people.

Take a look at Brian's smile—we haven't figured out a way to donate that joy yet. We are often told by those who know him, however, that Brian's sweetness is the sunshine of their day. His modest, but steady, developmental progress continues. He even does some 13-year-old things, like seeing what happens when you roll a desk chair down the steps from the second floor! He loves swimming, swings and bouncing balls.

Andrew has been busy with college applications, golf and writing for the school paper. It remains to be seen where he will get in, but he is interested in colleges in all parts of the country. He continues to have a passion for film, and a belief in limitless possibilities. (He threw out the first pitch at Fenway Park the night the Red Sox clinched a playoff spot.) It is scary how much he shares my belief in *connectedness*. Like me, he believes 'there is no such thing as coincidence.' (Who thinks it is coincidence that as I sit writing this letter, one of my favorite motivational speakers, Wayne Dyer, just came on PBS talking about one of my favorite motivational authors, Deepak Chopra . . . ?)

Nancy has been busy volunteering in our town, and at Lindsay's school. She put together a vacation for us in August that was a preview of our dream of owning a house on a lake someday. It was a fabulous week of fishing, swimming, canoeing, running in the woods, antiquing, martinis on the deck and cooking on the grill. Life at its best. She is masterful at taking care of us. Brian's care, of course, continues to be her greatest job. My job might bring in money, but what she does is truly priceless.

Speaking of jobs, my work of teaching professionals how to take better care of clients has evolved into more management consulting. I have also had several opportunities this year to do purely motivational speaking, and it has been a real joy. I am working on a collection of poems, and a book that has as many potential titles as it has themes . . . maybe it's just a form of therapy, but I still may try to publish it next year!

My great friend Fred sends me lots of interesting things to read and contemplate. He knows and lives the essence of true friendship. One of the most valuable things he shared with me is a Christmas story recounted on a PBS broadcast several years ago. It stays with me in an almost haunting way as a reminder of what is important in life.

I have summarized here a story that touches your heart in every way; it is told by a poor teenage boy describing his "greatest Christmas ever." His family didn't usually celebrate Christmas because they couldn't afford it. One year someone invited the rural families into town to pick up 'Christmas presents.' This young man's father came home with two chickens, and "stripety candy and apples and oranges; nuts, sacks of flour and real coffee." Mom and the kids were ecstatic. A sharecropper, who didn't go into town because he thought the treats "were only for white folks," stopped by with his family while they were unloading the "presents" from the wagon. They were promptly invited to Christmas dinner. As the mothers cooked, the children of both families played a joyous game of "Christmastime," which meant running to the kitchen door and smelling the wonderful aromas of a modest Christmas dinner, then falling down on the floor giggling wildly. When dinner was served "there was an apple, an orange and some stripety candy at everybody's place." When the boy's father asked his guest if he would say grace the sharecropper looked up and smiled and said, "Lord, I hope you having as nice a Christmas up there with your angels as we're having down here, because it sure is Christmastime down here. And I just wanted to say Merry Christmas to you, Lord."

If you ever have any doubt about whether we are living the 'good life,' think about this joyous celebration of great love, human kindness and simple gifts. It helps me cultivate an attitude of gratitude. And not just gratitude for the things we *have*, but also for those we know and have known. A heartfelt thanks to our friends Jane and Mark for hosting us for three fabulous days in Florida. A very special blessing also goes out to the Stetson family on the death of Steve's wonderful mom, and to Maureen upon the death of her dear mother. Congratulations to my mom and dad who reached their 70th birthdays, and their 50th wedding anniversary in the same year. A special thanks to Kathy O'Grady for her surprise visit over the Thanksgiving weekend. (She would do anything to see her name in print). And God bless Nancy's mom, who refuses to age and keeps giving so much of herself and her love to our family.

A final word from Storypeople. **"In my dream, the angel shrugged & said, 'If we fail this time, it will be a failure of imagination' & then she placed the world gently in the palm of my hand."**

Merry Christmas and Happy Chanukah and Happy New Year from the Watsons.

Speaking of sons impressing dads with their writing, this next little three-paragraph letter was written by my dad to his own father. Grandpa grew up paycheck-to-paycheck, so he was freaking out a bit when he learned that my dad had quit his dependable *real* job at a company to start his own business. The idea of not having a *real* job and the security of a regular paycheck probably scared a lot of people in my grandfather's generation. Dad had kept a copy of this hand-written note in a folder. I am not sure what information he sent along with the letter, but it was probably one of the articles that had been written in the trade press about Dad's new company.

Dad,

I never doubt that you are proud of me, but I know you sometimes worry about me.

When I went off to Harvard I know that, at first, you thought you were losing me. When I came home for the first time as the "same old me," your smile returned and your sense of relief was like that of a father with a newborn son.

These days, I am sure you have more confidence in me, and in my ability to run a new business. I suspect, however, that you still worry a little bit about me. After all, you are a dad! So I thought you would appreciate—as a sort of Father's Day present—some information about my new business. I hope you enjoy reading it; and thanks for giving me the values that will make this business a success.

Love,
Jim

A Great Letter of Recommendation

Dad did not write many letters recommending people for stuff, but when he did write one it was *really* good. He told me it was essential to be totally sincere when writing a letter of recommendation—so he only did it when he felt unequivocally that someone should get the job or be admitted to the school or program for which they were applying. Here is a copy of one letter of recommendation I found. Dad had written this for a dear friend who was applying to graduate school. I have changed the name and some facts to protect the person's privacy, but I have to share this particular letter, as it blew me away with its eloquent passion.

To Whom It May Concern:

Simply stated, Jack Evans is one of the most extraordinary strategic thinkers I have met, regardless of age or experience. His ability to absorb, recall and see patterns within data is remarkable. While modest, witty and immeasurably likeable, Jack possesses real genius in deconstructing complexity to isolate the core drivers of a given challenge.

I have known Jack since he was a college student at Vanderbilt. He was assigned to me as a summer intern when I was in charge of marketing for a professional services firm in Boston. Jack impressed me for a person so young: his work as a summer intern was better organized, researched and written than many full-time professional employees. He fit in beautifully with my team, and I found him to be mature and delightful to work with. Several years later I asked him to help me establish and run a new business, and he took it from concept to reality.

During the two-and-a-half years in which he ran my company, he created products that are still on the market today; he provided strategic plans and market analysis that were insightful and dead-on accurate, and we had a great time working together. From a management perspective, Jack can plan, organize information and pull the right people together masterfully. At a critical point he found great people to partner with us, develop our products and open up markets. His comfortable and professional presentation skills made meetings effective, useful and fun. I have no doubt that his vision for our company would have been reality, but I could not give the business the attention it needed for sales; and since I was largely the product, he was not able to complete his work.

When observing Jack engaging in projects both personally and professionally, I am consistently struck by his desire to take something and make it better for its own sake. Jack can genuinely see the underlying potential of any given subject, and he drives himself until the potential is realized. Jack is that rare individual who is primarily motivated by a set of ideals and the power of ideas—which puts him in the category of a "true believer." But he does not hang out in the 'la la land' of just being a great thinker. He comes alive when discussing impact and effectiveness. He is pragmatic, and great on follow through.

Add to his passion and intellect, an integrity that is exemplary. I asked him to be a mentor for my college-age son when I realized that they would be in the same city during my son's college years. I wanted Jack to be an example for Andrew. My son has not only learned a lot from him, but he also thinks of him as a trusted friend. Jack's involvement in Andrew's life thousands of miles away from home gave me great comfort. You can trust Jack to be totally ethical and uncompromising in doing what is right, and he will also pull together the people, data and ideas needed to answer difficult questions.

If he has a weakness, it is that he has been working alone for the past few years, and that isolation has caused him to rely on only a few people to develop his new ideas. I sense that one of his motivations for going to a world-class graduate school of business is to reconnect with the experience of being part of a team.

Jack's current enterprise, the non-profit [company name deleted], plays this out. When he first told me about his concept for reducing frivolous law suits, it struck me as an entirely original, simply elegant example of contrarian genius. He is onto something that, in my judgment, is destined to become a part of the solution to costly litigation. Now, it just has to be presented to a broader marketplace. I guarantee you that if you put a team around Jack, this company will be fully and effectively deployed. Nevertheless, the extent to which he has penetrated the relevant market, essentially on his own, is still impressive.

Jack's potential is virtually unlimited. His exceptional combination of intellect, integrity, energy, creativity and relational skills make him truly unique in my experience. His enthusiasm for learning is sincere and his curiosity is infectious. He is really unlike anyone I have ever met, and he would be an extraordinary asset to your school. I admire Jack Evans, and recommend him enthusiastically and without reservation.

Sincerely, and respectfully submitted,
Jim Watson

There were several other letters of recommendation sitting on the hard drive of Dad's computer – for former babysitters trying to get into colleges, and for close relatives and colleagues trying to get new jobs. There is just no way to share these letters without revealing who they are. In each letter however, he was true to his rule about recommendations: don't write it if you don't mean it.

There may not be a more challenging relationship than that between a man and his former wife's father. As you may recall, my dad got very close to Nancy's father; but what about my mom's father? He is, I can say from first-hand experience, one of the world's most amazing people. So, I was not surprised when I found the following handwritten letter that Dad had written to my other grandfather, but probably never delivered.

Dear Mack,

You were largely responsible for my marrying your daughter. Not in the traditional sense of holding a gun to my head, but by embodying so much goodness. You didn't "sell" the idea of dating your daughter any more than others who thought they saw a potential great match. You did, however, possess the values of honesty, fairness, and creativity that seemed to be so right. I believed that the eldest daughter of such a man must have adopted those same values, and that she would treat me with the same decency and respect that you did. She did, but a lot of stuff got in the way and now we all find ourselves worlds apart.

You may recall that you and I were friends long before your daughter and I were lovers. With glasses of scotch in hand we sat in your den and recreated moments of athletic glory with an enthusiasm that made us feel strong and capable again. We could solve a marketing dilemma or a Middle Eastern crisis. I understand that you now drink wine instead of scotch. Other things have changed, too. I have managed (with hard work and good fortune) to replace our shared moments of fantasy with real creativity and growing self esteem. You also have a new son-in-law. I hope you like him as much as I do. I think he is very good with your grandson.

Some changes are not so positive. Your father recently passed away. That is a loss that no words can eradicate, and I cringe at the thought that someday I will know the grief you surely experienced. I am sorry for your loss. I remember your father as a spirited man of many talents and few apologies. I remember him as a man who spoke his mind, but was fair to those who were fair to him. Sure, I only knew him in his latter years, but I recall him being a man who loved life and knew how to enjoy it. We should all take a lesson from that . . . .

The letter just ended there. Maybe it was just a little too difficult for Dad to reconnect with those emotions; we will never know.

Speaking of letters, this seems like a good place to share Dad's 2004 Holiday Letter. This is the letter in which he threatened to stop writing the annual issue, but the outcry of protest kept him writing. (Much to the chagrin, I am sure, of several of his college friends who found the letters to be painfully self-indulgent.) But the themes of love, connectedness and peace in Dad's letters resonated with a lot of people; and this letter, in particular, reflected my father's sincere desire to make a difference in people's lives.

Holiday Letter

After 10 years of sharing my family's exploits and my personal insights, I have decided that this will be my last Holiday Letter for a while. There is, after all, only so much that can be said about one's family members before it sounds self-indulgent. Wonderful things happen every year—not just to the Watsons, but to everyone. Indeed, wonderful things happen every minute, and I wish we could capture and package them all. Unfortunately, suffering happens too. The Buddhist view is that how we respond to suffering determines the richness of our lives. Jung says *neurosis* "must be understood, ultimately, as the suffering of a soul which has not discovered its meaning." Clearly, my preference has been not to report events, but to explore the meaning in events. My interest in the interplay between the cerebral and the spiritual has become almost an obsession—so I am going to take some time to chill.

Every now and then I look back at the Holiday Letters I have written over the years. It makes me grateful to remember Andrew's heroic action when Brian was sick, and to re-read the special words uttered by Lindsay as she witnessed her first shooting star; I like to be reminded of how lucky I have always felt to be married to Nancy, and I am humbled when I recall the experience of being in New York on 9/11. If there is a theme that runs through past missives, though, it is that the most important things in life are not necessarily the most profound. Just remembering to say "thank you" or "I appreciate that" or "how can I help," can mean every bit as much as scoring the winning touchdown, getting an "A" on a test or donating money to a charity. In a year of profound change in our household, I have needed to come back to this important place of awareness time and time again. We all need to 'let go and let God.'

In August Andrew headed off to college in Colorado. Leaving Andrew there was the hardest emotional test I have faced since Casey died 14 years ago. My dad said he felt a similar level of emotion when I left for college, and I bet his dad felt the same way when my dad left the farm in Arkansas to move to Michigan as a teenager. I guess it's just a parent's ritual of emotional passage, but it is a tough one. Fortunately, Andrew is in the right place; he has met great new friends, started snowboarding and is actually studying a lot. The enclosed photo is taken from Andrew's dorm room, with the kids standing on his balcony overlooking a beautiful mountain.

Lindsay is in 4th grade and continues to be our window into wonder and joy. During my frequent travels I would send her emails. Here are a few examples of our exchanges. Email from Dad: "Have a great day tomorrow." Lindsay's reply: "I will." From Dad: "You are the best girl a dad ever had." Lindsay's reply: "I know." From Dad: "How was your day today?" Lindsay's reply: "We made cookies." Her approach leaves me reeling with a hunger to know how her loving mind works. The simplicity and clarity of her insight and self-comfort is meditative. She sings in choirs, acts in plays, and teaches other kids how to play video games; in her first year of competitive field hockey the team was undefeated, but what most describes her is 'loving and imaginative.' She writes books, designs roller coasters and beats her big brother at video games for fun.

If Brian doesn't have a growth spurt soon we are going to have our own Simon Birch—John Irving's lovable character in *A Prayer for Owen Meany*. Brian still prefers to communicate with just a few words, but more and more he seems capable of putting some sentences together. He and I have connected at a new level. Perhaps being asked to speak at a dinner for the Association of Retarded Citizens gave me a greater appreciation for what he can teach us. We have all heard it said that "it takes special people to work with special kids," or "God does not give us greater burdens than we can handle," or "parents of special children are somehow uniquely qualified to handle these demands and challenges." There may be *some* truth in all this, but in my simple worldview we are all connected; and those who live and work with ARC Citizens could not do it without the incredible love and support we get from our families and friends.

After eight years of self-employment I made a bold decision in November to shut down a successful business and join a professional services company as its first Chief Marketing Officer. Sure, I will miss being on airplanes every day, sleeping in hotels, eating on the run, and meditating on takeoff (actually, I will miss that), but I will truly enjoy being a part of a great firm, with great people who have a long tradition of excellence. And it is nice to take the train to work every day, put the kids to bed at night, and have some quality time with Nancy. I have run out of words to describe Nancy, so this year I will just borrow the words of the 13th century Persian poet, Rumi: "The moment I heard my first love story I started looking for you, not knowing how blind that was. Lovers don't finally meet somewhere. They're in each other all along." She may volunteer for lots of good causes and play team tennis and be the world's greatest mom, but she has always been a part of me. We are all lucky to have her in our lives.

During the 5th inning of the Red Sox 7th game against the Yankees I sent Andrew a text message saying: "Do you believe?" His response: "I think I believe." Like Andrew, most Red Sox fans were afraid to feel the exhilaration and satisfaction of coming back from an impossible deficit; we were afraid to embrace the joy because we had been hurt too many times before. Ahhh, the lessons we can learn from sports. What part of our lives is still dominated by past pain and loss and fear? What part of us thinks there are limits because something has 'never been done before?' My father-in-law, Paul, born in 1919, believed for his whole life that the Red Sox could win again—he brought a wonderful optimism to every situation. Paul is one happy guardian angel this year.

In a book, *The Middle Passage*, I read that the child who was not hugged enough or the child who was overwhelmed with expectations, brings to midlife the defenses that were needed to cope as a child. Like a Red Sox fan, we can go through life afraid to love or to believe that everything will be okay. I am thankful to be surrounded by friends and a family that continually remind me that there is joy in each moment, and there is really no time or room for fear.

Upon learning that I had sent Andrew off to school with a *special* letter, my friend Steve responded best: "surprise surprise, you wrote something touchy feely." But Steve, whose heart is as big as Texas, also admitted that he had sent his terrific son off to college with a few words of wisdom the year before. One of the most important messages I tried to share with Andrew in the letter was that we often find ourselves thinking we need to work hard to earn love. "Please know," I said, "that you *are* love. There is within you all of the love you need. You can help heal someone's pain with a gentle touch or a few kind words—I have seen you do it. Don't forget to turn that compassion inward; give the same loving considerations to yourself that you would give to a friend. Self-criticism is not real; it is a conditioned response to a world of critics. If you start thinking you are failing in any way, call home, pray or talk to a friend who will remind you of what really matters."

Speaking of friends, happy 50th to Fred, whose genuine friendship lured a dozen of us to Orlando for golf and a great birthday celebration; and thank you to Kathy O'Grady who decorated our house beautifully for Halloween, complimenting the great work Lisa did to make our home warmer and wonderful. Thank you to brother-in-law, Cary, for paying off our baseball bet with Opus One, and to Pat Butler for his great wedding celebration. My life has been better because Pat has been a part of it; his will now be better because Debbie is in it. Thank you to our wonderful neighbors for hosting us for Thanksgiving and for hosting Nancy's birthday gathering on the Cape. Thank you to our fun-loving dog Sally for her greetings every time we walk in the door. (What is the human equivalent of wagging a tail?) Thank you to Jack Evans for being there for us and for Andrew in college—you are an amazing person.

As I kissed Lindsay goodnight and left her room the other night, she said: "I love you **sooo** much, Dad;" then she told me that when someone leaves we should always say what we would say if we knew we would not be seeing them again. What a beautiful philosophy to live by, and what a scary thought to know that I may have actually influenced this innocent creature with my existential obsessions.

I have come to accept that life is not perfect or even easy, but we are here for a reason—to make a difference in the world—one person, one cause, one good deed at a time. J.R.R. Tolkien said something like, 'All you have to do is decide what to do with the time that is given to you . . .' That's worth reflecting on. Tell people you love them; gather your family together to watch "It's a Wonderful Life." It will put everything we do and experience in perspective. Let's not stress about this holiday season, but find the meaning in all that it brings. I look forward to another year of joy and love, I just won't be writing about it. I want to say "thank you" to those who have encouraged (or simply indulged) me to write these letters over the years. I hope they have helped you in some way.

Have a Merry Christmas, a Happy Chanukah and a fabulous New Year.

When I found a document called a "Marital Contract" in one of Dad's writing folders, I asked my stepmother about it. She said she remembers Dad saying something about it, but she had never seen it. When I showed it to her, she said she felt that she and Dad lived by these principles, so they didn't really need a contract. She admitted, too, that she might have found it a little hokey if Dad had asked her to sign it. I know it is not a letter, but it seemed to fit into the collection of his writings right about here. With all of the talk about prenuptial agreements these days, it is nice to read something so positive and supportive of a lasting marriage.

The Right Kind of Marital Contract

Whereas James A. Watson and Nancy T. Reid (hereafter "J & N") have been brought together in this world;

Whereas J & N believe that they were destined to be together now and hereafter;

Whereas J & N desire, and have committed, to stay together forevermore.

Now, therefore, J & N hereby act and agree as follows:

1. They will always accept that which makes them different, as much as those things that make them alike;
2. They will look inward for faults and seek to correct them; they will look at each other with patience and appreciation;
3. They will end no days with anger and will minimize anger through communication;
4. They will know that their moods are not determined by one another, but that happiness and sadness comes from within;
5. They recognize and accept that there will be adversity in their lives, and they promise to support each other in every way;
6. They are committed always to focus and refocus on the rightness of their relationship; on the joy they can share and on the importance of hard work in making a relationship work.

Jim and Nancy vow to themselves and each other that, during the term of this Agreement, they will never give up on the other; that they will work together to make any wrongs right; neither will ever knowingly hurt the other in body, mind or spirit; and, any seemingly insurmountable hurdles will be referred to clergy and counseling, but in no event, to the courts.

These promises are made with a full and mature understanding of their implications and the love of commitment reflected herein.

To this Agreement we bring the benefit of our total life experience, our love and our ever-growing bond.

_____

Jim Watson

_____

Nancy Reid

_____

Witness

Chapter Six

ON MOTIVATIONAL SPEAKING

I'll never forget how excited my father would get when he watched or listened to a *good* motivational speaker (not the over-the-top, sweaty entertainers portrayed on TV). He said he always learned something new. "You must feed the brain like you feed the body; with healthy stuff, not just junk," he would say. But his excitement grew even greater whenever he talked about the possibility of speaking to a group of people himself about subjects that really mattered to him: love, compassion, gratitude, synchronicity, all possibilities and personal growth. Here is the brief description he used for one proposed presentation; it was essentially a "pitch" letter he used to be selected for a motivational speaking opportunity at a business conference:

Program Title: Burden or Purpose: What is Life Asking of You?

How we view our roles as marketers, lawyers or managers can have a tremendous impact on our level of personal and professional satisfaction. With so many challenges facing professionals, it is more important than ever to try to find the meaning and purpose in what we do. Jim Watson is uniquely qualified to address these important issues in a presentation that promises to be both entertaining and motivational. You will learn to appreciate the extensive impact many of your decisions have on people's lives, and how to bring a more human perspective to much of what you are called upon to do in your work lives.

Having come from a factory town, and a family in which no one before him had a high school diploma, Jim ended up at Harvard where he studied, worked (and played) his way into a new way of thinking. It was not, however, until he had to face the greatest loss—the death of a child—that he found the courage to start down his own path of self-discovery and real "success." He receives a great response from audiences whenever he shares his story and his life observations.

Speaking about issues ranging from "synchronicity" and passion, to common sense and love, Jim will leave the audience believing that they can live a more fulfilling and satisfying life—personally and professionally. Jim's work experiences include the door-to-door sale of insurance policies, working as a machinist in a factory, representing professional golfers, cleaning industrial grease vents, practicing law, running his own consulting business, and heading the marketing at a large company. He even had a stint working for a company that built websites for professional sports teams. This breadth of experience has given him a wealth of material on which to draw in discussing how professional challenges can teach, build character and make dreams come true.

Jim has impressed audiences around the world with his insightful and thought-provoking programs on relational sales, client service and personal growth. He is consistently ranked among the highest rated speakers at any conference.

This program description certainly made Dad sound like a professional motivational speaker . . . truth be told, he only did about four or five motivational speeches in his all-too-brief lifetime.

I found some random notes he had written on the subject of motivational speaking. It seems that he used these notes when he first "tested" his motivational subject matter at a Marketing Director Training Institute in Denver, Colorado over a decade before he died. His typical approach to a presentation was to write the text in full (long hand), but he almost never got around to finishing it, and he seldom referred to what he wrote anyway. So he usually just spoke from sketchy notes. Here are some of his notes from that first presentation, which he called: "Finding Your Right Livelihood."

"I have thought a great deal about how challenging this session is, because it is not your typical business fare—risky; too touchy feely; too soft; too personal. To adequately address the issue of 'right livelihood' requires me to touch on some vague emotional concepts, address some spiritual and metaphysical abstractions, and draw on a lot of personal experience.

It's also an area in which there are few concrete answers.

Maybe it's the uncertainty of today's session that makes it so exciting and so appealing to me. I agreed to lead this program because the conference organizer asked me to. I suspect that she asked me to do it because she is unwittingly complicit in some cosmically orchestrated evolution of my spirit. Speaking here today is a necessary 'next step' in the process of expanding my own horizons, and moving it beyond the realm of doing sales training.

But frankly, I'm okay with that. You can subscribe to agnosticism, atheism or any religion, but spiritual and metaphysical concepts, broadly defined, should be of some interest to us all—even at a business conference.

What I am about to share with you is evidence of a borderline obsession with self awareness—but I hope you will gain something from it nevertheless.

With so much written and produced on the subject of 'right livelihood,' and 'finding meaningful work,' how can I, or we, learn anything today that is different? Well, I hope each person here today will be motivated in some way to better his or her life. I would be especially pleased if you at least come away with a greater belief in yourself, in other people and in all possibilities; then I believe our time will have been worthwhile.

So, other than the fact that I read obsessively about self improvement, what qualifies me to be here today? Perhaps it is because I have had a couple of major personal milestones that have forced me to look deeply into personal development issues.

I have experienced the death of a child, and I was in New York City watching from my office window as planes full of people slammed into buildings full of people on 9/11. But let me say this—I don't think my life experience or my personal challenges have been exceptional. Everyone faces incredible challenges and knows real suffering. Many writers (and shrinks?) suggest, however, that it is often a particular trauma that starts us down a new path of enlightened thinking, introspection and life balance. Trauma can give us new appreciation for what we have, and the courage to look in a new direction altogether.

Have you asked yourself: "Do I truly love what I do?" "Is it the right work for me?" Often we *don't* ask these questions because if the answer is "no," then we must change something (or continue on in a state that we know to be less than optimal). If the answer is "no" we must either change jobs or change the job—something that is hard to do if we are trapped in our culture's definition of success.

Most of you go downtown every day to an office with a window, where you work with smart people, earn a nice income and get excellent benefits; there's capacity for professional growth, decent job security and a reasonable amount of respect for your role from your colleagues.

Sounds like *success* to me. But maybe this is not a description of success to those among us who see our jobs essentially as a way to finance what we actually love to do—such as a hobby or some unrelated work, like writing, painting, woodworking or music, for example.

You would expect me to like the book: *"Do What You Love and the Money Will Follow."* (I do fear sometimes that the job we love, not unlike romantic love, can come and go.) Like many of you, I am seeking to make my livelihood reflect more of what is important to me.

I guess you could say that my being here today is, indeed, another advance in my own evolution. I believe in synchronicity, testing new waters, exploring what is possible. My ultimate life goal, if I knew I could not fail (and if money were no object), would be to live in a house on a lake where I could write books and poems in the time between speaking engagements.

Let's just let that seed grow.

I could make considerably more money than I make right now . . . but money is not my scorecard. For some people it is, and that is fine. As a consultant, I sometimes decline a work engagement because it is going to take me away from my family more than I want to be away; I have also turned down work because I don't like the people or the culture of the firm, or because the work will simply consume too much of my time and energy. When I say "no" to this work and more money, I am saying "yes" to what matters to me.

Have I said "yes" when I didn't want to? Absolutely. But I notice it and try to learn something from it. And whenever I was locked into a job that required too many compromises, I made a change. I either changed the job or changed jobs.

There is no reason why you cannot do the same thing. I have no special capacity or secret for success. There is no family money to cushion the blow if I choose to move toward happiness and away from security.

Like the game of golf, the game of life has good days and bad days. To carry out that metaphor, you will inevitably get some birdies, some pars and some bogeys. In golf and life you sometimes hit it out of bounds. But that doesn't mean the match is over; you reload, take dead aim and swing again. Sometimes you might even achieve the ultimate accomplishment—a metaphorical hole-in-one; but guess what, you still have to play the next hole, as life goes on.

In golf you know what the goal is—to get the ball in the hole using as few strokes as possible. But for some of us there are different goals in golf, like enjoying the company of other players, getting some exercise, or enjoying the beautiful outdoors.

What are your goals? What is your scorecard?

Too much of life/work seems to be based on the assumption that society's scorecard must be our scorecard.

What I hope this session will do is help you look in the right places for the right answers about your right livelihood; and lead you to experience a more examined and purposeful life—a life more motivated by love, than by fear.

Clearly, Dad had managed to essentially write out the "introduction" for a presentation, but that left about 30-minutes for him to 'wing it.' What follows is the full *written* text of his next motivational speech. He didn't really follow the written script, however. I have heard the audiotape of the following presentation, and frankly, it has much greater impact as a live program. I once asked him to describe the scene where he delivered the program. He said he laid the written text on the podium and started walking around the stage. "I think I only looked at the text a few times during the 50-minute presentation . . . I spoke from the heart, but I actually managed to cover most of what I had written down."

So I am glad I found the full text of this presentation because, for the first time, Dad pulled together everything he believed in, everything he dreamed of, and everything he trusted in; and he had summoned up the courage to deliver it to a live audience. Parts of what he said here can be found in some of his sermons which appear later in the book, but this is a pretty amazing compilation of what my dad experienced, believed and cared about in life.

Striking a Balance:
Doing What You Love; Finding the Love in What You Do

This program should be titled: "The Fine Art of Saying 'Yes' . . . to Yourself." Let me start with one of my favorite quotes.

"I went to the woods because I wished to live deliberately, to front only the essential facts of life, and see if I should not learn what it had to teach, and not, when I came to die, discover that I had not lived. I did not wish to live what was not life, living is so dear . . ." *Henry David Thoreau*

This session is about living life, and not letting what we call life, control us. It's about being, not doing.

You could say this session is about empowerment, about making better choices, about being the best person you can be; about being the person your dog thinks you are.

When conductor Ben Zander is asked if he is a motivational speaker, he is quick to point out to his audiences that he is a "transformational" speaker: he says he tries to transform his audiences' ideas of 'what is possible.' It would be fabulous if we could accomplish a little of that in today's program.

Today's session is not your typical business fare—it is necessarily touchy feely; it is necessarily personal. But a dose of motivation can't hurt any of us in the middle of a business conference—or in the middle of a busy life.

What do we mean when we say we want to talk about work-life balance?

I spent two days at a work-life balance conference last week, where I learned that there are hundreds of programs, books, articles and tapes on the subject. Colleges have institutes on work-life balance; companies offer myriad programs intended to bring work-life balance into people's routines.

Work-life balance has become a big industry. Mostly, it is about finding ways for working couples to take care of their kids or their aging parents. But, sometimes it is about accommodating your outside interests—in a meaningful way.

It should not be about carving time out of a job that holds no meaning for you to spend time with your family or to study art or travel. Where is the balance in that? Flex time programs are a part of almost every firm's policies—that is a good thing. But most of us do not take advantage of them—because we are afraid that it will hurt our careers; or if we do take advantage of these programs, we still don't find significantly greater joy in our lives.

At the end of the day, though, no program or policy can change anything in that part of your heart that longs for balance. Change will come—balance will come—when you find that place inside you that is not "trying" constantly to achieve some form of illusory success, change will come when we are not seeking the approval of other people, and are not being motivated by a fear of failure. I think you will see from the program today that there are a couple of themes that are the keys to cutting through the clutter and chaos of life: love of self and sharing our gifts.

Work-life balance is achieved when we can start each day and go to bed each night with a sense that we are doing what we are supposed to be doing; that we are where we are supposed to be; that what we are doing in life is our purpose—not our burden.

So at this point you may be thinking this material is really out there! This guy is talking about stuff we see on public television fund-raising shows. But I can say from experience that there is a place in almost all of us that needs some healing and there are attitudes we all display that can have a profound impact on how we live.

As important as this discussion is, there are no clear or simple answers. The answers are different for each of us. This subject is quite a change from my usual experience of speaking to lawyers at retreats or in sales training programs—where I am expected to have an answer for everything! So bear with me here, as we explore new areas of life and questions without answers.

I said before that this program is necessarily personal. My own life experience doesn't make me special, but it has given me insights that might help you. You should know that by being here today you are making a contribution to my life journey. I promised myself many years ago that I would someday do some transformational speaking. This is a new program for me. Your willingness to let me help you on your journey is a blessing to me.

One of the challenges of this type of program is that I must reveal a lot about myself to address this subject adequately. But I truly believe that the life experiences I have had can be helpful to you as you carve your own path through this crazy life.

I am seldom at a loss for words. But recently, when I heard that an 18-year-old boy who attends our church died unexpectedly, I was speechless. Will Carter was the second teenage son in the same family to die suddenly and unexpectedly. In a physical and spiritual sense I remained speechless for a couple of days after learning of Will's death. I cried a lot, and couldn't imagine what I would say when I saw the parents. I was really concerned about 'what to say.' But in the hours just before I went to visit them I realized that what they needed wasn't words . . . what they needed were hugs; they needed compassion and support; they just needed love. So that's what I brought them.

I had gotten to know the family when they joined a bereavement group that my wife and I helped start after the death of our 3-month-old son, Casey, thirteen years ago. It was, in fact, Casey's death that sparked me to be more focused on the mission of my own life.

I had never been in a church pulpit before I delivered the Homily at Casey's memorial service. I always wanted to be up there, but I always had excuses to avoid speaking at church. I was always too busy; I wasn't sure if I could do it right or well. For a lot of reasons, I had stayed in the safe zone. I could always find a way to avoid doing the things my heart wanted me to do. With the zillion things going on in my training business, I could have easily passed on doing this presentation this morning. But I decided to trust my intuition on this one. Essentially, I borrowed an attitude I had heard about from a 12-step program: "Let go and let God." Let go and let Nature take its course. We can all benefit from more of this kind of thinking.

Well, let me make an important suggestion to each of you this morning. It took my son's death for me to try my hand at speaking about life and love and spiritual things. *Don't wait for some traumatic event in your life to motivate you to follow your heart; don't wait for some harsh personal pain to motivate you to give your time, your money, or your talents in the service of others. The world needs you to give and share compassion now.*

Our community rallied for the family of the young man who died. We brought them food, gave them hugs, and sent them cards. We offered them rides, sent them books to read and met them for coffee. This is all absolutely as it should be. The Carters are beloved members of our community—our extended family.

We do all of these things for them because we *know* about their pain. We are *aware* of their loss and we *can feel* their suffering.

But what about those whose pain and suffering we don't know first hand? What about those whose loss we can't feel today? What will we do for those beyond our awareness who are truly hungry or cold or thirsty or in prison? What will we do for strangers who need an education? What will we do for those who are not sure of their place in the world?

Just as we saw the Carters as a beloved part of our community family, we might try to see everyone we encounter as a part of a broader natural family.

A land-mine victim in Cambodia is a part of Nature's family, so are the homeless men and women who seek help from food kitchens and shelters; and the poor who rely on our donations for clothing are all a part of our extended natural family.

Some people I know are amazed and perplexed by how a particular pediatrician in our community can be so committed and so compassionate about helping a land-mine victim halfway around the world who needs a place to live. I know I was surprised when I first learned of his efforts.

To those of you who wonder how this doctor can care so much about helping a family find a home in Cambodia, I have a question: Do you think that when whatever spiritual force you believe in looks at the world he or she sees borders between countries or lines between cities or signs outside of places of worship? Do you think It sees the soul of an American in poverty and says: "this one in Florida gets a blessing, but forget about that struggling family in Southeast Asia living in a shack and working 18 hours a day to make ends meet?" I don't think that's how it works.

I don't think that those who are committed to helping others improve their lives are wasting their time . . . and I don't think Nature is laughing at people because they give up their nights and weekends to feed people they don't know. So why am I talking about charity and caring here?

In my own business I spend a lot of time trying to help lawyers be more relational. (Frankly, God is probably laughing at that one!) That doesn't sound like a very profound mission, does it? But listen to this email I received from a secretary after I spent some time working with the partners in her law firm in New Jersey.

> "On behalf of several of the partners' secretaries here at [the firm] who have asked me to e-mail you, I want to say: "Thank You." The change in the way we are being treated is such an encouragement. I think we all understand that this profession can be very stressful, and how we handle that stress and communicate with each other makes a tremendous difference.
>
> The discussion among us has been: "Have you noticed how nice so-and-so is being? It's wonderful." In fact, we drank a toast to one partner in particular, whose dramatic change has been visible to many.
>
> It's as if someone has opened the shades and the light has come into the room!
>
> Thank you, thank you, thank you.
>
> Jennifer"

I got paid for the work I did at that law firm, but I mean it when I say that getting this email made me happier than getting the check. Making this kind of difference is what keeps me going in a very challenging business.

What we need to think about this morning is how we can find a way to make a difference in the work we do. For many of us, the opportunities are there; we just need to discover them. How can we find more personal joy—and better life/work balance—by giving to others in (and outside) our work life? Don't we give too much already? Isn't that the problem that leads to imbalance? Or maybe the problem is that we are giving too many hours, and too much sweat, leading to too much anxiety—all without knowing the real value or meaning of the effort; without seeing our purpose.

You have all heard the story I am about to tell; it has been told by every minister and motivational speaker in history. I don't know the origin, but the message is a powerful one for people thinking about their personal *Mission*. I had to hear this story three or four times before the message really stuck.

"A couple is walking along a beach and thousands of starfish have washed up on the shore, each of which will surely die if not returned to the water. The woman reaches down and throws one back into the water. As they walk along she throws another one and then another back into the water. Looking at the thousands of starfish on the beach the man says: "What possible difference can you make by throwing a few back?" As she reached down, picked up another one and put it in the water, she smiled gently and said: **"for that one it makes a difference . . ."**

FOR THAT ONE IT MAKES A DIFFERENCE. Those words ring in my ears whenever I feel overwhelmed by the needs of the world—and wonder if what I am doing really matters. For a family in Cambodia, my friend the doctor has made a difference; to those less fortunate that we have fed and clothed, we have made a difference; to the secretaries in that New Jersey law firm I made a difference. For the families we comfort in times of grief, we make a difference. We cannot heal all of the pain and suffering in the world, but every single individual that we touch with love and compassion can profoundly benefit from our efforts.

We each have an inner voice that we hear once in a while, but we don't always listen to it because it bumps into something called "ego." Ego is that part of us that believes that achievement in this world is measured by having an impressive job title, wearing nice clothes, getting a name-brand education and driving a good car. Don't get me wrong; I happen to think Nature is pleased when we are able to live well, and that it is good to enjoy the fruits of financial success. But is that our only scorecard? Is our scorecard the size of our office, the title on our business card, or what we drive?

The next time you catch yourself denying that little voice in you that tells you to donate groceries to the food pantry or books to prisoners, or to read stories to special needs children, or coach a little league team, think about a man named Richard Alpert.

Richard was born into a wealthy New England family. He got the best education and enjoyed many of the world's finest benefits; and he had a lot of resources available to him. Nevertheless, he was kicked out of Harvard for experimenting with LSD. Richard went off to India and found a spiritual teacher who gave him a new name: Ram Dass. The name Ram Dass means "Servant of God." In the midst of this journey, Ram Dass asked his Maharaja how he could achieve enlightenment. His guru said simply: "Serve people; feed people."

Serve people; feed people.

Sometime later today—maybe when you get back to your hotel room—close your eyes, take a couple of deep breaths and see what message you get from that inner voice; see what image of *service* appears. Listen to the voice and contemplate the ways in which that voice may be your intuition showing you a glimpse (maybe a vision) of Nature's plan for you.

We all can't give up everything in our lives and head off to India to find enlightenment. (Although, many of our jobs and technical support operations seem to have found their way there!) But by being more open to the idea of listening to your inner voice, you will open up all possibilities.

What makes me so sure of this, and confident that it is okay to let our lives go in a direction that does not seem to fit the conventional rules of achievement?

First, check out all of the crazy stuff I read. I just walked around my house writing down the titles of some of the books I have read. If I have learned anything from reading these books, it is that we *can* control our attitudes, we *can* change the direction of our lives, and the less hard we try to insist on certain outcomes or *success* factors—when we stop pressing—good things happen.

Let's call this: "A Reading List that Can Move You"

- *My Grandfather's Blessings*
- *The Alchemist*
- *All I Really Need to Know I Learned in Kindergarten*
- *Minding the Body, Mending the Mind*
- *The Monk Who Sold His Ferrari*
- *Control Your Destiny or Someone Else Will*
- *The Good Life*
- *The Celestine Prophecy*
- *Your Sacred Self*
- *The Reconnection*
- *The Abilene Paradox*
- *The Artist's Way*
- *The Game of Life and How to Play It*
- *A Heart as Wide as the World*
- *The Path to Love*
- *The Re-Enchantment of Everyday Life*
- *You Will See It When You Believe It*
- *The Seven Habits of Highly Effective People*
- *The Art of Possibility*
- *The Fifth Discipline*
- *Inner Peace for Busy People*
- *The Drama of the Gifted Child*
- *The Architecture of All Abundance*
- *The Bible*

In many ways, I have had the experience of living the principles that these people have written about. And I have learned along the way that the definition of "achievement" is fleeting.

Let me share a taste of my personal journey as an illustration of faith. It may, at the same time, scare and inspire you. It starts out sounding like the first sentence of a bad novel.

I grew up in a small town where my dad worked in a factory for 35 years. As a junior in high school I had no plans to go to college. When a recruiter suggested that I apply to Harvard, I said: "Where is it?"

Fast-forward past Harvard. (One of the greatest parts of my education came from the fabulous people I met there.) I am willing to bet that I am the only Harvard graduate in history whose first job out of college was selling insurance policies door-to-door. I was making big money doing it, but I was also crying big tears as I sat alone in my car planning my route. I simply could not find the purpose in what I was doing.

With a couple more odd jobs under my belt, a year later I got into law school. I did well enough there to get a job at a major Boston law firm. (**Dream #1** had come true: I was Perry Mason.)

But I didn't like getting paid for spending a lot of billable time fighting with other lawyers. I always really wanted to be a sports lawyer anyway, so I got a job as a sports agent representing senior professional golfers. I took a major pay cut, left a 17th floor office with a view of Boston Harbor, and gave up a shot at partnership to work from what was essentially a living room in the Back Bay. (**Dream #2** had come true: I was a sports agent.) But a year and a half later my partner got cancer, we ran out of money and I had to find a new job. That's when I decided I wanted to be in the legal marketing industry. It was a rapidly growing profession, and I brought a unique set of skills to it. I went to a big law firm as its first marketing director, where I got experience in all aspects of legal marketing and marketing management.

Five years later I hung out a shingle as a legal consultant. With only my former firm as a modest client, only about $4,000 in the bank, and a belief that I could build something, it was both an irrational and exhilarating move. (**Dream #3** had come true: I was running my own business.)

Oh yeah, four years later, after establishing myself as a leading legal consultant, a headhunter called and asked me to work for a company that developed websites for professional sports teams. (**Dream #4:** I did work for one of my first loves, Major League Baseball.)

These are all examples of making changes to find my right livelihood, while balancing the right factors for my family.

But what was happening to me on the inside during this journey?

I mentioned that my child, Casey, died about 16 years ago. (When I was working as a sports agent.) When you hold the lifeless body of a baby in your arms, it changes you.

Three months later, I sat with my wife for 7 hours as Casey's twin brother, Brian, had open-heart surgery. He came through it great, but continues to have significant special needs. Nothing in business or life ever seems to be unbearable after that: I suspect that having faced these challenges gave me the courage to make some important changes in my life.

Unfortunately, I still sometimes wait for a traumatic experience before I do what I really want to do. I had to sit alone in my backyard one Saturday morning (for what seemed like an eternity) waiting for an ambulance to arrive as my father was having a heart attack. Before that I had never ever actually told him I loved him. What was I thinking before that moment??

For many people, September 11, 2001 was the traumatic event that made them re-assess what was important in their lives. Have you forgotten the things your inner voice said to you that day and in the days that followed? That would be a real shame . . . it may have been our most vulnerable and our most honest time of reflection.

I was working in a New York office on 9/11. My wife called me from Boston as I was entering the building to tell me that a small plane had hit the World Trade Center. By the time I got up to my office—which had a clear view of the twin towers—reports were starting to come in that it was no accident. Those of us in the office stood and watched helplessly as planes full of people slammed into buildings full of people. We held each other and screamed and wept as the buildings fell.

Soon after 9/11 my inner voice said to me, "even though this job and this experience will be a lot to give up, you don't want to be this far from your family every week." I called my boss to tell him this dream had to end for me. Ninety days later I was back in the legal consulting and training business (working out of my house).

Just so you know, I don't think any of my story is extraordinary . . . Nature didn't give me any special insight, emotional strength or capacity for drama that everyone doesn't have. **We all have challenges—the question is whether we see the challenges as part of our burden or our purpose.**

There are few things more challenging than raising a special needs child, but any of you who have experienced it know that it is much more of a purpose than a burden. I write an annual holiday message, which goes out with our Christmas cards. I am told by many who get it that it is an essential part of their holiday celebration—it started out as a burden, but writing that letter is clearly now a part of my purpose.

So the message I want you to leave with today is that achieving work-life balance isn't so much about saying "NO" to requests and demands; it is about saying "YES" to yourself and your heart. It is not so much about your work life; it is about your life work, and the impact you have on the world just by being a part of it.

When the Carters' first son died, they printed his favorite quote on the pamphlet for the memorial service. It was from a Steinbeck novel—it was about how we are all connected.

> "Whenever they's a fight so hungry people can eat, I'll be there. Whenever they's a cop beatin' up a guy, I'll be there . . . I'll be in the way guys yell when they're mad an' I'll be in the way kids laugh when they're hungry an' they know supper's ready. An' when our folks eat the stuff they raise an' live in the houses they build—why, I'll be there."

> John Steinbeck, *The Grapes of Wrath*

I believe in, and have experienced dozens of examples of, synchronicity—the many ways in which I have seen all of the events in my life connect—for me and for others, so this quote really connected with me.

Life should be all about knowing the importance of what you do with the gifts you are given, how to use those gifts, and how to use the circumstances you find yourself in. The events that followed my son Casey's death, for example, were full of synchronicity. A marketing director in Miami had an infant child die, and I was there for her; the people who joined our bereavement group were changed forever by our group interaction; a guy I worked with in New York needed my understanding and compassion when his baby died; a woman I sat next to on a plane to Bermuda whose baby had just died got off the plane with a copy of a poem I had written to Casey—she squeezed my hand and smiled for the first time in days; the parents of a kid whose death was reported in the newspaper thanked me effusively for sharing a copy of my Homily with them before the service for their child—complete strangers touched and affected by the death of my son. I DON'T GO AROUND LOOKING FOR THESE OPPORTUNITIES to connect—they are the synchronistic connections that life is made up of. [Dad elaborated on each of these synchronistic encounters in the live presentation.]

Seeing ourselves as playing an important role in an infinitely connected universe helps break down a lot of the barriers to being all that we aspire to be on this simple planet. One step we can all take toward getting in touch with our hearts and the world is to meditate. Meditation is often thought to be too weird or too hard, but that's because we judge it, instead of just doing it.

I have included in your handouts an example of one very simple approach to meditation; please promise yourself that you will try it. If you think you don't have time, you can do a few things to make the time: get up 10 minutes earlier, put it on your work schedule, take a yoga or meditation class; listen to a meditation tape instead of watching *one* TV show. Get a coach.

I use "triggers" for meditation: sitting at a red traffic light, airplane take-offs, and airplane landings prompt meditation. By the way, have you noticed that there is always sun above the clouds? No matter how cloudy life appears to be, there is always sunshine above the clouds. We have to stop those voices in our minds that say "you can't." Meditation is one way to do that.

One of my favorite poems, *The Journey*, by Mary Oliver, speaks volumes to me about how we often approach life as a burden, when it has the potential to be so peaceful and joyful.

It takes a certain amount of faith to think we can find Answers by just breathing and thinking about nothing; and it takes real courage to make meaningful changes in our lives, such as changing jobs, or changing what we don't like about our jobs.

But Nelson Mandela wrote something that might inspire us to have the courage to change. Many have heard this great message—now we must live it:

> "Our deepest fear is not that we are inadequate.
> Our deepest fear is that we are powerful beyond measure.
> It is our light, not our darkness, that most frightens us.
> We ask ourselves, who am I to be brilliant, gorgeous, talented and fabulous?

Actually, who are you not to be?
Your playing small doesn't serve the world.
There is nothing enlightened about shrinking so that
    other people won't feel insecure around you.
We are born to make manifest the glory of God that
    is within us.
It is not just in some of us, it's in everyone.
And as we let our light shine, we unconsciously give
    others permission to do the same.
As we are liberated from our own fear, our presence
    automatically liberates others."

Nelson Mandela
Inaugural Speech 1994

Regardless of how you feel about his politics, Mandela says something powerful here . . . WHAT'S WRONG WITH TREATING YOURSELF AND ENCOURAGING YOURSELF THE WAY YOU WOULD TREAT AND ENCOURAGE SOMEONE YOU LOVE? Does it feel like conceit or arrogance? Does it seem selfish? Does something inside us say we must suffer? Is there a voice from our past saying: Who do you think you are? If you ever have a chance to read another Mary Oliver poem called *Wild Geese*, it will help you deal with these inner voices of doubt.

Fifteen years ago I was in the audience when a speaker asked us to write on a small piece of paper what we would do if we knew we could not fail. If money were no object, and if self-doubt did not get in the way, how would we spend our time?

Right now I want each of you to take out a piece of paper. It can be any size, but I would recommend that you use a small piece of paper that will fit in your pocketbook or wallet.

Here is what I wrote in response to this question: "I would live in a house on a lake; write poems and books; make speeches on motivational subjects, and be connected with my family, friends and nature." These were aspirational concepts, not something I actually thought could happen.

And yet, that vision has started to unfold. I have outlined some chapters for a book, I have written almost 100 poems, and I have started looking at lake houses. I am still probably several years from achieving all of these goals, but I am speaking to you here today—that is something I could never have imagined doing 15 years ago.

Yes, I am here. I occasionally speak at my church; I coach little league, and I am on various charitable committees. I attend almost all of my daughter's plays and music programs, and I genuinely enjoy every minute I spend with my friends. I get exercise in hotels, am paid well for my work, and I have a fabulous relationship with my wife . . . sounds pretty good, huh?

But it's like playing a sport; we will have good days and bad days; when you bake a pie you will have some great crusts and some crumbly ones, but you bake another pie. Enjoy the playing, enjoy the cooking . . . life is not a game of perfect.

Let me leave you with a great story that has floated around on the Internet for years. I do not know where it originated, but it certainly speaks to knowing what is most important in our lives:

THE STORY OF "SMALL FISH"

The American investment banker was at the pier of a coastal Mexican village when a small boat with just one fisherman docked. Inside the boat were several large yellow-fin tuna. The American complimented the Mexican on the quality of his fish and asked how long it took to catch them.

The fisherman replied, "Only a little while."

The American then asked why he didn't stay out longer and catch more fish.

The fisherman said he had enough to support his family's immediate needs.

The American then asked, "But what do you do with the rest of your time?"

The fisherman said, "I sleep late, fish a little, play with my children, take siesta with my wife, Maria, stroll into the village each evening where I sip wine and play guitar with my amigos. I have a full and busy life."

The American scoffed, "I am a Harvard MBA and could help you. You should spend more time fishing, and with the proceeds buy a bigger boat; with the proceeds from the bigger boat you could buy several boats; eventually you would have a fleet of fishing boats. Instead of selling your catch to a middleman you would sell directly to the processor, eventually opening your own cannery. You would control the product, processing and distribution. You would need to leave this small coastal fishing village and move to Mexico City, then LA and eventually NYC where you will run your expanding enterprise."

The fisherman asked, "But, how long will this all take?"

To which the American replied, "15-20 years."

"But what then?"

The American laughed and said, "That's the best part. When the time is right you would announce an IPO and sell your company stock to the public and become very rich; you would make millions."

"Millions. Then what?"

The American said, "Then you would retire. Move to a small coastal fishing village where you would sleep late, fish a little, play with your grandkids, take siesta with your wife, stroll to the village in the evenings where you could sip wine and play your guitar with your amigos."

Ahhh, yes, maybe we are closer to what we want in life than we realize.

Thank you for spending this time with me today. I hope you will look in new places for new answers about life, work and your Lifework. Please say "yes" to yourself as you look at life from a place of love, not fear.

A final word from Storypeople:

"In my dream, the angel shrugged & said, 'If we fail this time, it will be a failure of imagination' & then she placed the world gently in the palm of my hand."

Dad had ended the 2003 Holiday Letter with that same quote. He believed that by unleashing the imagination and letting go of fear 'all things were possible,' and this phrase really captures that. In the same folder in which I found these written remarks, I found some pages that Dad called "optional additional sections." Having heard the tapes, I know he did not use this extra material in the presentation. Much of the material on these supplemental pages also appears in bits and pieces in various Holiday Letters. But there is some good stuff here, so I thought I would share one example of it, in particular. Dad told the following story in several of his presentations. It is one of those great pieces that gets passed around on the Internet. It might just be 'urban legend.' But it is a great message—especially for a family that has a mentally challenged boy.

"At a Church fundraising dinner, the father of a Church child delivered a speech that would never be forgotten by all who attended. After extolling the school and its dedicated staff, he cried out, 'Where is the perfection in my son Shaya? Everything God does is done with perfection. But my child cannot understand things as other children do. My child cannot remember facts and figures as other children do. Where is God's perfection?'

The audience was shocked by the question, pained by the father's anguish and stilled by the piercing query. 'I believe,' the father answered, 'that when God brings a child like this into the world, the perfection that He seeks is in the way people react to this child.'

One afternoon Shaya and his father walked past a park where some boys Shaya knew were playing baseball. Shaya asked, 'Do you think they will let me play?'

Shaya's father knew that his son was not at all athletic and that most boys would not want him on their team. But Shaya's father understood that if his son was chosen to play, it would give him a comfortable sense of belonging. Shaya's father approached one of the boys in the field and asked if Shaya could play. The boy looked around for guidance from his teammates. Getting none, he took matters into his own hands and said, 'We are losing by six runs and the game is in the eighth inning. I guess he can be on our team and we'll try to put him up to bat in the ninth inning.'

Shaya's father was ecstatic as Shaya smiled broadly. Shaya was told to put on a glove and go out to play short center field. In the bottom of the eighth inning, Shaya's team scored a few runs but was still behind by three. In the bottom of the ninth inning, Shaya's team scored again and now with two outs and the bases loaded with the potential winning run on base, Shaya was scheduled to be up. Would the team actually let Shaya bat at this juncture and give away their chance to win the game?

Surprisingly, Shaya was given the bat. Everyone knew that it was all but impossible because Shaya didn't even know how to hold the bat properly, let alone hit with it. However, as Shaya stepped up to the plate, the pitcher moved a few steps to lob the ball in softly so Shaya should at least be able to make contact. The first pitch came in and Shaya swung clumsily and missed. One of Shaya's teammates came up to Shaya and together they held the bat and faced the pitcher waiting for the next pitch.

The pitcher again took a few steps forward to toss the ball softly toward Shaya. As the pitch came in, Shaya and his teammate swung the bat and together they hit a slow ground ball to the pitcher. The pitcher picked up the soft grounder and could easily have thrown the ball to the first baseman.

Shaya would have been out and that would have ended the game. Instead, the pitcher took the ball and threw it on a high arc to right field, far beyond reach of the first baseman. Everyone started yelling, 'Shaya, run to first. Run to first!'

Never in his life had Shaya run to first. He scampered down the baseline wide-eyed and startled. By the time he reached first base, the right fielder had the ball. He could have thrown the ball to the second baseman who would tag out Shaya, who was still running. But the right fielder understood what the pitcher's intentions were, so he threw the ball high and far over the third baseman's head.

Everyone yelled, 'Run to second, run to second.' Shaya ran towards second base as the runners ahead of him deliriously circled the bases towards home. As Shaya reached second base, the opposing shortstop ran to him, turned him in the direction of third base and shouted, 'Run to third.'

As Shaya rounded third, the boys from both teams ran behind him screaming, 'Shaya run home!' Shaya ran home, stepped on home plate and all of the boys lifted him on their shoulders and made him the hero, as he had just hit a "grand slam" and won the game for his team.

'That day,' said the father softly with tears now rolling down his face, 'those 18 boys reached their level of God's perfection.'"

Dad always ended this story choked up, and he would say something like: "What a gift it is to help others feel bigger; to help them feel valued. Who among us couldn't use a helping hand when we go to bat from time to time? Who among the people with whom we work couldn't benefit from our guidance—personally or professionally from time to time? Too much of the life/work balance question is answered based on society's scorecard. Let's make what matters our own." Even without these extra materials, my father managed to pack a lot of motivation into his presentation. I wish he had recorded more of his speeches.

Before we move on to my father's writings about "the potential of poetry," I think it would be good to settle into Dad's Holiday Letter from 1998. This one was a little less sophisticated than some of the others; more like a "typical" holiday letter. But it is nice, nevertheless. And Dad's writing style is somehow soothing during the holidays.

Holiday Letter

At Christmas time I try to share with our friends and family the essence of what has transpired in the Watson household. Typically, I recount grades, events and developmental milestones; I also try to add a little inspiration. This year, however, I am struggling to find the right words, while at the same time feeling more emotions than ever. Is it possible that as we get older we get more in touch with, but less impressed by, important feelings? Maybe the events in our lives just get more profound than the words available to describe them.

My father-in-law died this summer; Andrew turned into a teenager at 12; Brian and Lindsay blossomed at 8 and 3 respectively; Nancy and I fell even more in love; and my mother-in-law became even more a part of our immediate family. I now fly first-class (because I have miles, not money). I am starting to make inspirational (not just business) speeches, and I spent a week in Sydney, Australia speaking and negotiating a license agreement for my CD-ROM product. Quite a year, indeed. But let's face it, without the joy and wonder of children and family, some of the richness of our more mature lives would be lost.

Whenever I walk in the door from a business trip, Lindsay shouts: "Daddy, I'm so glad you're home," as she runs across the room to throw her arms around my neck. She puts her soft cheek against mine and says: "Daddy, you have scratchy whiskers." Ahh, that's awfully close to heaven. Lindsay's pre-school teachers describe her as a sweetheart— she's everybody's best friend and her manners put most of us to shame. (Although, "excuse me" is really an inadequate follow-up to her adult-quality burps!) She sings freely the great songs she learns in school, and is comfortable expressing her emotions and her ideas. She operates the computer like a pro, and can navigate CD-ROM's the way we navigated coloring books at her age. Thankfully, she still asks to be held like a baby every once in a while. Watching how Lindsay hugs, guides, encourages and protects Brian is good old-fashioned, lump-in-your-throat heart warming. Like all of us, she seems to understand that having Brian in our lives is an immeasurable blessing.

As I sat in one of the classrooms at Brian's school recently, awaiting the arrival of Hillary Clinton who was supposed to pay a visit, I was flooded with emotion. Surrounded by other special needs students and their parents, each of whom Brian insisted on hugging and entertaining, I realized how lucky we are to have a child like Brian, and to live in a place where special kids get special attention.

With the ongoing help of his wonderful tutors, "I.E." and "Momo," Brian has started putting some words together, and his overall communication skills have improved considerably. He *really* is obsessed with hugging, but what a great obsession. (He also begs to be tickled!) He still loves *Barney, Wheel of Fortune*, and his all-time favorite show on his days off from school is *The Price is Right* (he loves "Ba Baka"). Brian was the hit of a 2-week summer camp where he was "mainstreamed" for the first time. His infectious smile and his love of life obviously resonated with his fellow campers as they do for us. (By the way, the First Lady stiffed us on that appearance, but that's another story!)

Andrew hasn't grown much . . . in the past 15 or 20 minutes. During the year, however, he has managed to go from 5'6" to almost 5'10". (Shoe size: 11½.) He continues to make us proud as a student (great grades, great reports and great friends), and as an athlete (he made the "A" travel team in basketball, hit a "walk off" home run to win a playoff game, and was the MVP of the 21st annual Starr-Wexler Turkey Bowl football game on Thanksgiving morning). He threw his first curveball in a baseball game—and it was a beauty—to fool a great hitter in a clutch situation, but he has thrown us no curves. He continues to be a model citizen, a wonderful big brother, and a delight to be around. In many ways, he is my best friend; so for me, watching him grow up so fast has been both exciting and saddening. We can now "pump iron" and go to "Pats" games together, but like any normal teenager, he no longer goes out of his way just to hang around with dad. Good for him; we are very proud of the young man that he is.

For my part, things are great. I have developed an interactive CD-ROM training program called: Just Think . . . about Clients™. My book, The Law Firm Marketer's Guide to Survival, was just published, and the consulting and speaking schedule for the first half of '99 is filling up fast. When people ask me how I do it, the answer is simple: Nancy.

If it were not for Nancy's incredible and unqualified support of all that I do (along with her masterful family management), there would be no book, no CD-ROM, fewer clients, and a lot more headaches. Amidst chaos she still manages to volunteer at The Community Women's Exchange, run several miles most days, improve her tennis game, and expand our network of great friends. She also has made our first Christmas season in our new home enchantingly beautiful. I can never thank her enough for all she does, but I will always keep trying.

God bless Fred and Shelly on the birth of A.J., and for introducing me to my fabulous assistant, Jennifer. God bless Steve Stetson on the loss of Larry, his dear friend and business partner. God bless Kathy for her awesome advice on how to design our new home's interior. God bless our great baby-sitters for "date night" and for the love they show our children. God bless the Cunninghams for keeping this wonderful old house held together. God bless the pilots on a recent Air Canada flight, who invited me into the cockpit to observe the landing in Boston. God bless Bob Jarmen for putting together the East/West Ryder Cup in Vegas during Final Four Weekend. God bless my folks, who love us so well across the miles. And God bless those who teach meditation, as it is in the silence between thoughts that God speaks to us.

When Nancy's dad died this summer, I thought it would be brutal to go on without him. He was so very special. But Paul was someone who lived by values of the highest order—honesty, openness, respect, sensitivity and humor. These values never die, so I see him everywhere I look. If virtues are our legacy, then a part of us lives on forever. Thank you, Paul, for these timeless gifts. You are evident in the best part of all of us. God bless you and your example.

We wish all of our friends and family a Merry Christmas, a Happy Chanukah, and a New Year filled with hope, joy, love, discovery and peace.

The Watsons

Chapter Seven

A FEW WORDS (ACTUALLY, A CHAPTER) ABOUT THE POTENTIAL OF POETRY

My dad loved poetry, but he always said that his poetry carried an asterisk with it. Other than a one-semester course in college, he never had any formal instruction in writing poetry. He said that he felt like a "fraudulent poet" because he didn't know any of the basic poetic forms or structures. He seemed determined to learn the rules, though. I once caught him asking my little sister for a copy of the course materials for a poetry class she was taking in 6th grade—about five years after he had asked me for a similar document from a poetry class I took in high school.

Dad was, it seemed, equally repulsed and challenged by the idea of trying to express his poetic thoughts within the confines of poetic rules and formulas. Yet the "challenge" seemed to be winning. I found that Dad made a photocopy of page 172 of Naomi Wolf's book, *The Treehouse*, in which she described various poetic forms and gave an example of a learning exercise. The paragraph he had circled started out saying:

"Like a carpenter showing a child how to build a birdhouse [my father] taught me the basic shapes one could work with [in poetry]; a quatrain (ABAB), a sonnet (ABAB, CDCD, EFEF, GG, for instance), a ballad (ABAB CDCD). He explained the beats of the words: iamb (du-DUH), trochee (DUH-da), spondee (duh-duh, equal inflection) . . ."

A note scribbled on the side of the page said, "sign up for a poetry class." Dad never quite made it to a class, however, and I am sure it was because he would have had absolutely no patience for these serious poetic rules. He would have called them "painful constraints." So my father's poetic form remained varied and undefined—commonly known as 'blank verse.'

Dad wrote dozens (probably hundreds) of poems. Once, in the early 90's, he put about 30 poems in a hand-made book and entered the collection in a contest. He was surprised by the favorable response people had to his writing. I remember him telling me that colleagues who read the collection called him to say that some of the poems had brought them to tears and others had made them smile. With this feedback, you would think that he might have shared more of his poetry over the years, but he seldom did. Sometimes, however, he wrote poems for friends who were celebrating something special or facing a particular challenge.

In fact, Dad had been writing poetry since he was a sophomore in high school. That was when he wrote his girlfriend a hokey love poem, and he still had the original poem (handwritten) in a folder 35 years later. He once told me that she laughed at it, so he took it back; and frankly, I don't know what 10th-grade girl would not have laughed . . . what was he thinking? Check this out:

First Love

What is this I have?
Is it not all I could ask for?

I am so very pleased,
and with a dash of pride
I say 'could a person ask for more?'

121

A question with depth: do I have
the unrestrained mannerisms
to follow up on such a blessing?

I have been told,
or in such a way informed
that this be not a fitting inquiry.
Dare I relinquish it
from confronting me?

This certainly is not something to which most teenage girls would respond favorably, but what a bold move to give something so cerebral to his young sweetheart.

Dad had a grand vision of using his poems to raise money for our church and for my sister's school. His brother and his best friend from high school ran a printing company, so he figured they could print a 50-page poetry book for about $2 or $3 each. His idea was to sell the books for $10-$15 with all of the proceeds being donated to the church or the school. He believed people would buy them just to be supportive, not because his poetry was any good.

Dad was the only person I ever knew who subscribed to *Poetry Magazine*. I know he wanted to have a poem published there, and he really did want to publish a poetry book, but he just never got around to it. Before he died he had collected 75 of his poems into a document that certainly had the potential to be a book; I will try to make Dad's poetry book a reality some day. A few of his poems appear here.

But before sharing some of his poems, here is one of my father's writings *about* poetry. The samples of his poems that follow this piece are drawn from the nearly 100 poems I found amidst the collection he had pulled together and a few others I found on random papers.

What is the Proper Place of Poetry in Life?

I still have a copy of the first poem I ever wrote. It seems oddly absurd, in some ways, that I actually wrote it. Something akin to a possessed voice stirred inside me, causing me to share my feelings for my girlfriend in the 10th grade (yes that would be in high school). My recollection is that she laughed and thought I was weird. Yes, my first real girlfriend more or less made light of my first real attempt at poetry.

I wonder what "the great ones" wrote first? Keats, Dickinson, Whitman, Stevenson, Shakespeare and others had to start somewhere! Not to suggest for a moment that I am, or ever will be, a great poet, but might their first efforts have been much better? Not an important fact, I suppose, but it would be fun to know.

So, what is it about poetry that keeps it out of primetime, anyway? Various sources tell us that there are roughly 300 million people in the U.S. I wonder what percentage of them would say they love poetry; how many would say they sometimes enjoy it, and what proportion of our country's population have little or no interest? I would expect that very few "love" poetry; but does this reflect a quality problem or marketing problem? Is it more about a lack of education in poetry, or incomplete human evolution? Consider this—a poem put to music and sung is a *song* and everyone loves songs. Hummmm . . . ?

Moreover, there are simple, wonderful poems that, when read by anyone, can soothe, impress, entertain, sadden or inspire. These simple poems seem to break through to even the most poetry-resistant. Would my modest attempt called *Fog* have any wide appeal? Who knows . . .

Fog

It drifted in secretly,
and I was unaware.

The haze slowly dulled my vision,
but I could still see.

I was afraid,
but I moved ahead in fear.

Contrast that poem with this next one, which is a more wistful rhyming love poem. Might this have more appeal for the masses?

A Fleeting Vision of Someone Special

Looking down the stairs I paused,
fixed upon a smile that caused
my blood to warm, my skin to blush.
Was this the girl I missed so much?

I moved ahead and down as well,
captured in a dreamy spell;
wishing now to see more clear
that loving face, my friend so dear.

My mind and eyes in combat stayed,
my heart's desire to embrace forbade.
But I could not help but look again,
to fan that flame of warmth within.

Feeling foolish now I slowed my smile,
viewing there another child.

Could I this gentle creature touch
and feel the love I felt so much
the night I knew her gentle cheek
and near the Charles our souls did speak?

The words that flowed that night so free
were words of love 'tween she and me.
And may they never fade away,
until again we touch one day.

Here is what my father wrote about the amazing poet Rumi. This is an honest appraisal of his response to his first exposure to Rumi's work. Later in his life I noticed a book about Rumi's life on one of his bookstands, but I don't know if he ever actually read it.

Interestingly, when I read a collection of poems by Rumi—considered one of the greatest poets of all time—I was not overly impressed with the first six poems I read in the book titled *Rumi: Fragments + Ecstasies*. Then I got to "Seven," and that's when I went "oh yes!" So maybe poetry is just too personal, or too complicated or too something, to have mass appeal. One of Rumi's poems, *My Beloved* (too long to reprint here), inspired me to write the following poem as a response.

Reflections Upon Reading My Beloved

Tell me, tell me again the meaning here?
The message, clear at inception; romance abounds

with a passion

beyond the most eloquent words.

Great love; that is, after all,
what speaks from the pages.

Great love

without distraction . . . until distraction wins.

Sharing; sharing words of great love;
Meant to stir love's response—or is it

just poetry?

(It is likely both; life needs love and poetry.)

Can others relate? Is the 'love described' brief
in life, but

long in fantasy?

Can love really linger so? Or again? Or always?

I hear "escape with me—go where great love goes."

I say "be patient with me as

new desires

visit old places. God will understand."

Know the heights of total peace, it says.
There is passion in reflection. There is,

delicious,

fulfillment in a menu of touching and smiling.
Romantic needs—candles and careless hearts,

a soft caress

that leads to nothing (or everything).

A rich, powerful connection—more
spirit than body—abstract love, powerful

love.

Lust without a plan; dreams more sensual than sexual.
Seeking simple peace (repose?) Warm hearts and

laughter

with My beloved, until My beloved is no more.

★ ★ ★ ★ ★

I really like the way my father wrote about poetry, and I think these are pretty good poems, too. So, I ask again—why did Dad not share more of his poetry? Remember that "lack of confidence thing" he exposed in his Homily at my brother's memorial service, and in the story he wrote on parenting? Indeed, the poem at the end of this chapter reveals how that personal battle was playing out for my father as he tried to overcome the sad voice of childhood. He carried around a lousy self image and a bruised ego that blocked his deepest expressions of talent.

Nevertheless, persevering and being ever the optimist, Dad often used poetry to speak of love and good things. When a new family moved into our neighborhood one winter, my father gave them this next poem as a welcome present. This loving family had left a familiar community (where they had deep roots), to follow the father's new career opportunity, and I think Dad sensed a little trepidation in the family about the move; he also learned soon after their arrival that they had a genuine appreciation for art and loving kindness.

Less than 5 years after my dad wrote this poem welcoming this beautiful family to our neighborhood, the young father died of a rare cancer. Dad was asked to read the poem at the memorial service for Maurice in the back yard of the family's Connecticut home (to which they returned upon learning of the diagnosis). Dad also made a reference to Maurice in his 2007 Holiday Letter.

To the Flanigans Upon Their First Christmas in Boston

Nature teaches that it is very
difficult to transplant a flower.
But with tender care, attention
and a shower of love,
the beauty of a special
plant can be moved to new soil.

We thank you for making our
garden your new home.
You have brought radiant
colors and vibrant life
to the place we view
as sacred ground—

our world.

We welcome you
with a promise to nurture the bouquet
that is your family.

Even though Dad wrote a lot of poems, he was particularly fond of one that he called: *A Leaf Outside My Window.* One day he was sitting in our den looking out the window at a leaf flapping in the wind . . . that, it seems, is all he needed for inspiration. He said that this poem felt more like "a real poem" than others he had written. I like that it had more imagery, and less slathering of emotion (and attempted therapy) that characterized so much of his writing. But even here, he could not resist taking a shot at the pain of the human condition!

A Leaf Outside My Window

Just outside the window
it sits in complex golden glory.

Forecasting a time of chilled
air and snow, perhaps, but not too soon.

With each flapping, a film of nature's life
and death plays out with passion;

Now a bird balancing, bouncing really,
on the thinnest branches,
reminds us of more life and of change and surprise;

The next surprise—which leaf will fall
from this flickering picture of autumn?

I try to guess
as I wait for detachment; for that is the natural order
in life—breaking loose.

Yet, how can dropping away
from that which has sustained us from a new-born bud
be a natural progression?

The wind continues
to make lovely dances
outside the window;
Few leaves actually fall;
it is not their time yet.

They hang on,
as most of us do, to what
we have always known.

Hard to imagine
what awaits the leaf
that falls from its perch—earth, snow, rakes, mulch?
Risky, it seems, the unknown.

And the host, so radiant today,
will soon be barren;
in turn, small tufts of snow
will appear and hold on;

Holding on until the sun comes,
until warm breezes replace cold winds,
and life is again renewed.

Life goes on . . . .

This next poem was a very special one for Dad. His lifelong
dream (he called it his "daydream and nightdream") was to live on
a peaceful lake in a cabin with a space that gave him a view of the
world outside; a place where he could sit and write. One summer we
rented a cottage 'sight unseen.' Soon after we arrived he announced
to us all as he looked out from the deck that he was seeing the precise
view he had always dreamed of. The next day he wrote this poem.

The View I Have Always Imagined

I usually assigned it to the morning;
that first look through the window, or off the deck,
to the soft serenity of blue and green.
A lake, ever calm, inviting me to do nothing
or to swim or to fish or just dream.

But there was always more;
this dream led to a place of peace, inside
a heart that longed for nothing more
(love perhaps), but this peace is really close.

In my mind, there seemed an abundance
of trees around the water.
But it was never clear—until now; eerily familiar
this Real Scene,
capturing the truth of an overactive imagination.

Tapping deep feelings, I resist any doubts.
This is the place (or a perfect form of it);
proving that what we dream does, in fact, exist.

Never becoming common or familiar,
each lingering gaze, confirming my long-held belief
that I belong here.

A lake surrounded by trees,
framed by a sky and pastoral shores;
a picture of quiet perfection
reminding all that nature can truly inspire (and heal).

Since I share my father's concern that poetry is not universally appreciated, I will not expound further on his lyric nature, but I have sprinkled a few throughout this book—I think that is what he would have done. It also seems right to share one of his most emotional and revealing writings here, since it was in a file called "poetry." But this one really seems—and sounds—more like therapy. I find this rather painful to read, as it reveals the inner struggle that was always lurking behind the scenes in Dad's life. I am buoyed, though, by the knowledge that he found a place of pure love and personal peace in later years. (God only knows where the #7 comes from!)

The Revelation of True Self #7

"Hello," I said, "where did you come from?"

"I've been here all along," he said. "I'm the person you don't like."

"You live with me?" I asked incredulously. "You are here with me all the time?" I said with a sense of inquiry and discovery.

That's correct," he said, in a tone that almost boasted. "So you may as well get to know me."

"Oh, I know you," I said. "I was introduced to you many years ago. As a child in fact, my parents told me how awful you are. They said you are despicable and worthless. I really don't like you."

"But you don't really know me," he said sadly, "so how can you feel such disdain for me?"

"I don't know," I said, seeming puzzled. "That's a really good question."

"I didn't know you were there with me all the time. I don't really know anything about you, but I feel this constant hatred for you."

"Do you feel this way about other people?" he asked. "Do you dislike most people?"

"I'm not sure," I replied. "I think I like most people—in fact, I want to love all people, but you keep getting in the way, don't you? Just when I start to feel love toward someone, my anger toward you gets in the way."

"So just love me," he said.

"I can't necessarily love, or even like you, just because I want to," I said with a sense of frustration. "It's odd, but even though I can imagine you as a loving caring person, I can't really feel love for you . . . you're just not loveable."

"We've got to figure this out," he said, "because I am not going away." "This is almost like an arranged marriage," he added. "We are together forever, so we can either go through life at odds or we can work toward becoming one."

"Sounds good," I shrugged, "because whenever I experience you as loveable and wonderful, I feel warm and content." I can feel your presence, even though I can't see you," I said. "I have a hunch that you would look very nice if I could see you."

"Keep trying," he said. "I've been invisible for a long time. It would be wonderful to be seen, understood, appreciated and loved," he added.

"Don't worry," I replied. "I will find you, I promise."

It's nice that Dad ended on a hopeful note! Let's stay connected to that positive attitude by inserting his 2005 Holiday Letter. In this one, Dad featured my sister's beautiful poetry. Of course, I call it "beautiful" because one of the poems she wrote was about me!

Holiday Letter

There wasn't going to be a letter this season, but throughout the year I found myself tossing little scraps of paper—with thoughts and observations—into piles around the house. It was ten years of behavior I couldn't change. Then one recent morning I heard the author of the book *Passion at Work* speak. When he was asked what his personal goals were, he said: "to touch as many people as possible in a positive way in the time I have on earth." It got me thinking. That was the same answer I wrote down in a "Seven Habits of Highly Effective People" seminar 15 years ago. So why wasn't I planning to write a letter this year? Writing an annual Holiday Letter had begun to feel like an obligation; not the labor of love it started out to be. I also began to feel oddly self-conscious about how many of you said you appreciated and looked forward to it. (I am sure that an equal number probably just toss it out.)

But then I started thinking about the people who needed to know we were praying for them, and how important it is to acknowledge our feelings for each other. I thought of Kathy O'Grady's great courage and attitude in the battle against breast cancer. I thought of Kathy Stuart's loss of her dear mother who was truly an extraordinary woman. (Kathy paid me the highest compliment when she told me one year that she had read my letter to her family.) I think of Maurice Flannigan who stares down a brain tumor with an irrepressible spirit of love and good humor. I think of Auntie Deborah, who has so many people who love her and are praying for her health. And I reflect on our friend Lori's dad passing away at Christmas time last year. They need our love. I read Lindsay's many beautiful poems and thought how unfortunate it would be not to share a couple with you. Here are two of my favorites (unedited). The first is about her big brother.

Andrew

"Don't worry, I'll be home from college soon."
Easy going, sweet, outgoing, caring;
beating him for the first time
in a video game, tall.

Easy going, sweet, outgoing, caring
him shouting "Yes!" after beating me, tall

Doesn't mind me hanging with him,
him shouting "Yes!" after beating me.

Watching him leave for College,
doesn't mind playing with me.
"When is the next time I will see you?"
Watching him leave for College,
beating him for the first time in a video game.
"When is the next time I will see you?"

Green

Green, the color of spring leaves.
When they sway, it moves the green grass with them.

The grass carries the flowers with them,
with what looks like a dance
for anyone who wants to stop and watch.

These things seem to shake the earth and everyone around them.

But when fall comes, the green
motion seems to fade away,
and the grass seems to stand still,
and the flowers stop dancing.

When winter comes,
the leaves vanish for good, the grass forced to stand still,
and many flowers, lost.

Winter ends, making room
for new leaves,
new grass, and new dances,
and the happiness returns too.

How many 10-year-olds could write that kind of poetry? Truly amazing. I am thinking of my family, our friends, our new Church home, my fulfilling job, Lindsay's poetry and of taking this opportunity to say that there is no greater joy than knowing that your college age son has turned out to be *exactly* the person you always hoped he would be. I am thinking about how great it is to know that your 15-year-old son, who faced death several times as a baby, is a blessing just by being alive; and that your 10-year-old daughter has made your dream of "having a girl" a universally more amazing experience than you could ever have imagined. Without writing, how else can we thank the unsung heroes in our lives. So many people do great things, and would do anything for us. If we all have a little Angel in us, then I guess that means we are surrounded by multitudes of Angels . . . cool.

I completed a book for lawyers this year called *The Essential Little Book of Great Lawyering*. The point of the book is that clients do not judge lawyers based on how smart they are, but on how the lawyers treat them. Does the lawyer listen, try to understand what keeps the client awake at night, help them solve problems and care as much about the client's success, as their own? This sounds a lot like the attitudes we should be bringing to all of our relationships—with our family members, business colleagues and friends. To constantly be reminded of these priorities, I fill my iPod with lots of stuff that makes my wife and children roll their eyes . . . Martina McBride ("In My Daughter's Eyes"); Elton John ("Can You Feel the Love Tonight"); Barbara Streisand ("At the Same Time"); John Lennon ("Beautiful Boy"); and even The Brooklyn Tabernacle Choir ("I'm Not Afraid"). It all just works together to remind me of what is important. But in the end I am moved most by a wonderful old hymn that says: "Let There Be Peace On Earth and Let it Begin with Me."

We wish you and your family peace, good cheer, love and joy this Holiday season.

And after the poems, a song!

Dad was convinced that he had a great idea for a country song. He said these lyrics "just came to him" while driving his old Toyota Celica down Clifton Road on his way to an afternoon law school class at Atlanta in 1983. He kept the handwritten lyrics all these years, and recently said that he could imagine it being sung by some classic country band like Alabama, or a more modern singer, like Carrie Underwood. Can you believe he kept these lyrics for over 25 years, never giving up hope that someone might actually put them to music, but he never sent them to a publisher. He believed the so-called "hook line" ("your love keeps changin' like the seasons") had the potential for mass-market appeal in the world of country music. You can draw your own conclusions . . .

Lyrics to
"Your Love Keeps Changin' Like the Seasons"

(A country song that has never been sung)

Written by Jim Watson

With *springtime* came the sunshine
and cool drops of rain.
I'd wake up to the sound of birds,
but nothing eased the pain.

I'd watch the world turn greener
as new life filled the air,
but I just couldn't see you
'cause I knew you didn't care.

I want to love the springtime,
but now it seems so far away.
My heart just keeps on trying,
but I can only say:

Your love keeps changin' like the seasons,
but girl there are no reasons
to believe that I could ever make you stay;
the clouds grow strong,
I've done no wrong,
but the sun still goes away;
help me know which way to turn
to keep the storms at bay.

Summer has its heat waves
and flowers all around,
but the time I spend without you
really gets me down.

A thunderstorm, the air is warm,
we seek the cool shade.

I need to learn just how to love you,
so this sweet time will not fade.

Your love keeps changin' like the seasons.
what will it be today?
The clouds grow strong, I do no wrong,
but the sun still goes away.
Help me know which way to go
To keep the clouds at bay.

The *fall* gets nice and crispy,
and the days they start to cool.
The leaves turn a brilliant red,
and again I play the fool.

As doubts creep in I'm chilled again,
but a jacket makes me fine.
I close my eyes, and bow my head,
and pray that you'll stay mine.

Your love keeps changin' like the seasons,
but girl there are no reasons
that will tell me why your love just fades away.
The clouds grow strong,
I've done no wrong,
but the sun still goes away;
help me know which way to go
to keep the storms at bay.

With *winter* now upon us
white flakes are falling down,
The coldest times I'll ever know
are when you're not around.

I see the snow, and it helps me know
that life is moving on;
I hope to God that I can find
the strength to carry on.

> Your love keeps changin' like the seasons,
> but girl there are no reasons
> to believe I could ever make you stay;
> the clouds grow strong,
> I've done no wrong,
> but the sun still goes away;
> help me know which way to turn
> to keep the storms at bay.

Speaking of song lyrics, I found a folder in my dad's office that had the lyrics from several popular songs printed out. There were no explanations to accompany any of them. You can tell a lot about a person by the kind of music they listen to, but you can tell a lot more by reading lyrics that someone finds important enough to print out and save.

These songs clearly reflect my dad's heart. In fact, he used a clip of the song, *Another Day in Paradise*, by Phil Collins in his last motivational speech. I know, because one of Dad's best friends was there, and told me Dad made the point of how lucky most of us are to have good jobs, great families, and our health. I encourage you to read the words from that song; I have reprinted my favorite two lines here. They capture so much of what we often experience in that moment when we encounter poverty or see misfortune in the eyes of someone on the street. You might be inclined to skim the words, since it is a song you have heard many times. But if you look up these lyrics and read them with care and openness, you may find some deeper meaning reflected in them. "He walks on, doesn't look back. He pretends he can't hear her." For many of us, another day with clothing, food, good health, and a job can truly feel like paradise.

Another song my father had printed out was a Chicago classic, *I've Been Searchin' So Long*. Again, the title alone reflects much about what was going on in his heart and mind. By reading the full song lyrics you might find a transformational message that is rather poignant for you. A song that talks about the long journey to finding real "meaning" in life was right in Dad's strike zone. And the upbeat way enlightenment seems to be discovered in the song can be motivational in itself. I think my father could have had a great time writing about and responding to phrases from this song like: "There's a strange new light in my eyes," and "Now I see myself as I am," just to name a few.

Dad used music to communicate a lot. When I was in college he once sent me the lyrics to *Beautiful Boy*, by John Lennon. The words delivered a powerful message about how much he cared for me. And he also gave me a tape of a little-known song by Lowen & Navarro called *All is Quiet*. The essence of the song was that as long as we stick together, we will get by. Good stuff.

Finally, I have to mention that Dad had printed out the lyrics from a song called *Tell It To My Heart*, by Taylor Dayne; knowing my father, he probably just loved the song's title. Interestingly, in the margin next to these lyrics Dad had written, "feel the rain on your skin, no one else can feel it for you, only you can let it in' . . . . like love and life." Clearly, a call out to the Natasha Bedingfield song, *Unwritten*. Since Dad was always trying to reclaim his own life—to not let the approval of others be the basis for his happiness—this would seem to be a reference to that important life-long journey in search of his authentic self.

Chapter Eight

SERVANT LEADERSHIP

"The ultimate aim of the *servant* leader's quest is to find the resources of character to meet his or her destiny—to find the wisdom and power to serve others."

Robert Greenleaf

Servant leadership was something my father very much believed in. Doing things that helped others (and being humble about it) was, to him, a form of leadership. Clearly, it was a form of "leading by example."

The following transcript is from one of my father's earliest presentations. It was intended to help the church raise money, and it is a wonderful example of his belief in Servant Leadership. Since this passage was typed from a tape of his spoken remarks (he did not use a written text that night), it has a less literary flow than the things he actually wrote.

The guests who were there told me it was a bizarre scene. People were drinking and having so much fun during cocktail "hour," that it turned into cocktail "hours." So, the dinner and the speeches started very late. Dad was the last speaker, so by the time it was his turn to present, people were tired and practically ready to leave. He held up his note cards and said: "if you just give me a few minutes, I will toss my prepared remarks aside." The gymnasium—a make-shift auditorium—erupted in applause, and people actually listened.

Keynote Presentation, St. John's Church Dinner:

All right, that much clapping means you've been drinking too much!

I heard a story recently that strikes me as being very appropriate for tonight. It is about a guy who died and was faced with St. Paul telling him he would have a choice about how he spends eternity. Yes, he was given a choice of whether he wanted to go to Heaven or Hell. St. Paul said, "How do you want to make your decision?" Of course, the man said, "I would like to have a glimpse of each if I might." "Okay, what do you want to see first?" "I would like to see Hell."

He went and looked upon what was Hell, and he saw a marvelous vat of vegetable soup with steaming broth—it was extraordinarily delicious looking. But it was surrounded by people starving and wailing. They each had attached to their hand a four-foot long spoon. These spoons could be dipped in the vats but they couldn't figure out how to get the long spoon up to their mouths—they were starving. The guy said, "I can't stand seeing this. Show me Heaven."

He then goes to see Heaven, and he sees another large vat of wonderful broth and soup. Everyone there also had four-feet long spoons attached to their hands. But here everyone was healthy, vibrant and feeling wonderful. The man said to St. Paul, "I don't understand. I saw the same scene in Hell, but the people in Heaven are so much healthier and happier. How is that?" His host said, "In Heaven, they have learned to feed each other."

I have never forgotten that story. I believe we are all feeding each other—or should be—as we go through this thing we call life. I am making that point in the first few minutes tonight, because we don't have a lot of time here, and I want the point to be made. If you remember nothing else from tonight, I hope you will remember and believe that we must, at all times, be feeding each other.

Now, what is interesting to me is that when I first heard that story I was on my way to speak at a retreat in northern Vermont. Having just flown back from New York, I was driving through the night to do an impossible task. I had been asked by a large Wall Street law firm to go to this resort and speak about teambuilding to a bunch of partners and associates who didn't like each other. Teambuilding is not popular in most law firms. But it was a real problem at this particular firm. So, I took the challenge. I said, "Yeah, I can do that."

I was struggling to stay awake during the late night drive, so I put on a tape that I hadn't listened to before. I am driving through the middle of nowhere in the middle of the night, listening to this guy I had never heard of before called Wayne Dyer. Some of you may have heard of him. This was long before he became a PBS icon. As I listened to him tell this story about Heaven and Hell—and other stories about teamwork, caring and interdependence—tears started rolling down my cheeks. I was on my way to make an incredibly challenging speech, but my speech was being written for me. I had not had a chance to prepare; I hadn't even had a chance to really focus on what I would say. My plan was to get to the resort at about six in the morning, and then spend two hours preparing my presentation. But there was rich material coming out of my speakers, and I realized that I would somehow be just fine the next day.

So, not only does the story of Heaven and Hell have in it elements of the importance of sharing, caring, and what is possible, but the way I heard it, it is also about connectedness. We are connected; whether we like it or not, we are connected to each other and to a vast, infinite, Universe. And through this connection we have this ability to experience all possibilities. That is what was going on during the drive that night. I didn't know where I was going, how I was going to get there, or what I would say when I got there, but it was being sent to me.

Another thing I learned from that "midnight" tape experience involves relationships. Our Minister said in a recent sermon: "It is through relationships that we experience the wonderful, life-giving and healing presence of God." Everything that we read about, talk about, and experience at the highest human levels, is about relationships. We are in relationships in every part of our lives—husband and wife; girlfriend and boyfriend; partners, children and parents, cousins, friends, professional colleagues, and casual daily encounters. We are in relationships in every aspect of our lives, so it's fun to think about being connected.

Being connected doesn't just mean we must give of ourselves; it also means we should appreciate the experience of receiving. Many of us are not good at receiving the gifts, the praise and the love of others. Yet, put yourself back in that original story—if the people in Heaven were unwilling to receive, they would have been in Hell. They were only able to experience the health, joy, and wonder of Heaven, by being willing to let other people feed them.

I really hope that in the course of this evening, we all can connect in a way that leads us to feeling comfortable both giving and *receiving* gifts from each other.

Further, if we trust in Universal connectedness, then we can stop trying so hard to *make* everything happen. Instead, we need to 'just let it happen'—be grounded in where we are; grounded in what's happening right now. There is a song and a video clip I want to play for you. This song is beautiful, and it reminds us to think about many things we should care about. The song has been used in a recent television ad, which is unfortunate, since it taints its specialness a bit. The next time you see the ad, just close your eyes and listen. I've seen the ad five times, and I don't even know what the ad is for. I think it has something to do with allergies, and how to get rid of them!

[A video plays, showing a montage of the original super-senior professional golfers who started the Senior PGA Tour. They are having fun and hitting great shots; Louis Armstrong is singing "What a Wonderful World" through the whole video. An audience member calls out: "That song was the wake-up call for the astronauts this morning."]

I did not know that. You know what is unbelievable? That song was also requested by a dear friend of ours who knew for a year that he was going to die of cancer. It was played at his memorial service, which hundreds of people attended because he was such a wonderful young man. You could have heard a pin drop amidst the teardrops—as the song played. I will never forget the power and the spirit in that service; such a joyful message at what was supposed to be such a sad time. With that song, Ken was sending us a message that he knew things were going to be okay; that we will all be together, and this is a wonderful world.

I shared that video clip with you tonight for a lot of reasons. Not just to hear the song, although I think that is important, but also because this particular video exemplifies for me the idea of being open to all possibilities. Twenty or thirty years ago—I don't know exactly when the Senior Tour started—the legendary senior golfers shown in the video had to believe their careers were over. They had had their days of glory. I know because I have worked with many of them. I had the good fortune of acting as a lawyer and agent for a bunch of the men in that video, including Sam Snead, Doug Ford, Bob Goalby and Gene Sarazen. They surely thought their careers were over when they got too old to play competitive golf on the regular PGA Tour. But somebody had an idea; somebody drove that idea forward, and a new opportunity opened up—something called the Senior PGA Tour.

Not all of these golfers envisioned this new tour or did anything to make it happen. But some had the Vision, and it happened. It was a profound, life-changing experience for thousands of golfers. What I am hoping we can come away with tonight is an acceptance that by trusting that we are in the right place in life—as hard as life may sometimes be, we can center ourselves around "What will be, will be; what is, is right now." This will help us find our way. These golfers had retired, and were having autograph parties to make a few dollars. But suddenly they had a wonderful new opportunity presented to them. They could once again play competitive golf, entertain millions of fans, and make a lot of money. To me, this is a great example of all possibilities, and a reminder that we can always restart our journey.

I have with me a poem from a New Zealand prayer book that ends with: "As we travel far and fast, lead our minds back to the wise men following [a] star, and forward to the day when we will all see your shining light."

For some time now I have been carrying a copy in my pocket. I travel a lot. When I wake up in a hotel room in the morning, I take stuff out of yesterday's shirt pocket and move it into today's shirt pocket—so I read it every day. To me, this prayer (too long to recite here) reflects a lot of what we need to think about daily. For you, it could be some other poem or anything that inspires you, but I think we need to feed our minds with good words, thoughts and images. We get fed plenty of bad stuff.

How many of you have screen savers on your computer? Do you have little creatures eating each other, or swirling stars and other strange stuff saving your screen? There is a feature on many computers that can be used to create any message you want to appear as your screen saver. If my office computer sits quietly long enough, it says, "The more you give, the more you receive." If our family's home computer sits idle long enough, it says, "Do what you love, and the money will follow." I haven't quite believed in that one yet, but I'm trying. Another computer screen-saver in our house says, "People are more important than money." These are messages to the mind, heart and soul.

Whether we are conscious of it or not, we are feeding this thing called a brain all the time; we may as well feed it good stuff! And when you are not feeding your mind, remember what our minister told us last Sunday, quiet your mind—meditate. Get grounded in the silence. Many of you have probably read something written by Deepak Chopra. He talks about how God works "in the silence between our desires." Due to time constraints, I am not going to read all of the special quotes and passages about meditation that I brought with me tonight, but, I do want to read one. "The cosmic psyche whispers to us softly in the gap between our thoughts. This is also what we call intuition. Time-bound awareness is in the intellect. It calculates. But timeless awareness is in the heart. It feels."

I am rushing through all of this because our time is constrained, and I want to end in a couple of minutes. This has been a very challenging experience for me. Many of you know me personally, so you know my flaws. You know that I am not good at a lot of things, so that makes it hard for me to talk about my life as some kind of model, and about "all possibilities!" The other thing is that there were expectations coming into tonight's program. A lot of you said something like, "I heard you speak at the church a couple of years ago, and I'm really looking forward to what you might say tonight." I don't like that. I like it better when you say, "Oh, I've never heard you speak before. Maybe you have something good to say." I am used to showing up and speaking at law firms where they are clueless about what I teach; so anything I say makes them think that I am brilliant. It is a real challenge when people think that maybe I actually have something to say.

Years ago, I started keeping a folder on my desk that said, "Life Change Seminar." I put articles and ideas into that folder that related to anything that might be helpful to people in their lives. I hoped to someday deliver a presentation intended to help people who might want change in their lives. Then I just let the thought go. I have been putting stuff in the folder for over seven years.

The first time I put some papers in the folder I visualized myself standing at the front of our church—not here in a school gymnasium. But I truly thought that this speech would happen some day at St.

John's. So when the church called and said, "Jim, we're having a church dinner and we would like you to speak about something motivational," I hung up the phone and said a quick prayer of thanks. I not only wanted this opportunity, I think I needed this opportunity. I needed to start moving my life in a new direction. The people at St. John's were there for Nancy and me many years ago when our child died. We were welcomed with open arms into a congregation that had never met us. It is all connected. Now, here we are, years later and you are again giving me something special. I don't know if any words tonight have been meaningful to you, but your willingness to let me say them is an enormous gift to me. I can only hope that they were in some way helpful to you.

Let me conclude with this. Recently, I had a business trip planned to Australia, but the night before I was supposed to leave, Nancy said to me, "Jim, are you sure you should go?" She could tell I was fretting. I had so many other things going on, I said, "I don't know if I can do this." She asked again: "Should you go?" And I said, "I think I should go. There is a reason for me to go to Australia."

I was feeling sad and lonely as I sat on the plane, thinking, "Why am I feeling this?" As the plane took off, it was a cloudy, dull Boston day, and I was saying a little prayer. We broke through the cloud, and the sun poured in through the windows. As I felt the warmth of that light, I said, "Yes. The light is shining on me now, and the light is always here. It is behind the clouds some days, but it is always here." And I swear to you, as I stand in front of you, the guy two seats from me turned to me and said, "Isn't it beautiful out there." No one has ever said that to me before, and I fly all the time. "Isn't it beautiful out there." I turned to him—I had some tears in my eyes—and I said, "You know what's beautiful? The sun is always shining. We don't always see it, but it is always there." He said, "Yeah, it is." That's what I'm always going to remember about that morning. The light is always there for us, just the way we are all here for each other.

Dad repeats that story (metaphor?) about rising above the clouds in a variety of writings. I have edited some of the references out of this collection to minimize redundancy, but you will find that it still appears in more than one place. It was such an important story to him, and in some contexts it just seems right to repeat it. It illustrates how much my dad saw hope and love and light in every situation.

One night Dad's quest for *servant leadership* allowed him to live a dream. He had always admired the Reverend Peter Gomes, whose messages from the pulpit in Harvard's Memorial Chapel had stirred Dad's soul over the years. When he learned that our church planned to have Reverend Gomes as the keynote speaker at a fundraising dinner, he asked if he could introduce him. I remember how excited he was telling me he would get to share the podium with one of his heroes. The night of the event he was even more excited because he got to sit with Peter during dinner, and, most importantly, Peter referred to Dad as "Brother Watson" during his keynote remarks. Here is what my father said that night.

Introducing the Reverend Peter Gomes at a Church Fundraising Dinner

The plan is for me to be the appetizer and the salad. Then we will clear the salad plates so you can enjoy the main course—our keynote speaker, the Reverend Peter Gomes.

For over a year now Nancy and I have been trying to figure out when to have a cocktail party at our house. We have been guests in the homes of many of you, and it would be appropriate for us to have a party of our own. After much contemplation and, realizing the limits of our house (and perhaps the limits of my entertainment skills), we just said: "Let's have our cocktail party at the Hilton and let the church pay for it . . ." So thank you all for coming tonight, and thank you to all the organizers who helped make our party possible.

By the way: has anyone besides me noticed that there are a lot of big houses in our town? There are a lot of rather large houses, not only around here, but in the surrounding communities as well. Someone might ask what that says about this part of the world, but I think there is an important observation to be made that transcends house size.

In my experience in this community—no matter how big or small your house is—the people in this church cannot fit all of their friends in their homes. I believe that this assembled group should be admired for the size of their hearts, not the size of their houses. It is nice (and more accurate, I think) to say that the true measure of our wealth is the extent of our friendships, not our financial or worldly wealth. But, what does all this have to do with tonight's theme: "A Time for St. John's"?

First, like many of you, this church—the *institution* of St. John's— has not only been a place of congregation for my family and friends, but it has also been a consistent source of strength, support and motivation.

It is amazing to me that I am standing here tonight having had the opportunity to attend Harvard and hear the Reverend Peter Gomes preach many times over the years. I will forever cherish the fact that my name appears in tonight's Program along with his. As I told Peter earlier, I had often sat in the pews in Memorial Church, being inspired by his words, and wondering what it would be like to meet him. It has been delightful beyond my imagination. As usual, St. John's has helped me realize a dream.

I was so moved by Peter's remarks at the Memorial Service during my 20th college reunion that I walked outside, sat down on the steps of Widener Library, and wrote a poem on the back of the service leaflet. (It is amazing to learn how many of our college classmates have passed away . . . .) I am pleased to say that that leaflet was still on my desk—dated June 12, 1997—when I started preparing for tonight's presentation. That was a long time ago. While it may not be great poetry, I want to share what I wrote that day, since it was Peter who inspired me to look back at my college experience in a different way.

On Going to Harvard

Did I lose my soul there, or find it more richly
than I ever would have known?

Why do I feel lost here now—fortunate,
but undeserving.
Hearing of those who have died before me
moves me to think.
There is, in some way, an absence of gratitude—blame?
No. Guilt, from a sense of not serving.

With the gifts I have been given,

and a fortitude true
to what got me here,
I should not wonder why I return, unswerving,
to the place where my heart and mind
were opened just a bit from fear.

I should make my mark
as one so lucky,
and offer more expressions
of the love that fills—and fulfills me.

I shall live with thankfulness,
knowing I am truly blessed.

But let's get back to "A Time for St. John's." If it is already a friendly place of worship, and a place that brings friends together, what more could we possibly need?

Well, many years ago I was asked to address a St. John's group during a fundraising dinner. I started my remarks with a story about the man who asked St. Peter for a peek into Heaven and Hell before he decided where he would go. That story ends with the observation that the only difference between Heaven and Hell is that "in Heaven they have learned to feed each other."

Our minister shared a story in a sermon a while back that is important to reflect on tonight. It was about a child with special needs who invited himself into a sandlot baseball game, and with the game on the line, the catcher showed him where to stand. The pitcher moved forward; another player came over to help the boy hold the bat, and they proceeded to help him triumphantly score the winning run. The father knew right then what it looks like to see God's love in action. God's love flows through people when they join together to help people succeed.

You don't need to be the parent of a special needs child to connect emotionally with that story. Who among us has not needed a little extra help from friends or strangers from time to time? Whether facing an illness, or getting through a day without alcohol, drugs or despair; maybe we just need a little help getting across a busy street. Who among us could not benefit on occasion from an uplifting gesture, a helping hand, encouraging words, or a sincere smile? And yet we count ourselves among the fortunate. Many of us are blessed with life's best benefits, but not everyone is so lucky. We must be mindful of what others might need for support.

I want to suggest that "A Time for St. John's" is really about establishing St. John's as a beacon to the greater community; a beacon of hope and caring for those who need support, guidance and sustenance. It seems like a good time for those of us with many friends to open up our hearts to those outside of our circle who need more encouragement, more education and more people to love them. In addition to opening our hearts, we need to open our church doors to them. And if we raise enough money, we will have more doors to open.

Let me conclude by mentioning a much misunderstood phrase from a movie you have all seen: "If you build it, they will come." I have heard some of you say in recent years that faith is not enough of a reason to build a new building that will cost millions of dollars. And you are right. As faithful as I think I am—that is a big leap. But it misses the point.

Those of you who have seen the movie know that *Field of Dreams* is not about building a baseball field in the middle of a cornfield—it is about creating a place where dreams come true, a place where you can experience hope and joy and magic; a place where you get a second chance to play catch with your long dead father.

Let's not have "A Time for St. John's" be about a building—let's make it about creating a place for miracles and hope and connection. This is the time for St. John's to be more thankful, more accessible, and more open to possibilities. Let's let "A Time for St. John's" be a time to rejoice, to reflect and to reconnect with each other and with a world that now, more than ever, needs our love.

God bless St. John's for being there for countless families over its long history. God bless us as a congregation as we grow larger, stronger and more faithful in the service of giving. And now, the main course. Please welcome the Reverend Peter Gomes.

Dad was pretty good at getting people's attention at fundraising events. His enthusiasm as a presenter was infectious, and he always seemed to find a way to touch that part of us that evoked compassion. He used this talent as a form of servant leadership by speaking occasionally (for no fee, of course) at a variety of fundraising events. A great example of this occurred at a fundraising dinner for the Southern Norfolk County Association of Retarded Citizens ("SNCARC"). Nancy was the co-chair of the event, and my brother Brian is, in fact, a SNCARC Citizen. I was not able to attend that night, but on many occasions people have commented to me on what a wonderful job my dad did. But I have to set the stage properly . . . .

Apparently, the outdoor tent that was set up to house the event did not lend itself to the makeshift speaker system they tried to employ; and the visual effects that were supposed to accompany everyone's remarks were not working. Moreover, the somewhat over-served crowd was growing increasingly boisterous as people sat around a dozen or so large round dinner tables. The event was slipping out of control and the formal program was at risk of not happening.

I am told that my dad just got up and went to the front of the tent, and without a microphone or his notes he got everyone's attention and spoke from the heart about why they were all there. I asked him once how much of his prepared material he shared, and he said "most of it, I think, but I really don't know." I found the words below in a SNCARC folder. They were obviously his planned remarks.

Dinner Remarks at a Fundraiser for Citizens With Special Needs

We are all here tonight for a reason. Probably not the same reason, but for a good reason I suspect.

We would like to think it is because we are all so aware of, and sensitive to, the many challenges of the Citizens of SNCARC. It is exciting to think we are all here because nothing could keep us away from an event that raises money for the special people SNCARC serves. But, in reality, some of us are here because it is a chance to spend time with our friends; and some are here because they would do just about anything to support the Committee members who have worked so hard to make this evening a success.

Maybe you are here because you know that there is an awesome auction item that you want to buy. That's certainly okay. In fact, it's all okay. No one is here to judge your motives. We simply want to thank you for your support and to educate you about the wonderful work SNCARC does. The Southern Norfolk County Association of Retarded Citizens provides programs for hundreds of people, and it supports and sponsors even more. Some of the wonderful citizens are pictured here. [They weren't actually pictured that night, because the video didn't work.]

I have heard people say things like, "It takes special people to serve special kids," or that "God does not give us greater burdens than we can handle," or that, "Parents of special children are somehow *uniquely* able to handle those demands and challenges." I think there could be some truth to these expressions, but there is more to it.

I believe we are all supporting each other in life, and that those of us with special SNCARC Citizens in our lives could not do what we do without the incredible support and strength we get from our families, our friends and the community. You particularly bless us with your presence here tonight.

Those of us involved with SNCARC Citizens know, however, that having a disabled or mentally challenged family member is not the only difficulty in life. Each of you faces myriad challenges of your own that have nothing to do with physical or mental disabilities. So as we gather tonight, please let us hear your needs; let us help you when you face your own challenges.

I read somewhere that what we do in this life ripples through eternity. Think of it like the ripples that form when you throw a pebble into a still pond. Every act of generosity that you give—that we give to each other—is felt far beyond the immediate moment. You gave up money and time to be here tonight. It means more than you can imagine to everyone in the SNCARC community.

I will think of your support every time I pull into the driveway at SNCARC to drop off or pick up Brian from a program. When I go into the SNCARC building to pick up our daughter from the sibling workshop, I will be mindful of your generosity. I will think of you when we attend the annual SNCARC holiday gathering.

I am humbled not just by the professionalism, but also by the love and joy that comes from the staff and volunteers at SNCARC. We should be impressed by the unqualified love they feel for (and from) those they serve.

We don't really know yet what Brian's educational, developmental or social future holds, but because SNCARC is there to help us . . . and because you are here to help SNCARC—we are hopeful that he will find his right place. SNCARC offers the gifts of support, comfort and optimism to those who need it greatly.

As some of you know, I send out an annual Holiday Letter that is partly about our family, and partly about life. I have tried in various ways to describe our Brian over the years—but it is hard to convey how truly special he is if you do not know him the way we do.

It is obviously a bit difficult for me to talk about these emotional issues, and I do not want this to be a sad or sorrowful evening. So let's let tonight be an inspiring celebration of all that is good in life. I hope these remarks will encourage those of you who are overwhelmed with requests to support many wonderful causes, to continue to save a few hours and a few dollars for this special organization. Actually, I am hoping that you will overspend enthusiastically for the cool auction items that will be offered later.

Mostly, though, we want to say thank you for being here. And thank you to those who have worked so hard to make tonight happen. As the husband of a Co-Chair of this event, I have seen up close how much effort goes into this. (Nancy, I would say something about how great you are, but I know you don't like being in the spotlight.)

Let us enjoy this evening, being thankful for SNCARC and thankful for each other.

Two years later Dad spoke extemporaneously at another SNCARC fundraiser. I found the following prepared remarks, but I have learned that he didn't even bring the notes with him when he went to the podium that night either. He, of course, probably found a way to remember some of what he planned to say, and added new thoughts that probably occurred to him while he was walking to the stage. I heard later (jokingly) from a friend that her mother was upset with my dad because he made her cry, which caused her makeup to run!

SNCARC Auction Dinner Remarks

Two years ago I stood before many in this audience and talked about the joys of being the parent of a child with special needs. I shared the story of Brian putting his hand over his heart immediately upon hearing the first few notes of our National Anthem. I told you that we can learn a lot from living with a child for whom simple pleasures bring great excitement—like watching Wheel of Fortune every night, bringing a package of cookies home for him from every business trip, and watching Bob Barker on days off from school. [Note: those stories were not part of his written remarks from the previous meeting . . . Dad loved to improvise.] These things become a part of your life because they are an important part of your special child's life—just like soccer, ballet, and piano lessons are a part of other children's lives.

So when I was asked to say a few words tonight, I decided to share some thoughts about what I have learned in the two years since our last SNCARC dinner.

I've learned that giving up a well paying, high-profile business position to be home with my family more is a blessing, not a sacrifice.

I've learned that the concept of "Work-life balance" is not a bunch of buzz-words, but something to truly strive for. Two years ago I rushed out of this dinner at 10pm into a waiting car to head off to one of my many weekend work engagements. My job at the time often required me to travel five or six days a week. I have learned that Brian needed more of me than that, so I changed jobs.

I have learned that having a teenager is hard, but having a teenager who doesn't really know he is a teenager is an extra special challenge. Brian is 14 now, and his excitement about moving into a high school based program is unbelievable. I have learned that sharing my shower with Brian a few mornings a week is not an imposition, but something to look forward to. (It's all in how you look at it.)

I have learned that Brian's habit of inviting everyone he meets to have dinner with us is probably a throwback to the pioneer days when everyone was always welcome for a meal in your home. One of his favorite phrases is "supper, me house?" I've learned that you cannot be too compassionate or too caring and that empathy is everything.

As many of you know, Nancy's mom passed away a few weeks ago—and one of the things that stood out at her service were the stories of all of the great things she had done for other people. She was committed to community service in a variety of ways. She set a great example for her daughter—my wife. I have been known to give Nancy a hard time for volunteering for so many important community service projects—like SNCARC—but I now understand that she, and all of you who give so much of yourselves to others, are setting a wonderful example for our children.

You will be asked to bid on some things here in a few minutes. Some items you may have waited a lifetime for—and some may just seem fun and frivolous. We hope that you will open your hearts, as well as your wallets, and think about the many ways in which the money you spend tonight changes lives. Nancy and I are taking a crazy long weekend vacation to Mexico next week, as a result of some bidding we did with friends at an auction in support of a scholarship fund. Not only do we get to do something fun with friends, but because of that bidding, some children will be able to attend a school they might not otherwise be able to afford.

What you do tonight will provide services for citizens facing a variety of challenges: transportation, counseling, job training and life skills programs are just a few examples of what your being here tonight supports. For all of that, we thank you—and our Citizens of SNCARC thank you.

I don't think you will want to be hearing from me again in two more years, but I REALLY hope I continue to learn as much over the next two years as I have during the past two years! Enjoy the evening.

This seems like a good place to put Dad's 2001 Holiday Letter. As he mentions in some of his other writings, he was in New York on September 11th, 2001. His reference at the end of the letter to the outpouring of light that he envisioned at Ground Zero eerily foreshadowed the plans that emerged years later for the World Trade Center Memorial. This letter fits well in this Chapter on Servant

Leadership, and it is also fitting that he leads off with a description of our own SNCARC Citizen.

Holiday Letter

Our first Christmas present came early this year in the form of a college admissions essay written by one of our babysitters, who, like her sister, has become an extension of our family. Her insights about Brian say ever so eloquently what he is all about. Here are some excerpts from her essay. We knew that Brian was a gift, but this reminder is to be cherished.

"At eleven years old, Brian is not learning how to play football or baseball, like most kids his age. He doesn't know how to multiply or divide. Instead, he works on learning how to eat holding his spoon the correct way. A speech therapist works with him weekly. Most boys look up to heroes like Superman and Batman. The costume Brian chooses every year for Halloween: the UPS man. Brian isn't like most boys. Yet he remains blissfully unaware of the fact. Most of us spend our lives comparing ourselves to others. But Brian doesn't even think to compare himself to others. He is happy if his daily report from school is an improvement from the day before. He has learned to take pleasure in all the little joys of daily life. Whenever I look at Brian, I can see the intelligence that glows in his eyes. It is heartbreaking to see the frustration on his face when he can't make you understand what he is trying to say. Although communicating is difficult, the love he feels for all those around him is evident . . . he hugs everyone within an arm's length. As I grow older, I strive to be like that eleven-year-old boy. I hope to compete with myself, not with others. I hope to find joy in all of life's little pleasures—those that we so often take for granted. I hope to be able to love unconditionally. Most importantly, I hope to never underestimate the value of a hug."

Our 6-year-old, Lindsay, asked one day: "Why does Brian have to have special needs? Can't the doctors fix it?" I suggested that it was unlikely. "Yes they CAN," she announced emphatically, "I know how to fix it; it's called *learning*. Isn't that a great idea?" A great idea indeed. Learning. As we watch her try to teach Brian; as we watch her try to protect and understand him; as Brian hugs her and says: "I love Baby," we think, just maybe, she holds a special key to her special brother's heart. Whether she is playing her violin, dancing with abandon or reciting the Lord's Prayer above the sound of the congregation, she sends a special message to all of us—one of hope and of learning.

We could all probably stand to *learn* more. For Brian it may be words or how to dress himself, but for the rest of us it might be tolerance, compassion, self-love, forgiveness and trust. I am guessing that we can learn a lot of this from our children just by watching them. They can show us how to touch the soul in so many ways.

One of Lindsay's favorite games is to look up to the sky and spot familiar shapes in the cloud formations. "Look, Daddy, there's a car," she might say. Or "there is an elephant," or a "teddy bear" or a "teapot". Seeing teapots where others see clouds—that's what Lindsay is all about. She insisted that we wake her in the wee hours of the morning because she heard that there was going to be an incredible display of shooting stars. What a magic time it was for Nancy, Lindsay and me to be wrapped up in blankets on the deck watching hundreds of streaks of light shooting through the clear, star-filled sky. (Andrew wanted to get up—really he did—but just try waking a 15-year-old at 5 a.m.)

Although he has grown even taller (6'2ish), we can report for the first time that Andrew's shoe size has not increased in the past year (13). His heart is still growing, however, demonstrated continuously by the love and patience he shows for Brian and Lindsay. His passion for sports continues, demonstrated in his starting role as quarterback for the JV team, and in throwing a touchdown pass in his debut in a varsity game. His maturity was reflected in his decision to stay home and play baseball on his AAU team, rather than attend the MLB All-Star Game with his father . . . this very grown-up decision turned his previously-mediocre season around.

Andrew, Nancy and I got to spend some special time together this summer. In a weak moment, Nancy let one of her usually enlightened friends talk her into booking us on a 4-day trip through the heart of the Grand Canyon. We would be hundreds of miles from phones, TVs, modern plumbing, radios or newspapers, in a place accessible only by small planes and even smaller helicopters. Well, we did it—a whitewater rafting trip that covered hundreds of miles! Sleeping under the stars on the banks of the Colorado River, waking at dawn to the smell of bacon and *cowboy* coffee? It was truly the trip of a lifetime. There is a lot of magic in playing catch, going to new ballparks and helping your teenager with homework, but to share the wonder of creation with Andrew was priceless.

Nancy got a little grief from us in the time leading up to this wilderness adventure, but it was just one more example of how she makes our lives special—along with the day-to-day nurturing, her constant (well, almost) good humor, and her constant (without fail) love for us. I am working on a poem to give her for Christmas, and would like to share a few lines here: "Those who see the real you, see radiance and love/a wonderful soul in body and spirit./Those who love you most, want to celebrate together the gift that is you." If there were more words of admiration in our language, they would be all about this wife and mother. Whether we are playing tennis or golf, sitting by a fire having a nice steak (and an even nicer bottle of wine), or playing hide and seek with the kids, there is no place on earth I would rather be than hanging around with Nancy.

This passion for Nancy's company has made my life a bit more challenging this year. Last February I accepted a position as Senior VP of a company based in New York City. We develop and manage websites for professional sports teams. This job gave me a chance to participate in the excitement of building an Internet company, to be part of professional sports, and to work with a great friend from college. It has been an amazing ten months. I spend three nights each week in an apartment in New York, and have racked up more Amtrak miles than some of the conductors. It's been an incredible professional experience, and we have all adjusted to the new routine. The kids call me every morning (Lindsay tells me what to have for breakfast). And we all look forward to Thursday night when the train arrives, where I work in my home office on Fridays.

What a time to be working in New York. On September 11th I stood in the office and watched from my window as planes slammed into buildings filled with people. I watched with dozens of co-workers as the World Trade Center towers collapsed and disappeared. Those images are forever etched in my mind, but in no greater proportion than the examples of love and compassion that have resulted from the horrific events of that day.

We were awakened today by Lindsay rushing into our room announcing that the world outside her window was covered with pristine white snow. What a contrast to the acts of terror I witnessed from my office window. This first snowfall of the season came on the 11th anniversary of the death of our son Casey, but the beauty and serenity of winter reminded us, in many ways, of all that is right with the world.

I think we will find that when they finally turn off the construction lights, remove the cranes and send the recovery teams home from Ground Zero, there will be an incredible outpouring of light from the ground where the towers once stood . . . light so powerful that people will stand in awe as they witness it. If you believe, as I do, that light means life, then this light will be a reminder that those whose earthly lives ended that day are now among the Angels that care for us.

Let's be prayerful, thankful and humble in this Holiday Season and the New Year, and share the blessings of life and love.

Chapter Nine

IN THE PULPIT

Dad thought it was cool that there was a famous preacher—apparently a very famous preacher at the time—named James Watson, who lived in the 17th century. (Something he discovered, no doubt, doing an Internet search of himself.) My father fancied himself a pretty good preacher, and my step-mom lived in fear that he would announce one day that he was going to Divinity School! (She never wanted to be the minister's wife.) But Dad got his "fix" by doing occasional guest sermons. The texts of some of his sermons are printed below. I left them in whatever format they were in when I found them. Apparently, he used words printed in capital letters (or bold font) to help him follow the text. But he usually spoke extemporaneously— he never actually read any presentation. (Personally, I think he was a better speaker than he was a writer.)

Dad had a folder titled: "Homilies I Have Known and Appreciated." Unfortunately, it was mostly empty, but it had a few notes in it. He mentioned that one of his favorite authors, Samuel Johnson, had written a number of sermons for local clergy to supplement his income. (I found a book with a collection of Johnson's sermons in Dad's library.)

Dad actually owned *A Book of Eulogies*. Depending on your mood, these eulogies can be quite interesting—maybe even enlightening— and, to me, compelling. Maybe it was this book that inspired Dad to write this note: "I think eulogies are like prayers—and I like a good prayer!"

The Homily that follows was delivered at a candle lighting service for families of children who had died. This service grew out of a bereavement group that formed in the wake of my brother Casey's death. It was a beautiful evening during which those who had lost a child were given a candle. At the appointed time there was a solemn reading of the names of the children who had died, and with the reading of each name, the family came forward to have the candle lit. The service was very powerful emotionally, and provided real healing for the families. It was held annually for several years, and Dad spoke again two years later. (Typically, he was asked back to speak almost everywhere he made a presentation.) The message in this homily may have been aimed at those who had had a child die, but like much of what Dad wrote, it applied to a lot of situations. Ironically, perhaps, this night marked Dad's return to the same pulpit in which he had delivered the Homily at Casey's memorial service.

First Homily to the Parents of Children Who Have Died

The first time I stood in front of a group of people in this church I was in a state of EMOTIONAL SHOCK and SPIRITUAL CHAOS.

I was in emotional shock because my 3-month-old child had just died. Yesterday was the 5th anniversary of his death. I was in a state of spiritual chaos because I was feeling the profound presence of God in a way that I had never known before.

TODAY, I stand before you with A STRANGE BALANCE OF EMOTIONAL STRENGTH AND A SPIRITUAL HUNGER that REALLY started when Casey died.

I also stand before you as a NON-BELIEVER.

Now, before our minister has a HEART ATTACK at such a suggestion FROM HIS PULPIT, let me explain what I mean by that:

I NO LONGER BELIEVE in COINCIDENCE, and I no longer believe in BAD LUCK or GOOD LUCK.

I do, however, believe that God can and does have an incredible influence on our lives. IF we have trust and are willing to open up our hearts and minds to the Universal energy around us, then I believe we can experience the fullness of Nature's power.

I COULD TELL you about dozens of examples of HOW the presence of the Divine has displaced coincidence and luck in NATURE and in LIFE, but let me focus on a couple of the most MEANINGFUL examples tonight.

Our reading for this service speaks of light in MANY WONDERFUL ways. John says in Verse 4, *"in him was life; and the life was the light of men."* Verse 9 refers to *"the true light which lighteth every man that cometh into the world."* We also heard: *". . . yet a little while is the light with you. Walk while ye have the light, lest darkness come upon you: for he that walketh in darkness knoweth not wither he goeth. While ye have light, believe in the light, that ye may be the children of light."* THERE ARE MANY SUCH REFERENCES throughout the Bible and other religious texts.

So why am I so interested in the many spiritual REFERENCES to "light"?

One night I visited the Memorial Garden outside of this church, as I do from time-to-time. Casey's ashes ARE buried there, and his name is carved into the beautiful, historic stone walls of this building; so I find it an important place to VISIT and a NICE PLACE to pray.

On this particular night the street light near the Memorial Garden was out, so it was unusually dark. But as I stood looking through the darkness in the garden, I suddenly saw AN OVERWHELMING DISPLAY OF LIGHT coming up out of the ground where dozens of urns of ashes have been buried over two centuries. I was SPELLBOUND.

I was seeing an incredible flickering of light, it looked like energy shooting up toward the sky. Literally, I rubbed my eyes and looked again, but the light was still there. I stood and enjoyed it for a few minutes—it may have only been seconds—but I was also a little afraid and overwhelmed. I left in a bit of a fog, knowing I had seen something very special.

I came back a few nights later WANTING SO MUCH TO SEE THE LIGHTS AGAIN; the street light was still out and the light was still there. Tears rolled down my cheeks as I reflected on how thankful I was for being able to see the light—light that I believed to be the spirit of life and love which flood the Universe. I have been back to the Memorial Garden many times since then, but I HAVE NEVER SEEN THOSE LIGHTS AGAIN. I believe I was receiving a gift and a message of hope just at the time I needed it.

LET ME GIVE YOU ONE OTHER EXAMPLE OF WHY I AM NOT A BELIEVER IN COINCIDENCE AND LUCK. [Dad recounted here the story of finding the words that he read at Casey's service in his cluttered home office.]

SO, was it coincidence that the STREET LIGHT was out on an evening when I needed to renew hope in many parts of my life?

Was it some kind of coincidence that I found the long-forgotten words of inspiration I needed IN THE MIDDLE OF HUNDREDS OF PAPERS in boxes that had been stored for years?

I THINK NOT.

Is it just luck that the Bible passage we heard tonight is the same passage that I memorized over 30 years ago and recited to the congregation in my childhood church AS PART OF A CONTEST IN WHICH I WON MY FIRST BIBLE?

And was it just coincidence that yesterday while preparing this Homily I stumbled upon a book titled *The Worst Loss: How Families Heal from the Death of a Child.* Nancy had purchased it over a year ago, and I had never seen it. But there it was IN A STACK OF UNRELATED books UNDER the bed!

Was it just bad luck that Casey died?

I THINK NOT.

IT SEEMS THAT THERE ARE MANY MESSAGES FOR US IN our experience of loss and in TONIGHT'S SERVICE.

We read a portion of the Wisdom tonight that said: *"they seem to have died . . . . but they are at peace . . . . their hope is full of immortality . . . . those who trust in God will understand truth and abide . . . in love."*

The other day I was given a book called: *The Message of Hope.* It paraphrases parts of the Bible, and fits nicely in my coat pocket. I was reading it on the train one night when I came to a passage that said:

"The people brought children to Jesus, hoping he might touch them. The disciples shooed them off. But Jesus was much displeased and let them know it: 'Don't push these children away. Don't ever get between them and me. These children are at the very center of life in the kingdom.'"

Now taking the Wisdom and these words from Mark together, it almost seems that we should celebrate the passing of a loved one as we are assured of a child's place in heaven, and of Nature's willingness to care for those of us who remain.

I don't mean "celebrate" in the generally understood sense of frivolity, but in its truest form. The word *"celebrate"* means: *"To observe a day or an event with ceremonies of respect; to perform a religious ceremony; to praise."*

Isn't this what we are doing here tonight? Celebrating the earthly death and spiritual resurrection of our children AND OTHER LOVED ONES, much the way we celebrate the earthly death and resurrection of Christ in the Eucharist.

Let this time together tonight remind us of all that was good about our relationship with our child. WHETHER WE KNEW THEM FOR a matter of hours or for decades, there was surely much to be appreciated. And, let this celebration remind us to give special attention to OUR other CHILDREN, and to children everywhere.

I AM PLEASED TO SAY THAT WE now have a daughter to join our two boys in the family. She bears an extraordinary resemblance to the brother she never knew. The brother whose brief life we celebrate tonight. A COINCIDENCE? I think not!

Why we were blessed with the wonderful gift of a daughter is a mystery of heavenly proportions, but I believe we are free to speculate. (Even if such speculation is merely an expression of our private hope.) So, I will suggest that Lindsay's coming to us reveals three messages to which we all can relate.

First, and perhaps foremost, it can be seen as a concrete symbol that there is life after death. A WORLDLY MANIFESTATION OF A SPIRITUAL WONDER.

Second, her birth is evidence that there can be joy after despair; evidence to each of us who has felt despair, or who continues to feel despair, that there can and should be joy in our lives after a child's death.

This joy need not just come in the form of new life. It can also come from:

- Helping another person
- Sitting on the shore of a tranquil lake
- Watching a child hit his or her first home run
- Or even getting your first hole-in-one

One way or another, life DOES go on.

Third, I see the blessing of Lindsay as a reminder of Casey. I believe that the Universe does not want us to forget what has happened, but to grow from it and build upon it.

So, I urge you to look for signs in your own lives that there is life after death. Look for opportunities to feel guiltless joy, and look for reminders of those who have died in the lives of those who live on. Celebrate life, the living, and the memories that will always be with us.

In dealing with your loss I ask you to resist blame, resist resentment and resist isolation, particularly from your spouses and other children. REMEMBER, THEY ARE EXPERIENCING THE SAME PAIN YOU ARE.

I recently told my Church School class that in this holiday season, one of the greatest gifts they can give to someone is forgiveness. The Bible says many things about forgiveness, but one of my favorite passages is in Ephesians, Chapter 4, Verse 32:

> *"And be ye kind one to another, tenderhearted, forgiving one another . . . ."*

And let me suggest that after we have forgiven others, we should also forgive ourselves.

Forgive missed opportunities or inattention;

Forgive yourself for words not spoken;

Forgive yourself for the treatment not pursued; and

Use these missed opportunities as motivation to attend, speak to, care for and hug those still with us.

Through forgiveness I am not suggesting that Grief will disappear, but I can say from experience that it will help the healing process.

I recall one time when I was talking to a dear friend about Casey and I started fighting back tears. I told him I was surprised that after so much time had passed, the grief was still so palpable. He described what he called the "Grief Balloon" which I have found to be quite helpful.

He said grief works as if there is a balloon inside us. It fills up gradually, but eventually it needs to be emptied—released. "Let it out," he said, "no matter where you are or what you are doing." It is not just okay to empty the balloon, it is actually important that you do so. As more time passes the balloon will fill more slowly, but it will always be with us. At first it fills up every few minutes, then over days, months and eventually, it fills up over years.

So, don't be surprised if it is suddenly full—it can happen at any time, and when it fills up, empty it. If you are in your office, close the door and let it out; if you are in a store, walk to a quiet aisle and release it; if you are driving, pull over and let the tears flow—you do not want the balloon to burst.

Let me conclude by sharing a poem.

It came to me recently while I was standing in the Memorial Garden after a Sunday morning service. I decided to start looking up at the sky rather than down at the ground where we had placed Casey's ashes. As I looked up I said these words out loud. When I got back to the car I decided to write them down. [Note: this is the third time my father has used this poem in a speech or a Holiday Letter. It clearly meant a lot to him.]

To Casey

I look up to the sky, as I stand near your name
In the Garden where we shared your ashes with the earth.
You are larger than life, larger than all of us;
A child in boundless spirit from birth.

You know the peace to which we all aspire,
and you know the joy we can only imagine.
You know the love that we all desire,
and the heaven we continually seek.

You know the Angels we dream to embrace,
And the thoughts of a genius unknown.
You know the secrets of this human race,
and the splendor of God on His throne.

Be now in our midst as a constant reminder
Of the hope and serenity of life everlasting,
And help us be mindful of the love we can find here
in a word that follows Nature's teaching.

As you light your candle tonight, and as you watch others light their candles, think of the light that I have seen in the Garden and of God's many expressions of light as HOPE, LOVE AND LIFE.

AMEN

In typical fashion, Dad was asked to speak at the candle lighting service a couple of years later. I always wondered how he could be in the same setting—dealing with the same subject matter—and find another way to interpret it. But he usually managed to find new meaning and lessons, and a way to touch the listeners differently. Clearly, he would use material from other presentations he had done, but there was always something new. (Interestingly, he ended this next Homily by once again sharing the story of seeing the lights he saw in the Memorial Garden. That experience was in the "miracle" category for Dad—but then he saw miracles everywhere.)

What follows are just excerpts from Dad's remarks, since several portions of what he said that night appear in other parts of this collection. In this presentation, however, I really like how he used everyday occurrences to make spiritual points.

Second Homily for the Families of Children Who Have Died

There is a special bond among those of us who have had a child die. Not unique perhaps, but very special. After all, there is a real bond among cancer survivors, widows and widowers, artists and addicts—even high school football players form a bond with their teammates that can last for a lifetime. But for those of us who have lost a child, there is a special bond indeed.

For example:

- I cannot hear about a military casualty without thinking of those among us who have had a child sacrifice her or his life for our country. It must be a mixed blessing for them to experience these patriotic times. But God bless them for having a child that gave us the ultimate gift so that we may be free and safe.

- Whenever I hear that a student has died in some athletic contest, I immediately say a prayer for the Carters, knowing that the news will flood them with difficult memories. (By the way, I also think of Jeffrey Carter every time I see a penny on the ground. He had a thing about flipping pennies and since he died, his mom keeps finding pennies in remarkable places. I do too.)
- When a child drowns, or dies in an accident, or has cancer or AIDS or any other illness, I immediately think about the people in this church whose children have died in a similar fashion.
- And whenever I hear about a miscarriage, I immediately think of my dear friends Fred and Sally—even before I think of the similar loss Nancy and I experienced.

Indeed the connection among those of us who have lost a child is very real and profound.

Those of you who have not had this experience might think about how you feel when the bus (or your child's ride) is really late, and you start to worry that something awful has happened; when your child's teacher leaves a message to "call us" during the day—and you think the worst; when you wake up and you don't find your children where they belong and there is that moment of panic that they might not be there. As you experience these feelings you can begin to know why those of us whose children have died need each other—and why we need this service. Yes, for us, these terrible fears—the child who didn't come home or wake up—were realized.

So how do we cope with these challenges?

It is not unlike the way the world is coping with the death and destruction that occurred on September 11.

You will find that I feel rather emotional tonight. More so than usual, because I witnessed the attacks on the World Trade Center first hand from my office window in New York three months ago. And like our minister said last Sunday after his trip to Ground Zero, the overwhelming emotion of being directly connected to that traumatic event, is now connecting people around the world.

As a result of what happened on September 11th, the world has opened up to love and acceptance, to generosity and to government cooperation like we have not seen in our lifetimes. There is a connection born of a common, shared tragedy.

Do you struggle, like I do, with the idea that too much pain and grief has to happen in order for us to refocus on what's important? Why do we need something bad to happen to remind us to love more, and to tolerate more and to change our lives in some meaningful way? Is that how it's supposed to work? Is there some cosmic or metaphysical equation that says for every bad thing that happens, two good things will result? For every hour of pain and suffering there will be two hours of joy? It seems to work that way—for me at least.

Just why things are the way they are is Nature's business, not mine. But for the loss we have suffered to be bearable, we must let it speak to us in some meaningful way. As we heard in the sermon last Sunday: "the crucifixion was an act of terror which no Angel descended from Heaven to stop . . ." And, yet, among my favorite words of hope are the words Christ uttered on the cross, as reported by Luke: "truly I tell you, today you will be with me in Paradise." Those Divine words, uttered to a common criminal hanging on a cross, make me imagine that our innocent children surely have been invited into an amazing Paradise.

I am forever changed by the death of my son Casey in many ways. His death put my life on a new course. It put our family in this church; it put me in this pulpit for his memorial service, which was eleven years ago almost to the day.

His dying brought me into a new life—a connected life that goes beyond what happens in this church and this group. Let me tell you what I mean by that.

August 22nd would have been Casey's 11th birthday. As I sat at my desk in New York, I got an email from an old college friend whose son had nearly died from drowning. He was reporting that some miraculous developments were making it look like his son was going to have a great recovery. Let me read a part of our email exchange.

This is how the thread started a couple of weeks before Casey's birthday:

169

"Last Tuesday, August 7th, at about 7pm, our twelve-year-old son was in a near fatal drowning accident at our club. Fortunately our daughter saw him at the bottom of the pool, pulled him up and got the lifeguard to begin CPR. The emergency medical team arrived quickly and had to restart his heart, which had stopped. They got him to the hospital and from there he was transported to Yale-New Haven Medical Center's pediatric intensive care unit.

Stephen's progress since Tuesday has been very good, but we are not out of the woods yet. He regained consciousness after about 24 hours, and on Saturday they took out the ventilator breathing tube and most of the other tubes. He is getting over a case of pneumonia . . . ."

The next email is the message that arrived on Casey's (and Brian's) birthday.

Friends and Family:

I wanted to give you an update on the progress our son has made in the past week. In summary, his recovery is nothing short of miraculous, and we thank all of you for your thoughts and prayers.

Our miracle child spent last week undergoing a series of different therapies and he has been responding very well. He can walk by himself; do some basic exercises and his speech is nearly back to what it was before the accident. The real question continues to be what cognitive deficiencies he may have. He can read and write; do some basic math problems; and is again beating his parents and siblings at many of the games we have played in the past. The best news is that he really has his old personality back.

The diagnosis for the cause of his heart stopping was an arrhythmic heart beat, which must have been congenital . . . . a defibrillator was implanted yesterday, and the surgery went well.

The plan is for him to be discharged from the hospital tomorrow, and from there we will take him to a children's rehab facility. From in-patient, he may move to a "day hospital" program, where kids come for therapy and school each day, but we also may be able to have him attend school in our town.

Again, the doctors have told us that the pace of the recovery is a miracle. We are trying to stay patient and not have too high expectations. He's so strong physically and mentally that we are hoping that he'll continue to make good progress.

All the best to everyone.

Martin

Here is my response to Martin:

Martin—

I just want you to know how thrilled I am with your son's recovery progress. I have no doubt that he has an incredible future—due in large part to what is clearly an awesome attitude and an awesome dad. My prayers and optimism will continue. Stay strong and thank you for reminding me of how precious my own children are every minute. As someone who lost an infant son, Casey, eleven years ago, I can honestly say I felt your pain. Today is Casey's birthday and your good news is truly an extraordinary gift to me. Much good has come from Casey's brief life, and much good will come from Stephen's long life and the comeback story that will inspire many.

Continued good luck, and thanks for the blessing

Jim

This exchange filled my grief balloon right to the top—I started sobbing in my office. So I decided to take a walk outside to get my composure. Now you must understand that I work in that part of New York that looks like the opening credits of the TV show *NYPD Blue*. It is not the glamorous midtown location people often identify with New York. So I went out the back door of the building into the somewhat desolate streets, where I knew I would not see a lot of people. I could just be with my sadness. I was missing Casey, feeling his loss and experiencing emotions I had not felt in years. As I walked and cried I found myself next to a construction site. There were no workers around, and no one else to be seen. Alone in this alley of debris, I saw a penny lying on the ground. I literally began to laugh out loud. I smiled like I had not smiled in a long time. I knew right then and there that this was a message; that Casey was just fine—"though I walk through the valley of the shadow of death, I will fear no evil, thy rod and thy staff they comfort me . . . ." It was so real and so powerful. I was renewed, "he restoreth my soul." Indeed, God does.

Let me share one more piece of magic with you. I was going to Bermuda to do some consulting work with a law firm. Because I fly so much, I am often upgraded to first class. On this particular trip it came down to the wire, but they said a seat opened up for me "up front" at the last minute. When I sat down in what was the last available seat, I noticed the woman next to me had a lovely stuffed bear on her lap. She was hugging it tightly. She seemed somewhat sad and distant, so I just smiled and nodded and went about my reading. After a while, I felt an urge to connect with this woman, so I made a comment about her stuffed animal; something like—is that lovely creature yours, or is it for someone else? She said meekly—"it belongs to my baby girl," she said, "but she died two days ago." I knew at that moment why I was sitting in that seat.

Expressing my sympathy, I asked how old her daughter was; "about a month old," she said. This lovely woman was Bermudan, and some unexpected complications at her daughter's birth required the girl to be flown to Boston for emergency care. When I told the woman that I had had a baby die, she and I had an instant bond. We talked a little bit about our feelings and frustrations, but the conversation was quite limited. Then I remembered that I had brought a folder of my poetry with me on this trip, because I thought I would have some free time in Bermuda to reacquaint myself with it. I have written about 50 poems since college, but had not read them or even carried them with me in years.

In the middle of my collection was a poem that I had written several years before about Casey. So I reached in my briefcase and said: "I don't know if this will help you, but it helps me when I think about my child who died." I gave her a copy of the poem about Casey. As she read it tears streamed down both of our faces. When she finished, she reached out and took my hand and we were silent for a long time. Finally she said, "May I have this?" and I said "of course." By now the flight attendants—who knew of the woman's plight before take off—were coming over and joining us in grieving. They said it was a miracle that we were seated beside each other. I just smiled; agreeing that it was a miracle, and knowing that miracles do happen.

What an incredible example of synchronicity . . . . in 300,000 miles of flying on airplanes, that poem had never been in my briefcase. There is no such thing as coincidence. Amen.

As you can see throughout these writings, my father had pretty much lost any inhibitions about revealing his heart, soul and personal history. On testimonial Sundays in many Christian churches, a few parishioners are asked to share their 'spiritual journeys' with the congregation. These are some of the most moving sermons you will ever hear. Those who struggle with addiction reveal their battle to the congregation; those with checkered paths talk about how they came to see the light; and others just share wonderfully moving stories about their lives and influences.

It is fair to say that my father's testimonial reveals a lot about how he followed hunches, trusted his intuition and listened to some great mentors on the spiritual journey he shares here. Enjoy the trip.

A Testimonial: My Spiritual Journey

I saw a television show the other night in which a guy gets a daily "newspaper" that tells him what will happen the next day. He uses this special knowledge to try to keep bad things from happening. It all seemed so contrived and predictable. At the outset I complained to my wife and son that this was not a show I would want to watch. But I am glad I stayed with it.

In this particular episode the guy with the ability to see the future was torn between saving a little girl from being hit by a car and stopping an airplane full of people from crashing. That seemed like a rather obvious one to me. After all, as horrific as it might be to know that an innocent child will be killed, the plane was surely full of children, parents, brothers and sisters, and many other people who are important to someone.

Well, a variety of obstacles got in the way of our hero's efforts to get to the airport, and the girl had been hit by the car before he could do anything about it, so he turned his attention to trying to help the little girl survive. As he sat down outside the girl's hospital room with a sense of despair for having failed to save the planeload of people, he looked up and saw a man in a pilot's uniform rush by looking for the little girl. It turns out that the girl's father was the pilot of the ill-fated plane. He was contacted just as he was about to start down the runway, so the plane never took off and everyone was safe.

What does this story have to do with my testimony?

It illustrates two things for me: *the connectedness of all* that we do, and *the importance of looking for God* in seemingly ordinary experiences in our lives.

We have all heard the verse: "All things work together for good to those that love God." This is my mantra. This is my response to those who would believe that life is just one unrelated coincidence after another. I will share some examples of how the Universal Spirit has manifested itself in my life, but first I would like to share briefly, the spiritual journey that brought me to St. John's, and put me in this pulpit for the fourth time.

My first memory of going to church was with Mrs. Keyes when I was in kindergarten or first grade. She was our upstairs landlady, and she used to take me with her to the Methodist church she attended on Sunday mornings. I have never asked whether it was her idea, my folks' idea, or mine. But I remember sitting in the pews, looking up at the preacher and feeling a sense of magic and mystery while frequently wondering how much time was left in the service.

We moved away from that apartment when I was in 2nd grade, and my next memory on the road to spirituality was getting on a bus and going to a vacation Bible school at the local Baptist church. I think my mom suggested it, but since my folks weren't churchgoing people at the time, I suspect now, that this was all part of a much greater plan.

I became very involved with that church as a young child. I was a regular attendee for many years, and I actually got my folks to start attending church. Then I got my relatives to start attending. I won contests for bringing the most visitors to the Sunday services, and I was the kid who always won the contest for memorizing the most Bible verses. Now all of this may sound a bit trivial, but I will never forget the feeling that I had as, one after another, a steady parade of people I cared about: my parents, my friends, my aunts and my uncles stood in a tank of water at the front of the church and got "dunked" in the ceremony of Baptism. All because I had invited them to attend months before.

You see, this was one of those good-old-fashioned fundamentalist churches where they preached hellfire and brimstone, proclaiming that the key to Heaven was a conversion experience. This message was not lost on me. I remember, vividly, thinking that I was destined to hell for all the bad kid stuff I did, and it scared me a little straight . . . I was constantly asking for forgiveness!

Although attending this church was a life-changing experience, it was just the *beginning* of a very long journey toward finding my spiritual self and defining my relationship with God. I did a lot of the right things then. I prayed, read the Bible faithfully, loved others more than myself, and dutifully gave 10% of my babysitting money to the church. I went to church every Sunday morning and most Sunday nights. I often attended prayer meetings on Wednesday nights, and I attended hymn-sings with the youth group whenever they were scheduled.

With such a powerful spiritual foundation, it might seem surprising that I let my passion for organized religion slip away in the latter part of my high school years. In fact, I did not go to church much in high school, in college, during law school or in the early years of my career as a lawyer. I did not read the Bible regularly, and I was probably more concerned about my own well-being than the well-being of others. I was often burdened with guilt, and motivated as much by a menacing fear of God, than I was by a sense of Universal love.

Through it all, though, one thing never changed. I never stopped praying. I never stopped believing that there was a Spirit that listened to us. Even though I was frequently disillusioned, I somehow knew that God had not abandoned me. In a sense, you could say that I ignored God publicly, but relied on a Godly presence privately.

This changed once and for all when my infant son, Casey, died. Most of you know the profound impact Casey's death had on my family's life. But I also hope you know that much of that impact has been channeled into many important efforts to touch others very positively. Which brings us back to connectedness and my rejection of the concept of coincidence. Let me explain.

Our family had moved to a new community and met the Taylor family in the years leading up to Casey's death. The first call we made the morning after he died was to Peter and Shelly Taylor. I told Peter on the phone what had happened, and I said we did not have a church at which we could hold a service. (The beloved minister of our church in Newton had recently retired.) Peter said: "Oh, but you do have a church." He arranged for us to meet here at St. John's with the minister that afternoon. Carl welcomed us as if we had been lifelong members, and each of you has embraced us like family ever since. Peter and Shelly should know forever that they have had a tremendous and wonderful impact on our lives. The way this congregation responded to our tragedy was among the most Christian gestures I will ever know. And our being in this community when Casey died was no coincidence.

★ ★ ★ ★ ★

Last week I was driving and listening to a tape in which Zig Ziglar said we should read the New Testament more. I thought that was a great idea. Two minutes later I stopped at a yard sale for no apparent reason—other than I love antiques (or "junk" as it is sometimes described in our house). I found a pocket-sized New Testament on the table for 25 cents. I paid the quarter and left the yard sale with a smile on my face, and a sense that I was led to that table.

And how coincidental is it that the scripture reading this morning was about a lawyer questioning Jesus in a way that demonstrated a lack of faith. As some of you know, I am a recovering attorney who recently started my own consulting business. I spend most of my time now training attorneys to better understand the importance of caring and relationships. I teach them that they must give more and expect less. Lawyers and faith—this combination speaks to me.

I find it almost embarrassing to suggest that God could actually be directly involved in the most mundane events of my life, because, let's face it, I am just one person in this big Universe with the same basic composition as everyone else. But this is not about me. I believe that a Universal Spirit is intimately involved in all of our lives. It is up to each of us to look for how that presence manifests itself. To be willing to see Nature's plan requires faith—faith and an understanding of what is possible. If we know what is possible, then we are more likely to achieve it.

For most of us, I think the Spirit is manifested mostly in how much of what we do actually makes a difference in this world. I can look back now and see how some of the things I did in my professional life have given hope to children of divorce, provided an education to kids who might have been denied one, and helped a struggling young man realize his potential. My work has helped attorneys who are depressed from the stress of their careers find more positive ways to look at what they do. I know several people who have gotten jobs because of my help. And a woman who was a victim of violence, has reminded me on several occasions that she would have taken her own life, but for my compassion and support. Knowing I actually made a difference is a tremendous blessing to me. And I hope by sharing my journey with you, you will all be reminded of the myriad things that each of you has done to change lives—and help the world be a better place.

I think my good fortune is due, in part, to my unwavering belief that we are enriched by giving. All that we give, we also receive. If there is one significant—profound—shift in the foundation of my spiritual life from those early childhood years, it is that I am now motivated by love, caring and compassion, not by guilt and the fear of a punishing God. It's all about love. At this moment in my life I see, more clearly than ever, how blessed I am.

Here are three thoughts to carry home with you this morning:

It is easier to smile than to frown.
It is easier to love than to hate.
It is easier to give than to take.

It was a tradition at St. John's to observe the "Stations of the Cross" on Good Friday. It is a 3-hour service of silence and brief homilies. Dad loved this service—he called it "inescapable meditation." One year he was asked to speak at the service. I found these notes that he had written for the homily. The station of the cross he was assigned to speak about was "Jesus is Laid in the Tomb." Again, I have reprinted it here with Dad's original formatting.

Homily on Good Friday:
Jesus is Laid in the Tomb

One of my favorite writers is not someone you likely know; his name is Norm DePuy, a retired pastor from a church of Newton, Massachusetts.

Norm writes a monthly newsletter, and in one of his recent issues there was an article that **inspired some of my thoughts** for today.

The article was **titled**: "With God there is always another one . . ."

In the article, he talks about one of the messages that dominate the Easter season—the message of HOPE. Norm talks about how the cynicism of the world would tell us we are **foolish to believe that with God there are no dead ends.**

The world would say that **hope is a delusion**, and that HOPE is **insensitive** to real suffering.

But Norm **reminds us of Samuel in the Old Testament**, and how Samuel, **in search of** an appropriate candidate to be king, was dejected after interviewing many candidates. So he said to Jesse: "HAVE YOU ANY MORE SONS?'

The response, in essence, was "yes . . . not likely to be king, but . . . ."

"Not likely, but . . ." What a wonderful definition for the word HOPE. "It's not likely, but." Where it would appear that there will be no miracle; where it would appear that there will be no job, no healing, no food on the table or no peace in the world, there is a chance. "Not likely, but . . ."

Of course Samuel learned that there was one more son. As Norm wrote so succinctly, "With God, there is one more chance. There is one more day." Before Good Friday, if someone had asked: 'Will Christ be raised from the dead?' the answer might well have been 'It may not seem likely, but.' That is truly about Hope.

Besides hope, there are other important themes in this season. One of them is **forgiveness**.

We should not overlook the incredible level of forgiveness Christ demonstrated throughout His torment; He forgave His tormentors, He forgave the weakness of His disciples, He forgave God for putting Him through this ordeal, and He reminds us that God will forgive us for our imperfections.

To be truly fulfilled during our time on this earth we must learn to forgive, because forgiveness is as important as breathing, eating and sleeping. It is fundamental to our health. Without the ability to forgive there would be no Easter story. Without forgiveness we, too, would be burdened and distracted from our divine purpose. We should follow Christ's example, because with forgiveness we replace seeds of hatred with seeds of love.

The theme of sacrifice is also very evident in the Easter story, but we could easily overlook the sacrifice that Joseph made by offering to let Christ have his tomb. While Joseph may not have been called upon to give up everything he had, he did give up a tomb that had been prepared for his own final rest. That strikes me as a rather significant sacrifice.

179

I would like to share one of my favorite stories about giving and sacrifice. It's called the *Rainbow Fish*—a terrific children's book. Among the fish in the sea was one more beautiful than all the rest—he had shiny scales that glittered as he swam about. Once when another fish asked if he could have one of the scales the Rainbow Fish said "no," and went about his business of swimming around looking beautiful; but he was lonely and unhappy.

Then he went to see the great, wise octopus—I think this was the equivalent of praying. She told the Rainbow Fish that he would not be truly happy until he gave others his most prized possessions. This did not thrill him, but he tried it. He gave a fish one of his beautiful scales . . . then he gave one to another fish, and another. Soon he had given away all but one of his beautiful scales. But when he looked around and saw all of the beauty swimming around him, he was finally happy.

In the passages we have read today, in this season, we can learn of **HOPE, FORGIVENESS, AND SACRIFICE.** But there is one more important theme in today's readings: **turning adversity into triumph,** or, put another way: "finding light in the darkness." IN OUR READING WE HEARD THAT JOSEPH HAD ROLLED A GREAT STONE IN FRONT OF THE DOOR OF THE TOMB.

Imagine yourself in that dark, damp and cold tomb. And yet the light of the heavens, INDEED the light of the world, was right outside the boulder that blocked the door.

As the story goes, the stone was moved. Not by the strength of mortal men or women, but by a higher power; that stone, the obstacle between Jesus' body and the light of the world, was moved.

And because it was moved, we too can overcome the obstacles that try to come between us and the light of the world—for us that light is the reward for our faith. It's TRIUMPH IN the face of ADVERSITY.

So let this scene at the tomb be a metaphor for faith and hope; let this scene be a driving force in your life. And the next time a challenge appears in your life remember that putting the obstacle in place—rolling the stone in front of the tomb's entrance—set the stage for triumph.

What symbolism. When life's obstacles are placed in front of us, that hardship sets the stage for victory. Norm Dupuy calls a lot of life's occurrences "our own little resurrections." In one of his newsletters he quotes from the April issue of *Homiletics*:

"Every time I see a man put down his bottle, there's a resurrection goin' on. Every time I see a man go back to school, there's a resurrection goin' on. Every time I see a man hug his son, there's a resurrection goin' on."

The Easter story shows us that in suffering, despair, pain, frailty, and unfairness, we can—through faith, hope and openness—find a greater good and demonstrate a greater strength than we have ever known.

When you feel like giving up; when the path seems too long and the suffering too great; when the hill seems too steep and the burden seems too heavy, remember that the stone was moved.

These remarks were particularly challenging for Dad, as he often struggled with how to talk about Biblical stories in a way that respected those with a fundamental approach to the Bible, while promoting an enlightened understanding of what he called "the Universal Spirit." He saw God in everything, in everyone, everywhere. He found a way to embrace Christianity, Judaism and Buddhism, without seeing a conflict. He even read a book on the Kaballah and Mystical Judaism, saying "it was all about love and awareness, how can we go wrong with that?"

Since Dad was on the Mission Committee at church, it made perfect sense that he would do the guest sermon on Mission Sunday. He used the opportunity to strike a chord about making a difference in the world. I heard this sermon in person, and again, his delivery made the message more powerful than the written words. But the words are still very much worth sharing here, although some of these stories appeared in one of Dad's motivational speeches recounted earlier.

Homily on Mission Sunday

I do not have time to lead the Mission Committee, to cook brownies for the St. John's shelter, to sew a quilt for the homeless, or prepare remarks for this Sunday morning. I have a mortgage to pay, a client to call, an assistant to train and children to raise. I have too much to do.

But listen to what Alexander Solzhenitsyn said in his 1978 Harvard Commencement address: "the freedom to get, and to do, and to have was insufficient in comparison with the freedom to be. We have placed too much hope in politics . . . being deprived of our most precious possession—our spiritual life."

I don't think it was a coincidence that I was scheduled to speak about Mission this morning—a morning that turned out to be just a couple of days after one of the children of our congregation died. Why? Because it was the death of my own 3-month-old son thirteen years ago that sparked me to be more focused on the Mission of my own life.

I had never been in a pulpit before I delivered the Homily at my son Casey's memorial service. I had always wanted to be up there, but I was "too busy;" and I wasn't sure if I could do it right or well. For a lot of reasons, I stayed in the safe zone. My wife has been away on a trip to Florida since Wednesday, so I have been home alone with the kids for five days. Later today I leave for Atlanta where I am expected to make an important business presentation tomorrow morning. If I had actually *thought* about it when I was asked to speak today, I would have said 'I can't possibly do a sermon this morning.' But I decided to trust my Intuition on this one. Essentially, I said: "Let go and let God." I think we can all benefit from more of this kind of thinking.

Well, let me start by making an important suggestion to each of you this morning. Don't wait for some traumatic event in your life to motivate you to follow your heart; don't wait for some harsh personal pain to motivate you to share your time, your money, your gifts and your talents. The world needs you to give and to share compassion now.

We rally for those around us when they face traumatic life events. We bring food and flowers, and give money . . . we do all of these things for them because we *know* about their pain. We are *aware* of their loss and we *can feel* their suffering.

But what about those whose pain and suffering we don't know first hand? What about those whose loss we can not feel today? What will we do for those beyond our current awareness who are truly hungry or cold or thirsty or in prison? What will we do for strangers who need an education?

Pov Thida, a young woman in Cambodia, is a part of our Universal family; the homeless men and women who come to the shelters we support, and those who rely on our Thrift Shop for clothing . . . they are all a part of our spiritual family.

Some of you are amazed, and some of you may even be perplexed, by how someone like our own parishioner, Lawrence Hermann, can be so committed and so compassionate about helping land mine victims halfway around the world. I know I was surprised when I first learned of his extraordinary efforts to support the family of Pov Thida.

To those of you who wonder how Larry can care so much about helping a family find a home in Cambodia, I have a question. Imagine yourself as God for a moment. Do you think that when you look at the world you will see borders between countries or lines between cities or the words on signs outside of churches? Do you think God sees the soul of an American in poverty and says: "this one gets a blessing, but forget about that struggling family in Southeast Asia living in a shack and working 18 hours a day to make ends meet?" I don't think that's how it works.

I don't think God thinks Larry is wasting his time . . . and I don't think God is laughing at Sue or Kathy or Don because they give up their nights and weekends to feed people they don't know in the shelters in our community. In a world full of hunger and pain, I am thinking the Universal Spirit is smiling approvingly on all of these actions.

In my own business I spend a lot of time trying to make lawyers treat clients more like people, and less like billing categories. (Frankly, God is probably laughing at that one!) But what matters more than making money, is making a difference. Nothing is more rewarding than to have someone say: "I really liked your training program, not just because it will make me be a better lawyer, but because I will be a better husband and father when I get home." I suspect that we are all much more motivated by making this kind of difference, than we are by making money.

[Dad then told the story of the couple that was walking along a beach finding hundreds of starfish that had washed up on the shore. The question: "What possible difference can you make by throwing one back in the water?" The response was Dad's constant mantra: **"for that one, it makes a difference . . ."**]

Those words ring in my ears whenever I feel overwhelmed by the needs of the world—whenever I wonder if what I am doing really matters. For Pov Thida our church's support has made a difference; for those we have fed and clothed, we have made a difference; to lawyers and secretaries in law firms where I have worked, I believe I have made a difference. We cannot heal all of the pain and suffering in the world, but each individual that we touch can feel profoundly benefited by our efforts.

In Matthew 25 we read that Jesus says: "You fed me when I was hungry, and you visited me in prison; when I was thirsty you gave me a drink." But those who heard Jesus say this were perplexed and said something like: "Lord, I don't remember doing those things." He responds by saying: "Oh yes you did. Whenever you did this for anyone in need you did it to me . . . ." We are talking about a part of scripture that is dealing with getting into the Kingdom here, so this is pretty important stuff!

Sometimes I wonder if God is looking around saying: "What part of 'do unto others' do you not understand folks?"

There are many in our church who give money; some give their time and their talents to make this a special place for all of us. There are gifts of music, of flower arrangements, and of stewardship just to name a few. Many also give generously to the greater community, and to God's family around the world. But the Mission Committee is hoping that we can get even more of us, to do even more of what needs to be done. Not because we want you to, or because the Episcopal Church wants you to, but because the Spirit of the World needs you to.

Since God is *in* all of us, we have an inner voice that we hear once in a while. We don't always listen to that voice because it bumps into that part of us called "ego." Ego believes that achievement in this world is measured by having a good job, wearing good clothes, getting a good education and driving a good car. Don't get me wrong; I happen to think God is quite pleased when we are able to live well, and that there is Universal delight in our success.

But when you are denying that little voice in you that says "donate to the food pantry, or give books to prisoners, or read stories to special needs children or deliver the homily this Sunday" think about the words of Ram Dass who, in the midst of his spiritual journey asked his

Maharaja how he could achieve enlightenment. His guru simply replied: "Serve People; feed people."

"Serve people, feed people."

Let's all go home after the service this morning, close our eyes, take some deep breaths and see what message we get from that inner voice; see what image of *service* appears. Listen to that voice and contemplate your mission—that spiritual vision that is in you and motivating you. If you find that you are moved by this vision and you would like some help acting on it, bring your vision to the Mission Committee; we want to serve you. But whether you come to us or not, trust your heart, follow your intuition and give yourself—and the world—the gift of your love.

Amen.

For a variety of reasons we changed churches a few years after Dad delivered this Homily. That was a hard decision in a lot of ways, since we were personally connected to a lot of people at St. John's. And, most importantly, perhaps, Casey's name was etched in the centuries-old stone wall of that church, near the spot where his ashes were buried in the Memorial Garden. But that little voice Dad spoke about in this Homily was at work. Something led him to visit a different church in town—one that Nancy had some fondness for since she had grown up in a traditional Congregational church.

As you might expect, we had only been at the new church for a few months when Dad was asked to speak. His brief 'stewardship' remarks that follow describe what was going on in his head the first time he visited the church. His words that morning evoked both laughter and tears in the congregation. (These words also inspired the theme for Dad's Holiday Letter that year, which was "Because of You.")

Stewardship Remarks

The first time I came to this church I sat in the back row in the corner. As the children came forward for the children's message before they went downstairs to Sunday School, a bearded man who usually sits right about there [Dad pointed at him] got up and began flapping

185

his arms like a bird in flight. He then told the children a story about how some wounded geese (and the geese who care for them) are not welcome to return to their old flock; they must find a new flock to join.

Tears came to my eyes. You see, I had had lunch earlier that week with Fred Ross, who, at that time, was the Rector at St. John's Church. My family and I had attended that church for almost 15 years. But Fred was wounded and would not be rejoining the St. John's flock. He wasn't going back, and I knew as I sat in the back row of this church that morning—hearing this story to which I could totally relate—that I was not going back to St. John's either. I was certain that my family would agree with me that we had found a new flock.

Brett and Linda Mather had told us for years about what a great church this was. They introduced us to the minister and his wife over dinner at their house in a delightful and memorable evening.

Yes, we came here because of that minister and his wife [who left the church soon after we joined]; but we stay here because of you. This congregation has provided my family and me with a rich, welcoming, nurturing experience.

Because of you:

- My son Brian wakes up every Sunday asking to go to church. That is pretty amazing in a world that still struggles with how to relate to and integrate children with special needs. He loves the babies who stay with him downstairs. And the loving people who work in the nursery make it look easy because they are so incredibly caring.
- Because of you, I got to hear my wife sing my favorite rock opera songs from Godspell as part of the church's Gospel Rock chorus.
- Because of you, Lindsay has a Bible with her name on it, and a passion for learning about our faith; you don't often see that in an 11-year-old. We had a little hiccup, though, when we told her that the minister was leaving to go to another church, she said "well, at least Jack will still be here . . . ." Ouch. [Jack, the youth leader, was leaving too.]

- Because of you, my 19-year-old son and I got to share a special time delivering presents to the children of prisoners as part of the Angel Tree Project. It was magical to be able to tell the beautiful little girl who greeted us at the door that we were bringing presents from her father who loved her. We spent a few minutes with that girl, her mother and her grandmother, sharing the Christmas cookies they offered to us. I even heard Andrew conversing with them in Spanish. I told Nancy I didn't need any more Christmas presents—that experience was the greatest gift.

Most of you would not know that our child Casey died almost 16 years ago; he was three months old. His ashes are in the Memorial Garden at St. John's Church. His name is etched in the historic stone wall of that church. It takes something special and powerful to move us away from that place of worship, but that would be love—the love that fills this building and flows from this congregation. There is a seemingly unlimited amount of love in this place, but the work we do here also requires money. There is not an unlimited amount of money. So, I encourage each of you to give from your wallets in the same way you always give from your hearts.

And thank you for giving so much to my family. We are thrilled and flattered and humbled to be a part of this church family.

This Chapter has been about Servant Leadership. Since Servant Leadership is largely about using your gifts for all the good they can bring to the world, I want to share Dad's 1999 Holiday Letter here. It focuses on unleashing those special gifts we all have that can make the world a better place. We have now completed the section of this book in which my father used his gifts in the pulpit, so this letter is a nice transition to some of his more eclectic writings.

Holiday Letter

Recently, I was reading a powerful book titled, *The Drama of the Gifted Child*. Although I'm tempted to say that this title describes our three wonderful children, I would rather share the book's simple theme as an insight for this holiday season: We are all gifted. My hope for the New Year is that we all spend some time discovering and nurturing those unique gifts that are in us. I believe that the blessing of gifts and the extent of human potential have been revealed in many ways in the Watson family this year.

Lindsay has demonstrated the capacity to enjoy a remarkable range of interests. She is equally fascinated by ballet, gymnastics, music, spelling, computers, "make-believe" and golf. Actually, the list goes on—she just loves to learn! At just four years old she continually challenges us with her insightful questions, like: *"Are there phones in Heaven?"* (she wanted to call Casey and her grandfather), and *"Mommy, why did you speed up instead of slowing down when the light turned yellow?"* She continues to expand her power and influence in the family through a combination of strong will and advanced persuasive skills. (From whom does she get these attributes?) Andrew likes to challenge her position of authority from time to time just to keep things in perspective. I marvel at the love and understanding Lindsay shows toward Brian. At different times she is his sister, his teacher, his defender and his playmate. It is also heartwarming to watch the way Nancy enjoys dressing, primping and loving Lindsay. We are very fortunate that we have become a part of the local Country Day School family. It provides Lindsay with a wonderful environment for personal growth and learning, and it has provided us with a lot of new friendships.

Brian has not lost his passion for hugs. It is a toss-up as to whether he says "hug" or "Mommy" more times in a day. (Each one is in the dozens, maybe the hundreds.) What continues to make Brian so special, however, is his unquenchable desire for hugs, along with the joy he finds in making people laugh (and clap). His new school is pushing him to develop better language and social skills; and his tutor, Erin, believes as we do, that there is incredible, untapped potential in Brian's busy little mind. He loves to be on the phone with Grandma and Grandpa "Gee Gee" (my folks); *Wheel of Fortune* and *The Price is Right* remain high on his list of viewing priorities. He is beginning to show some interest in, and capacity for, playing the cymbals—he likes to march around the house banging two saucepan covers at high volume and (almost) in perfect rhythm. Brian's nine years have been such a blessing to us, and we look forward to a lifetime of his hugs, his laughter and his growth.

Andrew's further maturity is palpable in a variety of ways. After another year of terrific human, sport and academic accomplishments, he continues to be the thoughtful, funny and wonderfully adaptable person he has always been. As many of you know, Andrew's mom is Jewish. Andrew undertook the years of rigorous training required to prepare for a Bar Mitzvah. Not only did this event mark a marvelous transition for Andrew into manhood, but it also reflected the connectedness of his two families.

Andrew's modesty is particularly admirable given his imposing physical stature at age 13 (6'1", size 13 shoe). He just keeps growing! His sense of humor and his easygoing attitude are refreshing. He enjoys and excels at sports, but looks for the fun in the contest, not just a fight. (The 40-yard pass completion he threw in the last game of the 8th grade football season brought the crowd to its feet.) His fantasy football team is ranked 31,076 out of 350,847 in the world; his fantasy baseball team did not fare so well. Together we are managing a fantasy stock portfolio that is doing pretty well, but we are counting on Cyberian Outpost to give us a major boost. (That happens to be one of our friend's latest hobbies . . . I mean challenges.)

As for Nancy and me, life is mostly about nurturing the development of our kids, and participating in their many enchanting experiences. Nancy has taken on more responsibility for our business, which continues to thrive. (Fortunately, there are a lot of lawyers who want to learn how to attract and keep clients.) Nancy could be the poster child for the do-it-all, make-it-look-easy, over-achieving, under-appreciated mom. She finds the capacity every day to take care of her family, her community, her physical health, her mind, and her friends.

Amidst the chaos of parenthood and business, however, Nancy and I always make time to just hang out together. We have been and continue to be best friends. Whether she accompanies me on a business trip to Bermuda, or watches a movie with me in the den after the kids go to bed, we always manage to have fun. I genuinely enjoy and appreciate my classmates, my clients, my colleagues and friends, but the love of my life and greatest companion is Nancy.

Now, I don't like writing about death in a Holiday Letter, but a couple of important people made the move to Angel status this year. Our dear friend, Kathy, laid her father to rest. Our prayers are for comfort in her family. My friend (and legendary golfer), Gene Sarazen,

189

also passed away. I continue to feel a close connection to the Sarazen family, and appreciate the love they have always extended to me. (Now maybe my late father-in-law will get those golf lessons he always talked about!)

But let's talk about life! As we were leaving for Andrew's Bar Mitzvah, my father suffered a serious heart attack. Until you have helped a loved one to the ground as he clutches his chest, and stand by helplessly as you wait for the EMT's to arrive, it is hard to appreciate fully the power of family love. I honestly don't know what was harder—delivering the Homily at Casey's memorial service, or participating in Andrew's Bar Mitzvah service—celebrating life and coming of age—while not knowing if my father was dead or alive. To those of you who have experienced anything like this, my heart goes out to you. To those of you who have not, don't wait until it is too late to say "I love you." Many of us grew up in an environment where those words were not uttered as freely as they are in many families today. Because my Dad survived, I got to tell him for the first time what a great dad he is, and to say, "I love you." Make every minute count!

I am reminded of some magic moments I spent standing on the 18th green at the conclusion of this year's Ryder Cup. Being sprayed with champagne, and singing the National Anthem was "goosebump city." But my lasting memory is of Payne Stewart graciously and magnanimously conceding his match to Colin Montgomerie. It was a selfless and humane gesture. At any moment it can all end . . . what is the last act by which each of us will be remembered?

Life is constantly changing. Nothing stands still. The green leaf you see on a tree today . . . . Too often we see our lives as static, limited, and almost predestined to involve little more than looking good, feeling good, and being pretty good at parenting, spousing and working. My hope is that our friends will join my family in moving into the next millennium with a sense of *all possibilities*. At this holiday time we wish for each of you an unlimited faith in the good you can do, the joy you can know and the love you can share by recognizing your gifts and using them in the service of others. Merry Christmas and Happy Hanukkah.

Chapter Ten

HUNTING

Let's make a major shift—from sermons to shooting! This next piece is an amazing chronicle of what it's like to spend hours in the woods hoping to bring fresh venison home for dinner.

Whenever we visit my grandparents in Michigan we go into the woods and shoot guns. My grandfather makes his "living" and feeds himself in retirement by hunting and fishing (and chopping wood). Hunting has always been a very important part of his life. The way my dad chronicled his first hunting trip in three decades is, in equal parts, poetic, funny, crude and insightful. The title that appears below is the title that was on the document when I found it.

Dad really wanted to see this story appear in *Esquire* magazine. Maybe I will submit it for publication. Much as he seems to make light of this particular hunting experience, he told me he loved it, and he hoped I would join him on a hunting trip some day.

Draft *Esquire* article:
"City Boy Goes Hunting"
or
"What Happens when a 'Type A' Ivy League Guy Finds Himself in the Woods with a Large Gun?"

After much urging by my father and my brother, I decided to spend a weekend in pursuit of the famed whitetail deer in the Michigan woods. It had been 30 years since the last time I had gone hunting. But the stars were in alignment for this trip to happen. I had no conflicting consulting engagements (a rarity), the hunting season started the day after my Dad's 69th birthday, and I really needed some meditative "down time."

As it turns out, the experience was incredibly rich. I am very glad, however, that I decided at the last minute, as we were about to leave the cabin for the woods, to put a pen and some notebook paper in the pocket of my hunting jacket (right next to the toilet paper). I thought it would be good to have a writing instrument and some paper in case any interesting thoughts or observations came to me in the woods. Little did I know that I would be so inspired that I would start writing soon after I sat down in the "blind" (a make-shift hut in which one hides from his prey). I have chosen to share my hunting notes essentially unedited, as there is something revealing about the spontaneous way these thoughts flew into my mind.

Day One:

6:20 A.M.—I close the rickety door of the blind and repeat over and over in my mind: "This is so cool!" Sitting in complete darkness wondering if I will be warm enough; pouring coffee from a thermos in the dark. Wondering what I will see when it gets light. I expect to hear more sounds in the darkness—but it is eerily quiet. You look at woods differently when you are hunting. Where are the shooting lanes?

6:45 A.M.—A bit of light appears, not nearly enough to see a deer though. I start planning my survival strategy—at 7am I will take off my thick orange jacket, and exchange the heavy orange glove on my trigger hand for a thin camouflage glove. I will also pee then, so I won't need to get out of the blind and make a stir as daylight emerges.

7:05 A.M.—I hear the first gunshot off in the distance. I think it is still too dark, and am hoping that the shooter is in a clearing on a hill with more light than I have.

7:15 A.M.—I don my knit camouflage hood that has holes for my eyes, nose and mouth.

7:30 A.M.—Another cup of coffee; another urination. A fairly loud and seemingly close gunshot—was it my cousin shooting? We should have cell phones or PDAs out here so we can keep track of each other.

7:45 A.M.—A gaggle of geese flies overhead; bluebirds and squirrels start to move around in the grass around me; I hear lots of noises that sound like they could be deer moving through the woods. I'm starting to doubt the wisdom of buying cheap boots.

7:55 A.M.—Another loud gunshot even closer to me. I am thinking it must be one of our hunting party. Another shot from the same place at 8:05.

8:25 A.M.—A shot from a new direction; that might be John. I swallow pride and put a hand-warmer in my left boot to warm my toes. Feeling another urge to pee! Did not drink that much coffee. Maybe I have a prostate problem . . . just for kicks decide to hold it until 9:00.

9:00 A.M.—Really need to pee, but don't want to scare deer that may be nearby, but out of sight. Then, I realize I am more likely to see a deer while urinating, than with my gun in ready position. That is just how it is. A woodpecker starts pecking away on the tree above me. So loud. I am hoping a deer can tell it is a woodpecker, not some guy playing *Wipeout* with two sticks on a tree stump.

9:05 A.M.—After third urination, I feel hungry. Checking my coat, I discover I do not have my Snickers or the $10 cigar I thought I brought. Shit!!!!! Feet are still cold . . . Boy will I get grief for wearing these inadequate yuppie boots.

9:30 A.M.—The squirrels and birds have quietly disappeared; the sun is out, but it seems to be colder. I re-replace my thin camouflage glove on my trigger hand with the heavy orange one. Would like to see just one deer even from afar—that would warm me up. It's windy; leaves are falling—lots of sounds everywhere, but nothing to shoot. I pour another cup of coffee—beginning to wish I had brought a magazine . . . wonder how my teenage son would like this experience?

9:33 A.M.—I couldn't possibly need to piss again. Could I? Hell the leaves aren't even getting dry in between! That's it, no more coffee! But I greatly enjoy the frozen Snickers that I finally find in one of the myriad pockets in my multiple layers of clothing.

Indeed, I had been prescient enough to put it in the pocket of my hunting vest last night.

10:05 A.M.—My body seems to have adjusted to the cold; now I just keep starting to nod off. I sit up straight and tell myself that this is no time to sleep. Simon Peter nodded off in the garden and Jesus was not amused. The 11th hour is nearly upon me. It is time for total concentration—extreme hunting focus at all costs.

10:43 A.M.—The tension is really mounting. I wonder if my brother has even started his promised trek through the woods in my direction; I must be alert and ready, as his movement is intended to push deer in my direction. It's windy and cold all of a sudden; I think about the *Sixth Sense* and wonder if it is an omen. My bladder is on the full side (again), but it will have to wait.

11:00 A.M.—I hear a rather loud noise right behind me—it gets louder and louder. My God, this must be a deer, I think. It sounds like it is practically in my blind. In a matter of seconds it is on top of me—literally. I realize that something is sitting on the flimsy roof of my blind; it looks in and startles me so much that I make an audible grunt and scare it off the roof. Now I have to leave the blind to see if "it" is gone. No sign of the critter, but the scare and the brief walk help warm my feet. Suspenders keep falling and constrain my arms to my sides! Not good for shooting. I take them off and let them hang. I pee again. I am going to see a doctor when I get home.

11:13 A.M.—I see a deer! It is slinking through the woods 70-80 yards away; even from that distance it looks like a rather large, solitary animal. Before I can even bring my gun up to "scope it," however, it disappears into a thicket. (My mind immediately jumps to a Sesame Street episode in which Kermit made my son laugh many years ago by telling Bert he saw "a cricket in a thicket.") I stare into the area for about 10-15 minutes, hoping for a glimpse of a companion or two, but there is none. Suddenly I find myself shivering. The excitement of seeing a deer had not, in fact, warmed me up. Somehow I was colder.

11:35 A.M.—I decide to walk down to another nearby blind about 100 yards further into the woods. I figured it would warm me up to walk, and maybe the other blind will give me better perspective when deer pass through the woods. There is something very cool about walking very slowly and carefully through the woods carrying a powerful rifle. I could not help but wonder how it would feel to be creeping through the woods as a soldier, rather than a hunter. I assume I would be more anxious and afraid than excited. Much as I liked the idea of hunting from a new perspective, I decide to return to my original blind until lunch. I would possibly spend the afternoon in the new blind.

11:50 A.M.—Arriving back at the original blind, I pee again. A shot rings out fairly close by. Now I am convinced that at least two of the hunters in our party have fired their guns.

11:58 A.M.—After a few minutes of intermittent dozing, my father and my cousin pull up in the truck to drive us over to the other side of Dad's land where we will all meet for lunch.

12:15 P.M.—Upon arrival at the designated meeting spot we found only two of the other four men in our hunting party. The guns and equipment of the other two were stacked neatly at the base of a tree, and one of the trucks was gone. A definite sign, I was told, that they had each likely shot a deer. Moments later the Avalanche pulls up; in back were two field-dressed bucks. But one, much to my brother's dismay, had horns less than the requisite 3-inch length. That means he had to tag it with his "doe" permit. It struck me as the ultimate indignity that this hearty male deer had to be labeled as a doe in death. It also caused me pause when, after hanging the deer from a tree to let them bleed and "cool down," my brother completed the field dressing by reaching inside the deer's already sliced open stomach to cut out the heart and lungs.

1:20 P.M.—After a lunch of sandwiches, chips, leftover fried chicken and brownies, we headed back out into the woods. During lunch I learned that despite having bagged two deer, very few deer had been seen that morning. I also learned that there is usually a lot more shooting around us on Opening Day. In the cabin the night before, I had heard story after story of how many deer had been shot in years gone by. My cousin had shown me a lot of collected antlers—souvenirs of good hunting days. I heard stories of seeing dozens of deer in a day; so my expectations were pretty high. (I also learned that hunting cabins have beer and cigars. Almost worth the trip alone.)

1:50 P.M.—I make my way into the alternative blind. Before settling into my new hiding place, however, I realize that there is something sensible about carrying toilet tissue . . . apparently a day in the woods can dislodge constipation. Soon after I settle into my condo-like blind (this one was probably 4 x 6), I hear a squirrel or maybe just a field mouse (it sounded smaller) playing on the roof of the blind. It does not really bother me this time. I am feeling like a hunter. It is a glorious, sunny and crisp November afternoon, and I am loving every minute of this experience—but I am starting to think I really want to get a deer.

3:05 P.M.—I can hear the faint sound of another shot off in the woods; it's coming from someone else's abutting hunting land. I can't help but wonder what impact (good or bad) that shooting might have on my hunting. (I also learned at lunch that someone else had peed five times this morning—I feel a little better.) I have been slowly scanning the woods for over an hour now, looking to the far left, beyond my peripheral vision, but not quite so far to the right. I missed my most recent physical therapy session for my stiff neck. It is hard to hunt with a stiff neck.

3:20 P.M—Maybe three shots have been fired (off in the distance, of course) all afternoon. Something is just not right in Whitetail Nation. I must say, though, that as I sit deep in the woods quietly observing and jotting some occasional notes, the silence, punctuated only by an occasional gust of breeze or animal scratching, makes me appreciate what Henry David Thoreau likely experienced. ("I went to the woods . . .").

3:35 P.M.—I urinate.

4:05 P.M.—It is getting a bit colder, and my toes are starting to get cold; but I announced at lunch that my insulated duck boots had withstood the test. (A slight fib.) Others in the group (with so-called "real" hunting boots) also had cold feet in the morning, so I felt less silly about my footwear choice. The woods are still ominously devoid of shooting.

4:25 P.M.—A shot is fired fairly close by, but I am virtually certain it is not one of us. I dip into the bag of M&Ms, peanuts and raisins that one of the guys gave me at lunch.

5:02 P.M.—It is that dusky time when shapes in the woods are deceiving; partially felled trees and shadows look like deer. Maybe I am just getting stir crazy. I start practicing my aim by pretending to shoot—fixing my scope on stumps and bushes. I really want to see a deer through this scope.

5:15 P.M.—I start nodding off. This is no time to fall asleep. It is that last hour before dark when the deer start to move . . . I sit up and fight sleep, I get another handful of M&Ms, peanuts and raisins.

5:45 P.M.—It's getting too dark to see. I make my way back to the truck, deerless, but not dejected.

Day Two:

4:30 A.M.—I wake up to the sound of a gurgling coffee pot. My dad is throwing some logs on the fire, and I roll over and go back to sleep until 5:00.

5:10 A.M.—Everyone is up, including my cousin who had donated almost everything in his body to the septic system the night before. He now says he feels great, but hungry; four pieces of toast later he is back in the bathroom. I would get to borrow his boots—my brother would sit in his blind.

5:40 A.M.—I am constipated. I load up on T.P. to bring into the woods.

6:02 A.M.—We climb in the trucks to head for the 120-acre parcel that my father owns exclusively as a place to hunt. It's colder today, so I am glad that I added an extra shirt to my ensemble.

6:30 A.M.—My brother and I take a long walk through complete darkness deep into the woods. He deposits me in a different blind; it is the one from which he shot the pre-adolescent buck the day before.

6:58 A.M.—As hints of daylight show themselves on the horizon, I experience the sensation of an incredible array of lights blinking throughout the forest—like strobe lights at a rock concert. I once had a similar, but more powerful, experience of light while standing in the Memorial Garden in which our son's ashes are buried. I marvel, but it passes.

7:00 A.M.—First shot fired in the distance (*Game on!*) I visualize deer walking up the long grassy stretch in front of me, like British soldiers marching to a slaughter.

7:15 A.M.—There's now sufficient daylight to see a deer. I pull down my camouflage mask, and replace the warm glove on my hand with the lighter glove that will make shooting easier. Surely this would be deer day, as the full daylight reveals this blind to be on a beautiful vantage point. I settle down into a comfortable swivel chair—recently retrieved from a remodeled office—and look slowly from right to left for the next hour and 15 minutes.

8:30 A.M.—I need to pee. I kneel in the corner of the blind so as not to draw attention to myself. (Maybe I think the deer are prudes, more than I think they will be spooked.) The experience helps warm me—especially my hand—it is so much warmer inside my hunting pants than it is outside! I pour another cup of coffee from my thermos and return to my vigil (which is now complicated by about a dozen squirrels playing in the leaves and trees around me). They make so much noise. And while you are sure it is the sound of a squirrel, you just can't help checking to make sure it is not a deer. Oddly, there are absolutely no gun shots around us. Like yesterday, I will probably hear at lunch that this is the quietest day of hunting in the history of the sport.

9:10 A.M.—Still no shooting anywhere. My knees are cold, my hands are cold. As I wiggle my slightly chilled toes in my cousin's boots, I envision him back at the cabin with a roaring fire, hot coffee (if his stomach is better) and his comfortable chair . . .

9:30 A.M.—Bladder is full, but it seems too cold to pee; then I remember that it warms me. After I pee I begin the process of alternating my hands in my crotch—it's really warm between my flannel-lined pants and my long underwear.

10:00 A.M.—I finish off the M&M's I find in my coat pocket left over from yesterday. (Wish I could wash my hands . . .) I think about taking a short walk to another nearby blind just to warm me; but I assume my brother will leave his blind early for lunch, and move through the woods in an effort to push a deer in my direction. So I pour a cup of semi-hot coffee and remain seemingly on ice in my perch.

11:20 A.M.—Either no one tried to push me a deer, or they tried and it did not work. (I would learn later during lunch that both my brother and one of my cousins had *thought* about doing it.) I start the long walk through the woods back to the truck. Again, it really feels powerful carrying a gun. I walk slowly and alertly lest a deer comes bounding into sight. At the truck we learn that three of us saw no deer, two saw one, and my dad saw four deer, but "no horns," so no shots were fired. Today we don't eat our lunch in the woods. We drive back to the cabin for some bacon, eggs, potatoes, toast . . . and naps. (I also treat myself to a Heineken.)

3:15 P.M.—We are back in the woods and I have made my way to the same blind in which I had spent the morning. It's much easier to find it in the daylight.

3:30 P.M.—I settle into the swivel chair, and notice immediately how mild the temperature is. The heavy winds of the morning have blown some dry leaves into the blind; I do a little housekeeping so they won't crunch under my feet. It is even more beautiful than yesterday afternoon. The sun is pouring through the trees, probably lighting up my shiny face like a light bulb. I guess it's time to don the camouflage mask, even though I don't need it for warmth. My search and destroy vigil has begun again, but it just doesn't feel like there are any deer anywhere. Some of my squirrel neighbors are still frolicking in the leaves around me. Otherwise, there is only the sound of a gentle breeze. No guns firing—not even off in the distance!

4:30 P.M.—This day in the woods is winding down—the sun is already starting to dip behind a big ridge. It's cooling off a bit, but it's still nice. If it weren't for the cold steel and wood of the gun, I wouldn't even need gloves. After a few near nod-offs I sit up straight, reminding myself that not only was this prime hunting time, but I was also running out of time. If I don't get a deer tonight, I only have tomorrow morning left to bag one. I start envisioning various successful scenarios. Reminiscent of De Niro in *Deer Hunter*, I imagine that a huge buck presents itself broadside and stationary awaiting my perfect shot. My fantasy (at the moment, anyway, and under these circumstances) was to have two nice bucks appear simultaneously—one in front of me and one off to the side. After dropping the first one with a precise blast, I spin to the side and kill the other as it tries to escape. My heart even races a bit as I think through this scenario. I am awake now, but there are no deer to be seen, and still not a shot to be heard all afternoon.

4:55 P.M.—I think about peeing, but decide to try and wait so as not to disturb the silence in that most precious of all hunting time—the hour before dark. I am near an area in which deer are known to come and feed in the evening, I actually believe that I might see one.

5:35 P.M.—No sign of deer. It is getting quite dark. I realize that I probably could not see a deer at 15 yards, so maybe it is time to start out of the woods. (After all, I have never made my way **out** of the woods with a flashlight—only into the blind in the morning darkness.) I look at a tree stump out off in the distance through the scope of my gun. To my amazement, it is a clear and detailed view. The magnification of the scope seems to add about a half hour of apparent daylight to one's hunting time.

5:45 P.M.—It's really dark now. I move slowly from the blind in the deep woods to higher ground. The fiery red patches of sky and the brilliant moon give me another ten minutes to hunt. I sit down on a stump and marvel at the beauty of the scene.

Day Three:

6:40 A.M.—I settle into the same blind as yesterday—in the darkness. There was much debate this morning about where I should sit (all of the real hunters wanted this interloper to at least see some deer, if not shoot one). I liked the deep woods solitude, as well as the hunting perspective of the place I occupied yesterday, so I went back. Making my way there alone in the morning darkness felt great. Since my cousin and I are leaving at noon today there is a plan. At 11:00 a.m. my Dad and my brother will start walking through the woods towards my cousin and me, in an effort to push deer in our direction.

7:15 A.M.—The first shot of the day is fired off in the distance. It is getting light. I pee and then perform the ritual donning of the camouflage mask. My feet are already cold; I am back in my preppy boots. I slide the last hand-warming packet into my left boot and begin the lookout for Bambi's older brother.

8:15 A.M.—I hear a shot fired somewhere near us, but it's still rather far away. I have heard over and over that there was more shooting within the first three hours of Opening Day last year than there has been in two-and-a-half days this year! One of my cousins, who is sitting in "his blind" only about 300 yards from me, said he saw 100 deer in five days last year. My squirrel friends are very active again this morning—and very noisy! Why do I have to sit so quietly when they are making so much noise? Only a few hours until the big deer drive will begin—when do I fit in the inevitable bowel movement? I pee and have a cup of coffee while I think about it. (The deer do not seem interested in showing up at inopportune times any more than opportune times.)

8:25 A.M.—Here comes the sun.

9:00 A.M.—The sun may be shining, but it is REALLY COLD this morning. To warm up, I decide to walk down to another blind that I can see at the bottom of the hill. I step carefully and quietly through the woods, and inspect this blind. It seems to offer yet another great perspective of the woods, but if there are no deer, it might as well be a picture on a postcard. I notice when I look back up at the blind in which I have been sitting that my orange coat is visible through the camouflage burlap that surrounds the blind. When I get back up there, I will turn my jacket inside out so the camouflage side is showing. I will also put my hands down my pants, as the walk has not warmed them at all. Only two hours until the deer push starts.

NOON—There would be a push, but no deer would be seen. I make my way out of the woods, give my dad a hug and hop into my cousin's car to start the 2-hour drive to the airport. My first hunting trip in over 30 years had ended with a whimper and a smile. I didn't have to shoot anything; I had a great experience.

I always enjoy shooting guns when I visit my grandfather, and reading this story actually made me consider deer hunting. We'll see . . . .

This is probably a good spot for Dad's 2002 Holiday Letter, since he references the hunting trip. I also like this letter because it features an essay I wrote about a scary experience I had with my brother during one of our visits to Michigan.

Holiday Letter

I guess I will start with Andrew's three favorite words in church. No, not "love thy neighbor," but "please be seated." Why should you be seated? Because we have a news flash—nothing profound happened in the Watson household this year! Sure, I gave up a great job in New York to restart my training and consulting business ('there's no place like home'); Andrew got his driver's license (and someone promptly drove into the side of his car); and we got a beautiful, fun-loving dog (a Wheaton Terrier named "Sally" because it's a word Brian can say). Let's see, what else happened—as unprofound as it may be?

Andrew showed typical good judgment and gave up football to join the golf team (on which he lettered); Lindsay started piano lessons (while she continues with the violin); she also played softball for the first time. (She particularly enjoyed making little dirt piles while playing second base.) Brian is in a terrific new school where they appreciate his adorable, special (and sometimes extraordinary) qualities, while working to unlock his limitations. He has somehow become masterful at operating TVs and VCRs. (Next year we hope his skills will include dressing himself and speaking in full sentences—nature works in mysterious ways.)

Nancy has discovered yoga and a forehand in tennis (a connection? Can you say "Zen"?); she has also discovered that her 7-year-old daughter has inherited many of my lifestyle attributes. (What's that song? . . . with a mess mess here and a mess mess there, here a mess there a mess . . . .) Nancy has also discovered that she should be as good to herself as she is to everyone else—that makes us all happy. I gave my first non-church-related motivational speech this year. It was about 'work/life balance,' and the conference organizers wanted to call it *The Fine Art of Saying "No."* I asked them to change it to *The Fine Art of Saying "Yes"—to Yourself!* Who among us can't benefit from being reminded of the importance of self-care from time-to-time? Anyway, where was I? Andrew has discovered independence, we all have rediscovered classical music, Nancy has discovered email, and I have discovered eBay auctions. (Can you say "obsession"?)

Lindsay and I took second place in the 3-hole parent-child golf tournament at our club. It was a beautiful moment when the assistant pro handed her a trophy, and the handful of members in attendance applauded spontaneously. Lindsay looked at them, smiled and said 'thank you' with warmth and confidence. Speaking of poise, my brother Rick and I won a dramatic 'shootout' in his Member-Guest golf tournament. My brother and I joined my father (on his 69th birthday) for some deer hunting in Michigan. Spending 8 or 9 hours a day in a Thoreau-like state in the middle of the woods is incredibly therapeutic. There were some other relatives in the hunting party, but I won't elaborate here since, like every family, we have a few scoundrels no one really likes to talk about. Seeing only one deer off in the distance, I understand why they call it "hunting," not "shooting."

We traveled to North Carolina for Thanksgiving this year. It was the first time we got on a plane for that holiday in 13 years, but the lure of family and good friends who live there was just too much to resist. It was a great time; the only missing piece was not having Nancy's wonderful mother there with us. It was her West Coast brother's turn to enjoy her company in California. God's blessing to Brenda on the death of her father on Thanksgiving eve. And God bless my brother and his wife as they prepare for a trip to China where they will be united with a precious daughter to bring home to their family.

Actually, something sort of profound DID happen this year. It is best conveyed by some excerpts from a beautiful essay (titled "Together") that Andrew wrote for English class. After describing in colorful detail the setting for our annual summer visit to my family in "small town," Michigan, Andrew went on to relate the events of one powerful evening there. This is what he wrote:

"I was left in charge of my brother and sister while my parents were out with my aunt and uncle. Truth be told, my only real project for the evening was entertaining my brother Brian who has special needs. It took a great deal of effort, and an even greater deal of tone-deaf singing, but Brian was finally in bed. Now I could kick back and enjoy my evening with a nice cold Faygo Red Pop. Or so I thought.

No more than ten minutes after I had put Brian to bed, he came strolling out of the bedroom. I took him by the hand and led him back to his room, but it didn't take me long to see that he was in a great deal of discomfort. He and I sat on the side of his bed as he gouged his left eye with his right hand, moaning with a sense of panic. It was no more than five minutes before things went from bad to worse.

His left eye was now swollen almost completely shut, and my heart really began to race. It was becoming very clear to me that Brian was having an allergic reaction. At this moment I had one goal: finding Brian's Epinephrine pen and somehow mustering the emotional strength to stick that gigantic needle into his leg. (The "Epi-pen" as we call it, is the antidote for an allergic reaction.)

I called on my cousin for assistance, and with the help of my Grandparents, we tore through every suitcase, but to no avail. At this point I carried Brian into the bedroom to cover his eye with a cloth. I used this time to compose myself enough to think of a plan. Calls to my Dad's cell phone went unanswered.

I sat there watching Brian's condition deteriorate; his face went from pained to helpless, and I couldn't stand it anymore . . . it was time to call 911. Right after my Grandfather hung up the phone, I heard the call go out on my Grandparents' police radio: "boy with special needs having allergic reaction". An overwhelming nausea overtook my body. I figured that Brian and I were on our way to some rural hospital. I told Brian "it will be ok, it'll be ok," trying to dispel his fears as well as mine. But he heard my wavering voice, and saw right through me. We were terrified together in the middle of nowhere, with nothing to hold onto but each other.

Our trance of fear was interrupted when my cousin came running into the room with the Epi-pen. Brian would live. The weight of the Universe was no longer resting solely on my shoulders. All that remained now was the challenge of sticking the needle in his leg; a challenge that proved to be too great for me. Brian wasn't the stuffed Ernie doll I had practiced on—this was my brother, and this may be the difference between life and death. Just then I heard the roar of the ambulance as it pulled into the driveway. Once again I breathed a sigh of relief. Trained professionals had arrived, I thought. I'm off the hook.

Carrying Brian out to the ambulance was not an easy task, though. When Brian heard the sirens, memories of a childhood spent in hospitals were revived, and he let out a howling cry. At this point I was holding back tears of my own. As they strapped Brian down to the ambulance bed and prepared to inject the shot, Brian and I looked at each other, wanting to be back home. Then, with a pop and a scream, it was done.

Brian fell asleep on my chest that night. I wouldn't have had it any other way."

It is said that "courage comes from deep love." You be the judge of how courageous Andrew was that night. What is our scorecard in life? I'm thinking that the most important scorecard is the one that measures how many friends we have and how many lives we have touched in some meaningful way. By this measure the Watsons feel truly wealthy. So many friends touch our lives in so many loving ways. We can never thank you enough, but our gift to you this year is a promise to try in every way to touch your lives with genuine love, compassion and support.

Lindsay surprised me one day when she said: "Yesterday is history, tomorrow is a mystery, but today is a gift. Mom learned that in Yoga," she said. Good going Mom! I try to think of these words every day.

God bless. Merry Christmas, Happy Hanukkah, and Happy New Year.

Chapter Eleven

DEALING WITH LOOSE ENDS

There were literally hundreds of Dad's writings, notes and outlines scattered all over the house, under car seats, on bathroom counters, and in the home office. Some were in folders, some were on computers, some were stuffed in books or pockets of jackets, and many were just in piles on the floor. What I have shared with you so far are the writings that were (somewhat) capable of being categorized. What follows is a more random collection of rather random pieces—some are in the form of short stories, while others are like magazine articles.

The first piece below is an autobiographical snapshot of what was going on in Dad's head at a single point in time; it reflects his thoughts one morning about 20 years ago. It would appear that he was alternately overwhelmed by and impressed with how much he was juggling in his life. He wrote this piece as an observer of someone else—not as if he were writing about himself. This is a technique that he used in some of the other literary endeavors that appear in this chapter. It was an untitled draft document, but let's call it: "A Day in a Life."

It's roughly 11 a.m., and even though he has been in and out of his office several times since 8 a.m., the light is still not turned on. The sports trivia calendar on his desk says it is Wednesday, May 13th. In fact, it is Monday, May 18th. He is still carrying around calendar pages he ripped off from days gone by so he could give them to his friends. The picture of his son, in a lovely (but smudged) brass frame sitting amidst the clutter on his desk, is months old. His son is nearly three times the age portrayed in the photo.

He has made phone calls to attorneys at the law firm from which he is on a temporary leave. He has calls in to clients of the firm who still want some attention, and he still owes a few other people calls— although he almost always returns phone calls the same day. He is not really on leave. He is working for the local legal aid office, representing indigent tenants at his law firm's expense. He is a corporate lawyer flirting with his dream to litigate—trying cases, arguing motions— helping those who need help the most. Of course, he also seems to be helping to shape the organization's policies and practices. He just can't help himself.

He takes a call from an acquaintance with whom he is working on an independent project for a sports marketing company—a possible path to getting into that business. This afternoon he will have lunch with a member of that company's sports marketing team. And next he will meet with a former member of the team who has started his own entertainment and sports marketing company. Residuals, that's where the money is. Or maybe the money is in brokering bodies. He has been fairly successful at putting people together. Maybe his law firm will be retained to handle the new company's public offering.

But why should he be concerned with a new career? He continues to cultivate and expand his client base and his role within the law firm. He plays a fairly prominent role in the firm's recruiting program, and has developed a highly-specialized and lucrative (for the firm) practice in international law. He speaks regularly at an extension course offered by a world-renowned university, and spoke recently at a well-known national bank. One of his published articles on export controls was forwarded to the President of the United States, and he got a response from a U.S. official in a position to act on it. Next month he will address a dozen Chinese business students at another prominent college to sort out for them the complex problem of selling U.S. products to their country. This presentation will likely be sandwiched between his third and fourth trials. The first was a taste of honey.

The volume and diversity of the reading material stuffed in his briefcase, scattered around his apartment and piled in his offices might suggest that he is an unfocused researcher—he would like to believe it reflects an obsession with learning. The collection includes: the *N.Y.*

Times, a business magazine, several international trade reports, articles on motivating employees, a summary of the new tax law, a handbook on buying and selling a business, a book titled *The Fundamentals of Trial Techniques,* pieces of *The Boston Globe,* and housing law materials addressing issues from condo conversions to evictions. (He was once fond of saying that his reading habits "showed a passion for knowing something about everything;" today he might call it curiosity looking for opportunity.)

Of course, there are also health club brochures he has gathered to help him negotiate a corporate membership deal for his firm (which recently moved into new headquarters). He has arranged two other corporate memberships for his firm—primarily, he will say, to accommodate his own aerobic, weightlifting and tennis needs. The more likely goal was to accommodate his budget. But he is distracted these days. The softball team he coaches and plays for may not have a field to play on. Yesterday he put out some feelers. He has to find a place to play. He bats clean-up.

He can't be too concerned with all of this right now, though. In two days he and his 13-month-old son will get on a plane for Michigan, where he will do three of his favorite things: spend time with his little boy, spend time with his family and go fishing. For a few restful days he will sit in a boat casting, reeling, drinking and relaxing. He will need to spend some time preparing for an upcoming presentation he has committed to give during his law school's orientation next fall. (Something about how to succeed in law school and in private practice.)

He will also think about whether his notes from that presentation could become a book; whether it is time to write another legal article (on export law); whether his article on commodities brokers will ever be published. He will also think about where he is going to live when he returns to Boston. For the past five months he has been going through a rather difficult separation from his Jekyll and Hyde relationship which may not end well; and mice recently (and literally) drove him out of his temporary student-like apartment.

During his trip, he will reflect on whether he has enough money to buy new golf clubs, a much needed summer suit, and to pay his rent when (and if) he finds a new apartment. He will contemplate which friends he can live with and for how long. He will attempt to jog around the picturesque lake to which he will escape during the Michigan visit, but must wait and see whether the joint he injured in his knee during last weekend's rugby game is healed. When it heals he is going to make the move to the over thirty rugby league; he says it will be fun to be one of the younger guys.

He thinks about how to deal with (and hang on to) his friends-turned-clients and his clients-turned-friends. He'll take them to baseball games, play some golf, accept their meal invitations, patronize their stores, share his problems and listen to theirs. One of these days he'll tell all of them about his separation—those who have not heard the details don't really understand why it is happening.

He is looking forward to his 10th college reunion and the onslaught of visitors that is only about two-and-a-half weeks away. Maybe he will meet someone there—or re-meet someone—who will take him away from all of this. One classmate (a political aspirant) has teased him with the idea of getting involved in a congressional campaign. Maybe an investor or inventor will ask him to join a bandwagon. Maybe he will just drink a lot.

He reads about narcissism and fears he is a victim. He dabbled with therapy, but convinced the doctor (and himself) that he didn't need it. He tried marriage counseling, but saw it going nowhere. He contemplates a new relationship and wonders whether that's the answer.

He can't spell or crunch numbers as well as his education would indicate, but he is working on those deficiencies. He wants to write, but can't decide about what. He carries around a Dictaphone to capture brilliant thoughts, but it never seems to be there when he needs it—if it's there, it has no tape in it. He doesn't know how much money he actually has or in which accounts it is kept. He only knows there is never enough.

All he ever wanted was to be a successful trial lawyer, a professional athlete, President of the United States, and a good father living in a house on a lake with a happy family. (Oh, and with a cooler always stocked with beer.) So, how is he doing at achieving his goals? Not so great, he thinks. But ask him again tomorrow.

★ ★ ★ ★ ★

It is clear that Dad was struggling with some tough personal issues here. I was the 13-month-old son that he refers to in this piece and, frankly, I am glad I was too young to feel that pain that clearly gripped him when he wrote this. I have little doubt the in some perverse psychological way, a few of the emotions he was experiencing at the time seeped into my soul. I must admit that I actually experience some of the feelings he expressed.

But he so often found a way to turn adversity into something good. The next essay is a good example of that. He was so mad when he got accused of going through an electronic toll booth too fast, that he called me at college to vent. He had told me since I first learned to drive that I *must* observe the speed limit rules at tolls, and I knew he always did! So I truly believed he had been wrongfully cited. Obviously, Dad often wrote as a way of dealing with emotions— good and bad—as is evidenced throughout this book. This next piece is a good example of writing as therapy.

How Getting Stopped by an Overzealous Police Officer Helped Enlighten Me

As I pulled away from getting the speeding ticket, I was so incensed I was shaking. The police officer did not have any evidence, and he didn't even give me a chance to explain myself. As I drove on I kept obsessing about how I was going to explain to a judge that I really wasn't "bad." Over and over I played out the inevitable judicial hearing in my mind. I couldn't let it go—until I realized that I was actually reliving my childhood.

The good boy, wrongly accused, was always trying to explain to those who were supposed to protect (and love) him that he really wasn't bad; and they really shouldn't punish him.

Having recently read a book titled *The Middle Passage*, I gained some clarity about the profound impact that childhood parental actions have on us well into adulthood. I saw clearly, for the first time, that most of the fear I continuously experience in life flows from fears that were programmed long ago—fear that I was not safe, fear that I was not understood and fear that I was not appreciated. I had grown up with the belief that if I made a mistake I would get called out. Now I was supposedly grown up, but still harbored the same fears.

While reading *The Middle Passage* and becoming aware of the way I was being controlled by old, negative beliefs, I started listening to a series of meditative CDs during my commute to and from the office on the train. I was taking the train to a new job—a job in which I was viewed by virtually everyone as a real asset to the firm. (They actually thought I was a highly capable marketer . . . .)

This meditative time helped me work on what I now understood to be the process of "killing the ego;" an ego that projected "wrong," fear-filled images to my heart and soul. This reflective process also helped me deal with what turned out to be some overwhelming challenges in the new job.

Bringing this increased awareness to my new position allowed me to see myself as a more valuable contributor to the organization than I believed myself to be in the past. Others always seemed to see me in a much better light than I saw myself.

Moreover, the meditative experience on the train had the effect of opening up space in me for "whatever," and for "what is possible." I started seeing that there is both a Universe of Joy and a Universe of Possibilities available within my Spirit. I was finding it easier to let go of "outcome-focused" approaches to everything. "Pay attention" became my mantra. "Loving kindness" became my goal, not just as something I would give to others, but for myself, as well.

Simply stated, I found myself shifting away from a life lived with the subconscious belief that anything bad that happened to me was deserved. And, yet, my old ego still made me think it was critical to defend myself passionately whenever I was criticized about anything. Then along comes an overzealous police officer who triggers every one of the painful thoughts and negative habits I was fighting. After a few miles of agonized driving, during which I had thought it through and worked some things out, a "smile" came to my face as I let it go.

So, I propose a toast to a new understanding that "shit happens;" that there is suffering in life, and to knowing that it is not always aimed at me (or caused by me).

My new measures of success will be: how I respond to suffering, how much loving kindness I can extend (to myself and others), and how much I pay attention (and can be present in the moment). Did

211

someone pull me over and give me a citation for no reason? Oh well, it happens.

I found some loose notes in a folder labeled "Pathways to a Connected Life." They presented a lot of interesting little – or big – thoughts. What follows really are "loose ends," so don't expect much in the way of continuity in the next few pages. But these random writings provide some fun reading. Let's start with this:

Pathways to a Connected Life

Have you ever thought about what your message would be to your family if you knew you were going to die? Am I the only one who thinks about these things?

To my wife I might say: "Love again. You have so much to give, but don't give too much next time. You have almost done that in your devotion to us, and you need more time for yourself. Know that I am always with you; a part of me is in you and the kids."

To my eldest son Andrew: "Don't ever stop being a part of this family. Know how vital you are to its fabric even though you are older, and not here all the time." I would also remind Andrew of the time we played in a parent-child golf tournament, and the other father in one of our matches lied about his score—it was a learning moment. Andrew's big brown eyes looked up at me in confusion when the man announced his score. I put my hand on his shoulder and whispered that we could talk about it later. I would remind him of what I told him that afternoon: "no victory is worth cheating for."

I would say to anyone who would listen, "Happiness is hidden everywhere, you just have to look for it and be open to it."

I believe that Nature has given me an incredible capacity for understanding people, situations and connectedness, as well as for helping people feel better about themselves, their opportunities, or even their tragedies. I want to use these gifts to fulfill my role in the world.

I believe that 'what we do in life echoes in eternity.' I read that somewhere, but can't recall where.

How many dads have a copy of *A Book of Eulogies* in their reading collection? Of course, mine did. I mentioned previously that I was surprised by how much my dad thought about death. In the "Pathways" folder Dad had even copied an excerpt from Thoreau's unpublished works found in an elegant eulogy of Henry David.

I also found a page of obituaries in that folder from *Harvard Magazine*, and two death notices were circled from the class of 1977—that was Dad's graduating class. A note in the margin said: "didn't know them—check photos in Reunion book to make them real. Pray for their families—especially children—appreciate your own." My sense is that Dad used reports of mortality as a constant reminder of what he saw as the preciousness of life. Here is another random piece from that folder.

Notes for a Screenplay You Won't Likely See on Screen

A teen boy has an idea for an online business enterprise. He wants to get teenage kids to subscribe to a site where he collects video parodies of famous movie scenes performed by the teenagers. This is not without some risk, as God knows what some kids would create in short, three-minute, scenes. (And there may be some copyright issues.)

The site launches. A cult following starts to develop—the boy wants to start charging a fee for submissions, and give a cash prize to the person submitting the best parody (size of prize based on number of member registrations at $5.00).

With this background established in the early scenes, the boy starts fooling around on the dad's laptop one night, and two parallel threads develop: the kid discovers a world of illegal activities on his dad's hard drive, but he also realizes he can use his dad's account to get into . . . .

That is just plain crazy stuff! Can you believe that such a rich story idea ended so abruptly after just a few sentences? What a shame, since this "screenplay" sounded very promising. And then there was this rather odd, unfinished, motivational piece in the "Pathways" folder.

In her book, *Do What You Love*, Marsha Sinetar highlights the Big "R" (*Resistance*) and the Big "S" (*Should*). They are really two sides to the same coin.

We resist doing what we love because years of programming cause us to doubt ourselves, and to believe that what we can truly accomplish is limited. At its best this limit comes from Resistance—at its worst, it is an acute problem of negative self image. Ahh, the ever-lurking problem of self-image.

The "Shoulds" flow from the same defective emotional program: we are told that we should do what we are trained to do, we should be loyal employees (and make as few career changes as possible); we should make as much money as possible, we should be careful not to take risk, we should drive a nice car . . . .

Right below these introductory sentences, Dad scribbled something that might be called an "emotional timeline." It looked like this:

Sink…Struggle to stay afloat…Swim…Swim long distance…Walk on water

_____ | _____ | _____ | _____ | _____ |

His mind was just so full of analysis and observation. I REALLY wish my father could have more completely explained this line (literally) of thinking. It seems "pregnant with potential" (one of his favorite phrases). I guess this illustration really just reflects life. What we do and what happens mostly falls somewhere in between sinking and walking on water! Dad was pretty obsessed with the movie, *Being There*, in which Chauncey Gardiner walks on water because no one ever told him he couldn't! This is referenced in one of his Holiday Letters, and in this next somewhat disjointed excerpt from the folder.

Thank God for Chauncey Gardiner whose story is like an intervention in my war against Resistance and Should. Without the little inspirational snippets that I find in movies or wherever, I would be losing my footing.

The opposite of the metaphor "losing your footing" would be finding your footing, walking on water or learning to fly. Without these alternatives we would simply sink or fall into the abyss metaphysically speaking. Many of us, except perhaps those most acutely afflicted with emotional dysfunction, believe (or would like to believe) that existence happens somewhere in between flying and falling—between sinking into water and walking on it. Yet we often act as if our options are only those extreme and disparate choices at each end of the spectrum. Why do we fail to see all of the options? More importantly, why do we fail to see that by failing to consider all of the choices we turn life into a game of survival—not just living?

I think Chauncey Gardiner illustrates the reality of the Big R and Big S more then any number of psychiatric terms I could list. Living sheltered and essentially alone into his adult life, he could neither read nor write. He went through life "not knowing any better." His simple approach to life, people and politics—he equated everything to the concept of raising a garden—caused him to emerge into national political fame without effort or ambition. No one told Chauncey he couldn't advise the President; no one told him he shouldn't say what he truly believed; no one clouded his honesty with doubting questions.

The ultimate statement about life is made at the movie's conclusion. Not knowing that it is typical to mourn and linger a bit over the grave at a funeral, he walks off into the woods while others are still at the grave site. He props up some windblown plants and then, without a second thought, he walks across a small unfrozen body of water to his home. That's right, no one ever told him he couldn't walk on water.

These are all of the writings I could salvage from the "Pathways" folder, except the following "poem." Using the concept of 'walking on water" for transition, here, I present: *Who Else Might Be My Angel?* (I guess we could argue that Angels walk on water.) I like this piece; Dad had always believed that we were surrounded by Angels.

Who Else Might Be My Angel?

Without a doubt my Grandma is there,
watching my every move.

Surely, too, my late son so dear,
is teaching me to love.

I think my Grandpa has a role;
some uncles, aunts, a cousin, a teacher past.
Or perhaps it's Jane who lifts me.

But who else lights my path and way?
Who guides me now and then,
without me knowing how, why,
what or even when?

I'll see the face, but then it's gone;
was that an Angel light that moved?
Who gives me strength, a friend unknown,
who lives beyond the dawn?

And here on earth, does Harry count?
Are Angels in my home?
Is the life we know connected,
so all are not alone?

I'll think about and wish always,
for Angel-warmth from sun.
I'll offer love to all who long,
for an Angel's touch each day.

'Cause maybe I'm just passing through,
a spirit on the way;
but then again, I have a hunch
my son showed me the way.

As others help me, show me, move me;
as others lead me through,
I'll give back all I have to give
and be an Angel too.

A couple of things jump out here. The reference to Jane was surprising. I remember him telling me once that his first real childhood experience of death (other than his grandmother, when he was two years old) was when his friend Jane drove a snowmobile under a single wire fence and was killed (in a way as horrific as you might imagine). This happened when he was in junior high. They had spent years together in a drum and bugle corps performing and competing. But this was not a part of his life that Dad talked about much. Clearly, it was more important to him than any of us knew—giving an old friend Angel status is not a benign gesture.

I also wonder about his reference to his "son." I am pretty sure it was not a reference to me. It could be either Casey who died, or Brian with his special needs. I think my dad sometimes worried that he wasn't connecting enough with Brian. It was obvious that he wanted to be a great dad, but found it hard to know how he was doing with a mentally challenged child who could demonstrate only a few emotions and desires. Dad really wanted to bring special needs awareness to my sister's private school, but he never really got around to it. You may also recall that he had drafted the letter to Oprah that he never sent. (I really should bring all of this to Oprah's attention!)

So, the concept of a "spirit" passing through life, as expressed in this poem, could go either way, referring to the brother whose continuing existence is a blessing, or to the brother whose death profoundly changed Dad's life. I will just leave it at that.

A number of things Dad wrote had the word "chapter" in the heading. One such note said: "A chapter for a book: On Having A Special Needs Child." That would have been a great chapter, but there was no text. In some ways that chapter is incorporated into much of this book. Another title I found, which clearly would have appealed to a limited audience was: "Bathroom Humor: How Samuel Johnson might describe a morning bowel movement—An incomplete, but important first step." I don't even want to go there . . . .

I want to shift gears for a minute. My dad didn't talk much about having "heroes," but he was very fond of Gene Sarazen. He used to talk about him a lot. There was the time he called me to simply say he was sitting in Gene's living room on Marco Island watching a PGA Tournament with "The Squire." "It doesn't get any better than this," Dad said. But it did get better. He was Gene's guest at The Masters golf tournament on several occasions; he drove around Augusta in Mr. Sarazen's "Champion's Car" (as he referred to it). He also got to read personal, hand-written letters exchanged by Sarazen and Bobby Jones. Dad's idea for a book based on these letters came to pass about a year after Gene died.

My father's favorite moments (and one of his best stories about his relationship with Gene Sarazen) occurred the night before the Pro-Am at the first Sarazen World Open Championship at The Legends golf course at Chateau Elan. My dad had represented Gene, Sam Snead and Kathy Whitworth in connection with their contracts to design and endorse that golf course. It was a reasonably lucrative and fun project for all involved. But, more importantly, Gene had always dreamed of hosting a golf tournament in which the "Open" winners from countries all over the world would compete against each other. Yes, the winner of the Zimbabwe Open, and the Brazilian Open, and every other Open Championship. (Many countries have their own version of the U.S. Open Championship.)

Working closely with the golf course owners, whom my father described as among "the world's most amazing people," the tournament became a reality. I heard my father tell the story of going to Gene's hotel room to take him to the "pairing party" where the sponsors would learn who they would play with in the Pro Am. When Gene opened the door he was with a representative of Wilson Sports, and Gene introduced my father to this man as "my good friend, Jim Watson, who made my dream come true."

Nothing pleased my father more than helping other people realize their dreams, but he especially loved helping an 80-year-old golf legend see his dream come true. I did some research and learned that the tournament was played for several years. Ernie Els won it twice. For some reason, though, The Sarazen World Open Championship was taken off the PGA's schedule.

I know it is completely obvious, but I must mention again that my dad was a bit of a pop psychology nut. So it was no surprise at all that I found a folder titled "Therapy." With all of the ups and downs he had experienced, his myriad interests, and the plethora of ideas and missions Dad had, it is no wonder that there are themes of "therapy" in many of his writings. No doubt he needed it, and, of course, he regularly dispensed it (without a license). The "Therapy" folder had the following pieces in it.

On Therapy

Correct me if I am wrong, but isn't it a therapist's job to make every patient think they are the most important (or impressive or wonderful) person they work with?

So, knowing that, how can you trust a therapist? How can you believe it when they tell you how gifted or special or blessed or appreciated you REALLY are? Of course, they will say that they (and others) can see it readily, and that only you (and probably your mother) do not see the beauty and wonder that you are.

It should not be surprising that most people do not seek out therapists until years after they sense dysfunction. How hard it must be for a therapist to get a patient—someone who is paying them to make them feel good—to actually believe it when they tell them about their inner (or outer) beauty . . . ! I was lucky to find someone who knew how to connect with me—someone I trusted and believed in.

Dad titled the following poem "Writing Therapy," so I guess in writing it, he was dealing with some important issues.

Writing Therapy

I didn't want to go.
It was—or seemed—far away;
And I had been away
A lot lately.

But I went, finding new time
with an old friend there.
I was reminded from his sorrow
Of all that was good with me.

Flying back
I was imagining love;
Love and appreciation
All around at home.

The primary object of my hope
Barely looked up from her book,
As I reentered the world
I had so missed.

The youngest children slept;
One, older, was sleepwalking
through his own life.

A cocoon of loneliness
transformed me back
to another home
Devoid of the love
I so desperately needed.

Feeling alone, I was,
As a child, in fear
Of the next parental outburst.

I prayed,
Asking God for peace;

"Let me feel love" was
part of the intercession.

"Hold on," Nature breathed.
"Love is there around you.
Look past the evidence
and the walls."

Maybe it was all just anxiety;
Since one of my little ones
would be
facing a little surgery soon.

Apologies, to my other son;
A job well done
deserves more
than fleeting reference.

I had lost perspective;
retreating into "victim" (and self-preservation),
I had lost loving kindness.

But perspective is returning,
clients be damned;
parents be damned.
A passing glance
at a Holocaust reference

Snaps me back to what is,
and a belief in what can be,
If I chose to pursue only love.

There is so much about fear and loneliness in Dad's writing. It makes me wonder how he always (well, almost always) had such a great disposition. But he certainly found great love and optimism in his year-end writing. Get a load of the first paragraph of the next Holiday Letter . . .

Holiday Letter

Each year at this time, I am overwhelmed with appreciation for the richness of life and the joy of family and friends. We, like all of you, face plenty of stress and challenges, but I don't think I can write enough Holiday Letters to acknowledge all of our blessings. (I will try, of course. But, fortunately, for you, Nancy limits me to one piece of paper!)

Our house is for sale! After two years of looking for the perfect new home, we found it. (Actually, Nancy found it and bought it while I was in Toronto!) In late January we plan to close on a beautifully restored Greek Revival (c. 1847). Finally, we will have a guest room (actually, a guest "suite"), so please come visit! (Are you listening New Hampshire cousins, college classmates, Watsons and friends everywhere?) What makes this new house even more special is that it is on the same street as the Memorial Garden where Casey's name is forever etched in stone on the wall of St. John's Church. It just makes sense . . . .

We have had an amazing year. I actually got my handicap down a few points, but Nancy played more golf than I did! We made our customary visit to Michigan this summer where our kids learn about hunting, fishing, swimming and 3-wheeling, while my folks learn about Barney, Arthur, wiffle ball, and the art of grilling venison. (Nancy just doesn't like her steak fried!) We made a bonus trip to Grand Rapids this fall during which we got to spend some quality time with the whole clan at cousin Jeannie's beautiful wedding.

Nancy's parents continue to be a wonderful extension of our family. It brings Brian and Lindsay to a veritable frenzy whenever "Mimi" and "Ahbie" arrive. Paul continues to fight the good fight for good health. Any of you who have been touched in any way by the challenge of cancer, please know that our prayers for Paul are also prayers for your health and comfort. Nancy and I feel very fortunate to have our parents to learn from and hang around with—but it is especially nice to have Paul carrying the burden of our Rotisserie baseball team!

And then there are the kids . . . Brian has a lust for life that I envy. He really appreciates every little thing, and his teachers love his sense of humor. His best new word is "hug," and he gives hugs freely. He loves to watch ice skating, gymnastics and Wheel of Fortune (two mom shows and a dad show?) He also likes watching hockey with Andrew, and he loves holding hands with anyone who will let him. He is truly a special kid. He now has two private tutors who see real potential for language development, increased attention span, and improved motor skills.

Speaking of special people, Andrew continues to amaze us with his warmth, wit and wisdom. "What a charming son you have," someone said at our recent open house. "Where is he in High School?" Imagine the look on the woman's face when we said he was only 11 years old (5'4½", 110 lbs., shoe size 9½-10)! He just got an awesome first report card; earlier this year he hit his first "over-the-fence" home run; he pitched five innings of no-hit baseball in the first game of the playoffs; and he made the "travel" team for basketball.

Andrew may be one of the most balanced people in the world. He has great friends; he is really smart (but not a nerd); he is caring and helpful (but not overly sensitive); he is a terrific big brother (but he gets appropriately annoyed with his siblings); and he loves sports (but is not obsessed with them). His Turkey Bowl role continues to increase. This year he intercepted a pass while playing middle linebacker (à la his hero, Ted Johnson). He completed several passes as quarterback, but he also threw an interception (which proves that he has at least some of my genes). A special guest appearance by Tony Brown made this year's Turkey Bowl extra special!

Lindsay—now 2¾—has discovered—I should say "mastered"—the computer. Thanks to a Dr. Seuss CD-ROM, she knows all of her upper and lower case letters, and she can count to 19 (the next number is "oh-teen"). Lindsay labors under the illusion that cookies and ice cream taste better than chicken and carrots. Recently, she has taken to asking for popsicles for breakfast! (She has also taken a keen interest in "the clicker"—maybe this is not a gender thing . . .) Most importantly, perhaps, she sprints from the back porch to my open arms as soon as I open the car door, yelling "Daddy's home, Daddy's home!" This is a totally lump-in-your-throat, awesome experience. (And check out those cheeks in the picture!)

The business of teaching lawyers how to get—and keep—clients has proven to be enormously satisfying. I like the fact that my business message is essentially the "Golden Rule." My "mission" is to totally reform the lawyer-client relationship by teaching better communication. Call me crazy, but when my work is finished, lawyer jokes will be a thing of the past! A special thanks goes to my assistant, Jennifer and my associates, Harry and Holly. They all make me better at what I do, and they also make it fun.

Speaking of fun . . . I am married to the most delightful and supportive woman in the world. (Did I mention that she is also very smart and terribly sexy?) It is hard to describe the incredible impact she has on me, our family, and our friends. She is my perfect teammate. Understandably, Lindsay is crazy about her. There is never a substitute for "mummy." Will it always be so? I think not! I'm sure I will learn a lot from observing this mother-daughter thing, but on the list of great mothers, Nancy will be at the top.

Some random thoughts: Kudos to Fred and Sally for bringing so many good friends together this summer for a phenomenal wedding week; always wear seat belts—even in the back seat; read stuff that makes your mind healthier and your spirit stronger; redefine "coincidence" as "part of the plan;" thank you to Billy for always being there; and ultimately, we need to remember that the more we give, the more we get.

I want to conclude with a passage from a life-changing book that many of you may have read, *Embraced By The Light*. Upon returning from a near-death experience, the author's message from the other side of life was that unequivocal love brings incredible peace and happiness.

"I saw a loving Being . . . [who] has invested us with God-like qualities, such as the power of imagination and creation, free will, intelligence, and most of all, the power to love. I understood that he actually wants us to draw on the powers of heaven, and that by believing that we are capable of doing so, we can." Amen!

We will all become someone's Angel some day—they are all around us. Let your Angels help you do good and enjoy life. Let this holiday season be about giving, appreciation and cooperation. An extra hug goes out to our Jewish friends. After all, Chanukah and Christmas coincide this year. But with a God of harmony trying to help us sort out some of the chaos down here, that, too, just makes sense . . . . Coincidence? No, just part of the plan.

Happy Holidays,
Jim, Nancy, Andrew, Brian and Lindsay

Here is one of Dad's random poems that I particularly like. It had no title, but I might call it "Logical Therapy." I am sure this form of poem does not conform to any established poetic structures.

There are

>   moments when we think (and truly feel) that we
>   know all there is to know;

Only to

>   awaken to a reality that brings fear (and
>   awareness) into our wishes;

Our true wish

>   for peace of mind (and a spirit without doubt or
>   complication) gets buried unless we;

Shut down

>   those thoughts that trouble us, finding in
>   silence (and stillness) the joy of acceptance;

Pray more

>   for the courage (and the humility) that makes us
>   dare to let go of familiar pain; and

Know that

>   in the moment when we fell (and began to
>   doubt), we actually knew all there was to know
>   to be at peace.

I will never forget the morning of my Bar Mitzvah. (My mother is Jewish, and Dad was always supportive of my dual religious upbringing.) My most vivid memory is not, however, just of the beautiful service and my flawless readings. Rather, it is of the courage my father demonstrated by showing up, sitting in the front row and doing his assigned reading. That may not sound so courageous, but moments before he arrived at the Temple he had kissed his father on the cheek as the paramedics put him in the back of an ambulance.

Unbeknownst to me, my grandfather had suffered a serious heart attack as he was heading out the door to attend my ceremony. Dad did not want to disrupt my special morning, so he had a friend sit in the back of the Temple and monitor his father's health on a silent cell phone. His friend came down front and sat with Dad mid-service just long enough to say that Grandpa had been airlifted to a Boston hospital. Dad said later that all he wanted to hear at that moment was that his father was still alive; once he got that news he was actually able to enjoy the service.

There was much to admire that morning about how my dad balanced his love for his father with his love for me. But, mostly I admire (and thoroughly enjoyed) the fact that Dad was able to leave the hospital (once Grandpa was stable and out of the woods) in time to offer a toast at the bar mitzvah reception.

With amazing composure Dad told the gathering of family and friends that I had saved my grandfather's life! You see, Grandpa's annual fishing trip to a remote northern Michigan island was scheduled for the same weekend as my ceremony. Grandpa had skipped the fishing trip to come to my service. We learned later that there had been symptoms of heart disease for months; "hints" of an impending heart attack were presenting themselves right up until he left. But Grandpa had decided to ignore these signs "until after the trip."

Thirty-plus years of heavy smoking had destined him to collapse that day. But instead of being hundreds of miles away from medical care in a wilderness fishing camp, Grandpa was in Boston just minutes away from the greatest healthcare in the world. (And he came within a few breaths of dying, even under those circumstances!) Typically, with his toast on this day, my father turned something potentially tragic into something positive and inspiring.

There were few dry eyes in the room as he thanked me from the bottom of his heart for being such a great son (apparently paternal love has some blind spots), and for saving his father's life. He also made a point of telling the assembly that one of the things he was most thankful for was my stepfather . . . Now I am getting choked up, so I will just leave it at that.

Is there such a thing as too much inspiration? I think not. With just a few words it seems like Dad could change someone's attitude—or even their life direction. Let me share with you a little "poem" that I found in one of Dad's many piles of words.

Everyday Connections

Don't be disappointed in the world; love it.
Don't be disappointed in yourself; love you.
Don't devalue the gifts you've been given; use them.
Don't just seek to achieve; seek always to love.

I believe someone could read these four lines and shift their attitude toward life in a meaningful way. The essay that follows is inspirational in a different way. It strikes me as a bit bizarre, but entertaining. You will see that a book called *The Golfer and the Millionaire* seemed to have a profound impact on Dad. This piece actually appears to be a first draft of something more, but in some ways, it is just a collection of moderately related thoughts revealing (again) some of Dad's tortured soul. He says little about the content of the book that apparently inspired him to write. (It makes me want to read the book . . . .)

Random Reflections on the Book: "The Golfer and the Millionaire" and on Life Itself . . .

Certain friends, like Harry, Chris and others, have given me the gift of the millionaire. That means they believe in me.

227

Since reading this book I have accelerated the process of "seeing" my negative thoughts and influences, and replacing them with positive supportive thoughts and ideas.

My emotional childhood experiences were, for the most part, negative; I was often made to feel inadequate and anything short of being perfect was unacceptable—somehow, I think, even perfect would have come up short. In those days God punished, God did not love; that was my childhood belief.

I must now consider abandoning the money and security of being a marketing expert, for the love—pure joy—of being a motivational speaker.

My greatest challenge is to stay in the zone of acceptance, and to not let childhood influences and attitudes influence me. I must trust the Infinite Spirit and Universal Love (which are one and the same) to take care of everything for me.

I must stop thinking that I can, or that I must, fix and do everything myself.

Creative expression and encouragement of others are my "reasons to be." It is a joy to do creative, motivational thinking, and a joy to share my thoughts and feelings.

I am not good at communicating openly and honestly with those I love most, because I had no models in my life to show me unequivocal, non-judgmental love. I know the value of meditation, but cannot bring myself to do it. I am not good at "just being"—or just letting the moment be what it is; I am not good at having no agenda. I need to be working on, thinking about, or doing something all the time, it seems.

I have, and now recognize that I have, been blessed with *elements* of genius (no, let's just say special skills) in the areas of intuition, teaching, and recognizing the connectedness of people everywhere.

Yet, I fall into patterns of isolation, of non-communication and loneliness, because I have found comfort there for so long. It is a state (loneliness) that interferes with relationships and connectedness; I need to engage, feel and connect!

Another proposed chapter title my father had written was: "Begin with the End in Mind." This was the title of one of Stephen Covey's books, and the notes that follow were written in a course book from a Covey seminar that Dad attended many years ago. The question posed in the program booklet was "What might people say at your memorial service?" The participants were apparently asked to consider what might be said from the point of view of family, friends, colleagues, employees and bosses. Dad was pretty candid about what he hoped people would say about him, but I doubt that he thought anyone would ever see these reflections. Since the idea of the course was to encourage people to live their lives in ways that will lead others to say these things, it seems like it was actually a great exercise. Here are Dad's notes—writing about himself.

<u>How was he as a family member?</u> Nancy's possible reflections: He always made us—me and the children—feel that we were the most important things in his life. He told us he appreciated us, and that he loved us unconditionally.

<u>How was he as a teacher?</u> Andrew's possible reflections: He made the time to help me learn anything I ever wanted to learn. He pushed me without hurting me; he encouraged me to excel; he admitted his own limits; and found ways to help me go farther.

<u>How was he as a boss?</u> His administrative assistant's possible reflections: He taught me skills, with positive feedback and an understanding of my sensitivities. He invested more time in helping me than the job justified; he cared that much. He respected my personal skills, weaknesses and needs. I watched him teach everyone around him—he loved what he called "growing" others.

<u>How was he as a friend?</u> A college friend reflecting: He supported me through thick and thin; he made me feel that I had value; he trusted me with important responsibilities; he appreciated me for what I could do; and tried to help me when I needed it. He honored me by asking for my help when he needed it.

<u>How was he as a confidante?</u> Harry's possible reflections: He gave me attention when I needed an ear; he was a good listener, who took time to understand, so he could help people in tough times. He could be trusted to be sensitive, empathetic, helpful and discreet.

<u>How was he as an employee?</u> A boss's possible reflections: He took responsibility for important projects and made them successful. He respected my style and concerns when we collaborated. He

was creative, hardworking, pleasant and effective. He made my job easier.

How was he as a teammate? A co-worker's possible reflections: He didn't ask for credit in success, nor did he shy away from responsibility in failure. He contributed more than he was asked, he pushed others to be better, and was fair and fun to work with.

A long time ago my father bought a packaged Tony Robbins program. He had found some inspiration in the tapes and books, but he was disappointed at the commercialism he found in the one live program he attended. He told me that the guy had helped a lot of people achieve their dreams, though, so he didn't want to be too critical. I found the following questions and Dad's answers in a booklet from the course.

The character qualities I admire most in others are: honesty, trustworthiness, creativity, self-acceptance, and generosity.

The people I know who seem to be happy are happy because: they are in good relationships; they are loving, they work hard and they play hard.

If my resources were such that I did not have to work for a salary, and I could do anything I wanted, I would: live on a lake, write books and poems, hang around with my family a lot, travel to visit friends more, preach a bit, and donate time and money to those in need.

The reason I would do that is: it would allow me to relax, reflect, be creative, have fun and be spiritual.

The moments of greatest happiness and satisfaction come to me when: my family members are especially happy; when I help someone with any struggle or difficult decision, and when I perform at a very high level in any activity I undertake.

At this point in my life, the most admirable thing about me is: my caring for my family and others, and my constant efforts to improve myself.

There are no real surprises here. If you have read the book to this point, you pretty much understand that this is who my dad is: A passionate, relational, compassionate and spiritual being. But, then again, there was a tortured soul underlying all of this. These next few short pieces are a glimpse into that soul. Each note was scribbled on a random piece of paper. But first, here is the letter from 2006 which, again, focused on the message of how we affect each other in daily life. It also foreshadowed the birth of this book.

Holiday Letter

When I was asked to speak at our church a few weeks ago, I fell upon a simple theme that got me thinking. The theme was **"Because of You,"** and it seemed to flow naturally and sincerely. I found myself saying things to the congregation like:

- Because of you, our son Brian wakes up every Sunday asking to go to church.
- Because of you, I got to hear my wife sing my favorite songs from *Godspell.*
- Because of you, Lindsay has a Bible with her name on it. And a passion for learning about religion that you don't often see in an 11-year-old.
- Because of you, my oldest son and I shared a special time delivering presents to the children of prisoners.

This theme, 'because of you,' reflects not only the spirit of love we have found in the Congregational Church, but also the concept of Universal connection that governs our lives every day. In looking back at 2006 it was clear that the Watson's lives had largely been shaped—and most certainly had been touched—in some way by everyone we know (and probably a bunch of people we don't know). When you let gratitude flow . . . and just think about everything good that has happened in your life, you quickly recognize that it is all because someone put an expression of love or caring in motion. No matter how unremarkable it seems at the time, everything pretty much flows from there.

I had already started the mental debate about whether to write something this holiday season when Nancy told me Lindsay wanted me to write a letter. I was just about to leave the house to run an errand when she mentioned this little tidbit in passing. As I drove down our street, thoughts started flooding my mind; so I pulled over and grabbed a piece of paper. Every thought seemed to center around what our friends and family members had done for us this year, and how much they truly meant to us. So with that in mind I started listing all of the possible endings to a sentence that starts with: "Because of you." (Not to be confused with the Kelly Clarkson song of the same name, which is not so positive!) I shared the list with Nancy and Lindsay, and we think you will see a lot of yourselves and your own experiences in these heartfelt reflections of gratitude—and I particularly like that the word 'you' is so often used in its plural form here!

Because of you Nancy walked 60 miles in three days to help cure breast cancer. **Because of you** we had a beautiful and loving Thanksgiving on the Cape; and **because of you** the sadness of Nancy's mother's sudden death turned into a time of connection. **Because of you** Regina's memorial service was a joyous celebration of life, friends and family. **Because of you** our children are cared for with heartwarming love when we sneak away for a date night or a long weekend; **because of you** Brian looks forward to going to school every day; and his special needs only make him more special.

Because of you Lindsay loves learning, singing and writing poetry; Andrew is having a fabulous experience of life and education; and my parents were able to attend their first-ever playoff games at Comerica Park in Detroit (to witness the Yankee demise). **Because of you** Nancy and I enjoy golf, walks on the beach and deep friendship in Florida; we feel family love when we are in Keene; and our Salvatore has a wonderful new playmate called Rocky. **Because of you** Nancy's eyes brighten when she gets those short (almost) daily phone calls; humor—leading to laughter—is a regular feature on our email; and we have a beautiful new church home. **Because of you** I love my job and going to the office every day; we carry on the rich tradition of Christmas Eve; and we look forward to Christmas Day cheer. **Because of you** our Boston world is filled with fond (midwestern) memories of your time living with us; Brian's recovery from foot surgery was followed by hot meals, comforting words, selfless childcare and comforting hugs; and *SuperNanny* means more than just another television show. **Because of you** we believe in miracle healing, the power of prayer and the resilience of the human spirit; SNCARC has money to serve special children; and my daughter's school can offer more scholarships. **Because of you** Nancy and I experienced paradise with friends in Cuernavaca; we know the joy of social tennis; and I can appreciate a good cigar on the golf course. **Because of you** I get to experience brotherly love in the midst of a golf tournament; time with high school friends is still special, and there is warmth in the heart of Chicago.

Because of you this year's Harvard-Yale game was a blast—despite the score; I witnessed my first poetry slam; and Andrew's love of baseball turned into a summer job. **Because of you** the season of Advent is celebrated throughout our house; trips to the airport are spiritual adventures; and community gatherings are warm and festive. **Because of you** Lindsay has wonderful friends; Nancy loves playing tennis; Brian has someone special to look forward to on Fridays; and we have a special place to visit every summer. **Because of you** we have terrific nephews and beautiful nieces!

The paradox is clear: "What you give out comes back. What you give away is yours to keep. All that you give you give to yourself." (Douglas Bloch) That should make everyone feel pretty good, since what you have given to us alone is immeasurable. There is one more thing you can do, though. You can give me some help in making a dream come true. Truth be told, I would rather write than almost anything else I do . . . . Some time next year I will ask you to go to a website where you will find a manuscript—currently a very rough draft of an idea I have for a book. It is essentially a novelistic way of presenting a collection of things I have written over the years. I hope some of you will spend a few minutes reading and critiquing this little hobby of mine, tentatively titled: *My Father's Writings: Glimpses of Life on the Inside.*

I forgot to mention one detail about when I pulled the car over to write down my ideas for this letter. I found myself parked right next to the Memorial Garden where our infant son Casey's ashes were buried and his name was carved in the wall 16 years ago today (December 9th). It made me remember the poem I wrote to Casey almost 10 years ago.

*I so vividly remember the outpouring of love in those difficult days, and am reminded again that **because of you** it really is a wonderful life.*

Thank you. Merry Christmas. Happy Chanukah and a wonderful
New Year to you all.

I have mentioned in other parts of this book how fond my father
was of his paternal grandmother. In the first of a series of brief notes
I found, and have reprinted here, Dad described that bond. I guess
he was experiencing the same needs, and sensing the same feelings
we all have for total acceptance. These short pieces reveal a level of
personal pain that makes me sad.

About My Grandmother . . . .
The Power of Unconditional Love

I had a profound, almost irrational, somewhat tragic response to
the death of my grandmother. For many, this would not be surprising
since their grandparents were very much a part of their lives. For me,
the depth of sorrow came out of nowhere. This was a woman I saw only
one week a year while growing up. In my early adult years, I had only
seen her once every couple of years. We didn't talk over the phone,
or exchange letters—although I would write her once in a while. Upon
reflection, however, it became clear that she was among the few family
members (or people on earth) who seemed to love me unconditionally.
She never said it. People from her old-fashioned world didn't share
feelings in words—but my grandmother truly did in her deeds. I felt it.
I could feel unconditional love in the quiet support she gave me, and
the warmth she extended to me whenever I saw her.

An Untitled Prayer

Lord,

When I see what is possible, I immediately set out to accomplish
it—my heart and my body say, "we will try," because we can do this
and we should. But despite all of the wonderful blessings you have
given me, I can only physically accomplish "so much." Spiritually, I
know I can accomplish more, because love, caring and respect know

no bounds. Help me to constantly remember this, and to seek out what is possible in Spirit; and for everything else, help me to smile and say "someday."

Ideas From a Tortured Soul

Six little words with the power of locks and chains: *"Who do you think you are?"*

This simple question—these six simple words—can only be asked in a few circumstances that I can think of.

When someone is coming out of a coma or struggling to recover from a brain injury or mental disease, a caretaker might ask the question— hoping for a coherent reply to demonstrate cognitive capability. And even this use of the question is a stretch. Typically, I would think the doctor or caregiver would simply ask, "who are you?"

So that leaves us with another more common—and potentially damaging—use of those six harmless-sounding words. By asking the question, or by just sending it as a subtle message: "Who do you think you are" can put someone in their place, cut them down to size, or be used to humble the arrogant and stifle the aggressive. Unfortunately, these words can also make a gifted child feel small . . .

I am not sure if Dad thought he was a gifted child or if he was just making an observation. But if feeling small made him write, then I hope I have made him bigger in memory.

235

Conclusion

So much of Dad's writing was abbreviated—ending before it was finished. But then so it was with my dad; it *all* ended too soon.

The fact that some of my father's notes survived the plane crash allowed me to know that his last (well, almost last) thoughts were creative. He really loved to write, so it is reassuring to know he was writing, and that he was thinking about me, and about his dad, and about our whole family during the flight. What a wonderful certainty to hold in our hearts.

We have no certainty, however, of what his thoughts were in the final seconds, when he knew the plane was going down. On the one hand, Dad was the type of guy who would assume he would survive. He was a bit of a risk taker and a survivor in his life and in his heart. But if there were an instant in which he sensed and accepted that he was going to die, knowing him as I did, he would likely have already reached out and grabbed God by the hand before impact. To soften the blow? Maybe. But more likely because of the peace he would have found in his profound faith at that instant; he had an unfailing belief that we will all move on to a place of total love.

While others may have been screaming and crying he may well have been smiling. I know he would have been praying for our family and to not let his death be a horrible cancer in our lives. He would pray for us to see signs of assurance that he is our personal Angel. He saw the Angel in everyone, but he also believed he had his own Angels all around him.

I think about the poem he wrote to Casey in the Memorial Garden (it appears a couple of times in this collection). It was filled with a belief in everlasting life. I think about the homily he wrote called: "There is No Such Thing as Coincidence." He just had so much to say, and I am thankful that I found his words and was able to share them. There was a proposed chapter title written on one of his scraps of paper that said: "The 3 hardest words: I Love You." I am not sure why these words were so hard, because everything he wrote suggested that love was the most important ingredient in life. Fortunately, I told my dad on many occasions that I loved him. As you may now know, there was a lot to love.

★ ★ ★ ★ ★

It just seems fitting to end this book with the very first Holiday Letter Dad ever wrote; it was written in 1994. It is a pretty ordinary message of what was going on in our family's life, but it made him want to write more . . . and it gave him a forum to share more of what was going on in his not-easy-to-understand mind, and his increasingly coming-to-life heart.

Holiday Letter

Life is good, Nancy is 6½ months pregnant, Brian is now 4, running around celebrating two years of constantly improving health and development. Andrew is a wonderful 8-year-old (going on 18, or so it seems), and I have the pleasure of being the husband and father of this lovable crew.

Nancy is the "total mom" and homemaker. She takes incredible care of us, makes our home warm and color-coordinated, while continuing to be on the silly side. She recently played an important role in organizing a memorial service at our church for families of children who have died. This beautiful candle-lighting ceremony was an important tribute to our son Casey, whose brief life and death four years ago touched our lives profoundly.

Brian has only a few words in his vocabulary, but they are *really* good ones! "Bubba" means "daddy," "Muma" means "mommy," "baby" means "Baby," "Raffi" means "sing to me," "Ker" is Andrew and "Mimi" means "nana." There are others, but the important thing is that he is communicating with us very well and we expect to see continued development. Brian has charmed the preschool teachers and has an incredible fascination with big trucks—he loves garbage collection day! He also loves to look in the mirror—a trait he surely inherited from his mother. Brian loves to swing, get tickled, watch tapes and blow kisses. He is a real sweetheart.

Andrew and I went to Fenway Park on his birthday—it happened to be on Opening Day. Red Sox first base coach, Frank White, threw him a ball they had just used for infield practice—that's just one example of why Andrew has a passion for Boston sports. He is vehemently opposed to the demolition and replacement of the Boston Garden; he has shaken the hands of Dave Cowens, Cam Neely and "the Chief." He has been to Foxboro to see the Patriots more times in the last two years then I have in 39¾ years. Andrew played in his first Turkey Bowl on Thanksgiving morning and we played in our first parent/child golf tournament. Andrew's teacher says he is a "delight" to have in class and we think he is a delight to be around as well. We sometimes tease him about his shoe size (7 mens), his short attention span (he wants to shoot hoops and practice cursive writing while doing his math homework), and his fondness for grown-up TV (he likes Seinfeld a lot). We never tease him about his big heart however; he is a very caring young man.

My thoughts often turn, as they do here, to dear friends who have faced difficult personal and family challenges this past year. Our prayers go out to them and will continue to until we know that they are safe and well. I thank God every night for the family I have and the joy it brings to me. Together each member of our family wishes you a warm and wonderful holiday, a new year filled with hope and a world of dreams fulfilled.

Epilogue

Observations on the Concept of Legacy by the Author

The word "legacy" is used a lot to refer to how we might be remembered after we die.

While I think a little bit about my own legacy, my concern is much more about what kind of impact I can have on the world while I am here! That impact might consist of little more than lifting the spirits of people I encounter in everyday life; or it could be to write something that might help thousands of people who need some inspiration, motivation, appreciation, or simple guidance.

But because so much has been written to fill that need, I questioned whether there was anything to add. Then I started thinking that there could actually be some value in the hundreds of pages I had written over the past few decades. There were sermons, homilies, personal letters, holiday letters, and motivational speeches, as well as poems, half-finished book chapters, unpublished articles, and some (very short) short stories.

People have always responded favorably to those writings of mine which actually saw the light of day. But the idea of just filling up a book with a random collection of essentially unrelated writings did not appeal to me. (And probably wouldn't to others.) So I came upon the idea of putting the writings in a context—and here's where the *legacy* thing kicks in.

I thought about how great it would be if my son were able to pull together all of my myriad papers after my death and publish them in a book. He happens to be a great writer; he knows the real story behind almost everything I have written (so he could string the reflections together in a meaningful context), and he would probably enjoy the project. But I didn't want to wait until I died to share my writings—so I put myself in my son's shoes and completed the project as if I were him. I think I needed to write about my writings in the third person to be comfortable with the inevitable, deeply personal revelations that flow from these words. So I hope you were able to suspend reality for a few hours and join me on this mystical journey to the heart.

I was tempted not to disclose myself as the true author. Indeed, the book probably works better in some respects as a ruse. But an article I stumbled upon in the *Wall Street Journal* said there is a serious debate about whether or not it is ok for an author to claim to be someone else. So I am who I am, and I have written what I have written. I hope that putting a little fiction around it made it more palatable. Forgive the informality and imprecision of much of the writing, but it seemed right to leave many phrases and structure in a more vernacular tone. Thank you for reading.

Second Epilogue

The Real Son of the Author gets the Final Word

I am the real son of the man who wrote this book—a man who is very much alive. Like the "son" in this book, Dad asks me to read a lot of articles, an occasional book chapter and short paperbacks, but rarely does he ask me to read a real book!

Throughout my college years he literally sent me an envelope every couple of weeks stuffed with things he had torn out of newspapers and magazines; things he had copied or printed from the Internet. (I saved much of it for my own book some day.) We called it my "bathroom library." I mostly did read the stuff, but when he asked me to read this manuscript I was hesitant. What 26-year-old wants to read over 200 pages of something his not-famous father has written?

But then I remembered some of the many motivational things he had sent me. Things about "signs," like the butterfly that just appeared at the back door of a home while the people were grieving the death of a loved one—they all knew the deceased was obsessed with butterflies. And the pennies that kept appearing in Dad's life, and started appearing in my life, after Dad shared with me the story of their magic. When he asked me to read this manuscript I had just moved to Cape Cod to work for the summer—and I was lonely. What better way to fill some time, I thought, and to feel like my dad was there with me. So I read the words he had written and I smiled.

I approve these messages. What would my title for this book have been? Something like: "Oedipus Trips Over Freud and is Inspired to Write a Semi-Autobiographical Tome, to Educate Others,

Communicate with Loved Ones, Offer Therapy, Cleanse His Soul, and Get Out From Under His Guilt, Fear and Ego, So His Light Can Shine More Brightly." Hey, maybe I did learn something from all of those things he sent me to read in college. And I hope I can learn from the following simple phrase that my dad has taped to the inside of his wallet: "BREATHING IN, I receive . . . BREATHING OUT . . . I let go."

I hope I can keep coming back to this.

CPSIA information can be obtained at www.ICGtesting.com
Printed in the USA
BVOW072302070113

310019BV00001B/2/P